The Toyota Production System Journey

The Toyota Production System (TPS) is regarded as a sophisticated concept that helps us understand the world of manufacturing. It evolved from the system of mass-producing cars, established by the Ford Motor Company, and the Japanese have since endeavored to make their own universal production system. Though much has been accomplished, TPS' progress is a continuous process. The theme of this book is how to understand and learn TPS.

There is a TPS concept that seems to elude many, and that is that manufacturers should be able to make a product available at the very moment a customer comes and asks for it. There are various ways and tools that can be used to pursue the ideal state, and therefore we need to focus on the basic principles of TPS. This book tries to explain those Toyota Production System concepts that may otherwise be elusive.

This book focuses on the factory to help readers understand the fundamental ideology of TPS. In the narrative of the book, the lead character started his career as a Technical Expert in the R&D Division of an Automotive Company and eventually becomes an Instructor of TPS. His broad career in companies is used to vividly describe the form of the Toyota Production System. To explain the growth of apprentices of various titles and positions, this story is woven with several short stories presented from the perspective of the main character, who grows from being a Group Leader to Section Leader, to Manager, and then to General Manager.

Essentially, this book describes the Toyota Production System, which is based on the philosophy, "Always sketching out and pursuing the ideal state of manufacturing."

The Toyota Production System Journey

The Continuously Changing Features of TPS and Lean Thinking

A Novel by Noboru Takeuchi

Translated from Japanese by Takehito Kimura

Routledge
Taylor & Francis Group

A PRODUCTIVITY PRESS BOOK

First published 2023
by Routledge
605 Third Avenue, New York, NY 10158

and by Routledge
4 Park Square, Milton Park, Abingdon, Oxon, OX14 4RN

Routledge is an imprint of the Taylor & Francis Group, an informa business

ISBN: 9781032346786 (hbk)
ISBN: 9781032346779 (pbk)
ISBN: 9781003323310 (ebk)

DOI: 10.4324/9781003323310

Typeset in Minion
by KnowledgeWorks Global Ltd.

Contents

JOURNEY THREE: Implementation Journey

JOURNEY FOUR: Deepening Journey

Preface to the English Edition

I feel greatly honored to be able to present the contents of this book to all of you, and it is my hope that the story will provide some insight into the Toyota Production System, if even a little.

In this book, the Toyota Production System is referred to as TPS, not simply because it is the acronym, but affectionately so as the three letters conjure up thoughts about those elements that make the Toyota Production System so revered in the world of manufacturing. Yet there are some who feel some degree of hesitation in using the name "Toyota." In fact, the TPS acronym originated back in the 1970s during the oil crisis, but it was from the name of a company's production system, a company whose name also started with the letter "T." In those days, a company that perhaps had a name starting with "N" would have called its production system "NPS," or "D" company would have called theirs "DPS," "IPS" for company "I," and so forth. This style of applying an acronym became a trend among companies back then. Still, even if they had their own system, the Total Production System was acknowledged and used to some degree. It was so common in manufacturing that the name "TPS" became itself a proper noun. In manufacturing today, there is no mistaking that TPS stands for the Toyota Production System, and this is due to its fundamental ideologies and the impact they have had on manufacturing.

TPS is regarded as a sophisticated concept that helps us understand the world of manufacturing. It evolved from the system of mass-producing cars, established by Ford, and the Japanese have since endeavored to make their own universal production system. Though much has been accomplished, TPS' progress is a continuous process.

A system called "Lean" was a version of TPS that was introduced in the West, but the approach and ideology are different. We should also not say that TPS is superior to Lean. Still, in the West, there are many discussions on social media regarding the methods, techniques, and statistical data of TPS. This is, of course, natural. However, the previous methods, techniques, and statistical data of TPS may not always have been informative. If TPS is to be followed, then implementing it should not be rushed, and focus should always be on the fundamentals. If we are too particular about methodology, we may fail or do things that run counter to what TPS is intended to do.

The subtitle, "The Continuously Changing Features of TPS and Lean Thinking," is reflective of the metamorphosis of certain creatures, whereby the shape is completely transformed, yet the genetic information is unchanged. The features of the Toyota Production System among different companies appear different. Even if the fundamentals are the same, the features differ at each TPS level. In addition, our actions as dictated by TPS should vary according to our situation and environment.

I was an engineer, but it was difficult to understand TPS at the beginning.

The first reason was that I couldn't understand the fundamental concept. Though I had studied the basic ideology of Just-In-Time and *Jidoka* (autonomation) since I was young, I came to realize that I was not able to actually understand it at the time. I was still trying to grasp the ideal ideology without being bothered by the minor details.

The second reason was that there was a lot of jargon used by TPS practitioners. It was challenging for me, even though I was a Japanese native, and it took a long time to understand the meaning of the various terminology thrown about in the world of TPS. Actually, it was expected that an understanding of the fundamentals of TPS be established before practice, but I had felt that the best way to grasp TPS was only by practicing.

In addition, the nuance and the vagueness of Japanese jargon adds to the difficulty of non-natives who are trying to understand TPS.

If looked at from a different perspective, TPS is a company-wide activity. There is TPS interpreted broadly, and that surrounds more narrow interpretations of certain TPS elements, such as Just-In-Time and *Jidoka*. As well, more can be achieved if cooperation is enhanced between the top-down management and the bottom-up activities of the employees. What is also certain is that companies have found or should find ways of advancing TPS.

The theme of this book is how to understand and learn TPS.

The main character in the book works in an automotive components manufacturing plant. A novel woven with several short stories describes his experiences, and changes happened in his TPS understanding as he matures from a group specific leader to a company-wide leader. He has learned TPS through practices developed by himself, and improved his understanding to where he was able to lead with conviction. Depending on your level of TPS understanding, certainly feel free to skip difficult parts or just skim through the book.

English readers might feel it unnatural that this book uses terminology which differs from other books on TPS. Here, I would like to address this.

Sometimes, the Japanese-derived terms of TPS are used at production sites in the West. *Kaizen* is a TPS term that means continuous or never-ending improvement. The concept may also be referred to as *Andon, Muda, Kanban, Poka-yoke, Jidoka, Heijyunka, Sensei,* and so forth. Many attempts have been made to explain these words, not only in this book but also in others.

The word *Monodzukuri* means making things, and it is often used in Japan, at companies and elsewhere. For me, the most apt description is manufacturing with Japanese soul. When Japanese people hear the word *Monodzukuri*, we feel a sense of tradition whereby Japanese craftsmanship is blended with techniques of mass production to powerfully influence the world. In this book, *Monodzukuri* is translated as "Manufacturing," with a capital.

Genba means the actual workplace or shop floor or workshop, and it has a certain nuance in Japan. Though I do use the word *Genba* occasionally in this book, I prefer to use the word *Seisan-Shokuba* (production workplace).

When I did use *Genba*, I spelled it with an "n" at the center, but in the West, an "m" is used. In the English prefix, we understand there is an etymological rule of "m," used before the letters "b," "m," and "p." But Japanese people feel this spelling is slightly strange. When English natives checked our pronunciation of *Genba*, we decided "n" was better phonetically. Though even if spelled as "gen," the pronunciation may slightly change depending on the words or letters following. As an example, the word *Genchi-Gembutsu* has been used frequently recently. Using both "n" and "m" with Japanese actual pronunciation, *Genchi-Gembutsu* means the actual thing in the actual place, and it is sometimes translated into the slogan, "Go and study, and see what a team can achieve."

In order to help readers easily understand TPS, this book was written through a novel like TPS story. The first half of the book, Journeys One and Two, was translated into English by Mr. Takehito Kimura. The second half of the book with more technical parts, Journeys Three and Four, was translated into English by the author.

I am very grateful to many people who supported me in creating this English edition. I'd like to thank Mr. Takehito Kimura who translated this book, as well as Mr. Peter Chin who further assisted with translations.

Also, thank you to Mr. Nilesh Raveendran, Mr. Jason Lippa, Dr. Hiroshi Ozawa (Nagoya University), and Dr. Rei Hino (Nagoya University). I particularly express my thanks to Mr. Michael Sinocchi (Routledge) and Ms. Cole Bowman (KnowledgeWorks Global), without whose support this book could not have been.

Even though some (or a lot) of the content may be challenging to grasp as far as understanding TPS is concerned, I hope you will not be too bothered reading the story in its entirety. It is also my hope that upon finishing this book, you will have gained some deeper insight into TPS. If such is not achieved, then the fault lies with me as the author. Any thoughts you could graciously share with me will be greatly appreciated.

Noboru Takeuchi
Nagoya, Aichi, Japan
December 2021

Preface

The Toyota Production System is often referred to simply as "TPS." When a novice in TPS tries to study it, the objectively and systematically written books become useful to understand the basics of TPS. However, there are a lot of books which present individual cases and methods in the production workplace. This may also be helpful to understand TPS with reference to the process in action. But there are some books which seem to have been written without a good understanding of TPS, with a perspective given only from outside the production workplace, often from the perspective of the so-called headquarters' operations of a company. And then there are some books which just look at one aspect of TPS and remind us of the parable of the blind men and the elephant, which originated in the ancient Indian continent. It's important for us to understand the fundamental basis of TPS, and we shouldn't stick only to methods or tools which are trivial details, because TPS doesn't work if we only imitate the external aspects of TPS, without also considering the production workplace.

It's necessary to keep developing the right TPS ideology in order to get a more favorable outcome from the Toyota Production System. When this is accomplished, we can shed the falsely understood ideology of TPS and pursue the ideal that will bring the desired results in manufacturing.

Companies should manufacture products as much as possible with the ideal state in mind, which becomes the source of new competitive strength. Meanwhile R&D efforts that keep producing new attractive products are also certainly critical. On the other hand, keeping manufacturing in developed countries is increasingly difficult because the cost of labor in developing countries is relatively inexpensive. Under such circumstances, the effective management of companies becomes even more crucial. Discussions and planning around this issue is very important for Japanese manufacturers to have.

With manufacturing increasingly being shipped abroad, TPS teaches us to continue to pursue those features of the manufacturing process that lead to ideal outcomes, and only companies which have the competency to develop and continue this process can survive.

There is a TPS concept that seems to elude many, and that is that manufacturers should be able to make a product available at the moment a customer comes and asks for it. There are various ways and tools that can be used to pursue the ideal state, and therefore we need to focus on the basic principles of TPS. This book tries to explain those Toyota Production System concepts that may otherwise be elusive. So, this book might not be useful as such from a technical or managerial standpoint, as the use of a lot of related lingo is avoided.

The features of the Toyota Production System sometimes seem to be different among various companies. Even if the TPS's fundamentals are the same, the features appear different depending on each company's level of TPS understanding and implementation. The processes which we should implement are also different from the viewpoint of each practitioner. TPS is primarily a company-wide process which starts from "Our Customers" and ends with "Our Customers." It handles the whole supply chain process that passes through Marketing, Receiving, Production, Shipment, and Customer.

This novel focuses on the factory in order to help readers understand the fundamental ideology of TPS. The main character started his career as a Technical Expert of the R&D Division in the East Automotive Company, and eventually becomes an Instructor of TPS. His broad career in companies is used to vividly describe the form of the TPS.

In order to explain the growth of apprentices of various titles and positions, this novel is woven with several short stories and described from the perspective of the main character, who grows from being a Group Leader to Section Leader, to Manager, to General Manager, and then to Leader. This literary style uses the present tense in narrating the process of this journey so that you can perhaps be better able to compare instances in your own production situations. To further aid understanding, the main story runs parallel with the supplemental stories, which explain the TPS ideologies or technical aspects. This format therefore enables you to delve into those stories that may be most closely related to the areas for which you would like to focus.

Journey One, Growth Journey, presents a Toyota Production System motif. The main character learns the Toyota Production System and develops to where he can offer advice on *Kaizen* activities. The main character's activities are described from the perspective of an apprentice, a female Team Leader at a food company. As a result of the main character's experiences at the workplace, he realizes some important work principles of TPS.

Journey Two, Meditation Journey, depicts the main character as a Technical Expert of the R&D division, where he experiences an incident which triggers a desire to learn TPS. The occasionally impertinent main character faces struggles to put his invented product in the market. Facing difficulties in the production workplace, he begins his novice learning of TPS. He realizes TPS may be the solution, even though he is yet to understand it fully.

Journey Three, Implementation Journey, depicts the main character as a person participating in a TPS autonomous study meeting (*Jishuken*) and who develops into a *Kaizen* practitioner of manufacturing. He gets the opportunity to study ideologies or tools of TPS in *Jishuken*.

Journey Four, Deepening Journey, depicts him as an Instructor who struggles to lead TPS. One day, an idea about *Kaizen* comes to him, which instills him with confidence. This story will help you see how TPS can be used for problem finding, target making, and executing solutions in order to create a more ideal and comfortable workplace.

Principally, this book with the above-mentioned stories intends to describe the Toyota Production System, which is based on the philosophy, "Always sketching out and pursuing the ideal state of manufacturing."

Mr. Taiichi Ohno, who systematized TPS and published it in a book, stated that the Toyota Production System has to be continually changing. Even now, the Toyota Production System is constantly evolving. Therefore, our understanding of TPS is inadequate if our learning is limited to past or even currently developed methodology. Such methodological books can't lead to an understanding of TPS if their content is examined from such points of view. So this book simply explains the fundamentals of manufacturing in TPS in order to try to frame the elements which comprise the Toyota Production System. This story is set in relatively big organizations, which may cause readers to think that it is not applicable to their own situations if they do not work in a large organization or have a large staff. Such differences should be ignored, while the focus instead should be on grasping the fundamental ideology, which may allow this book to be used as a resource for enabling understanding of more technical books.

When I was younger, I once experienced a new product launch at a factory, where production started from scratch. At that time, I eagerly hoped someone would eventually teach me TPS, and that there would be a good TPS book helpful for engineers. So this book intends to include my innermost thoughts that might encourage the technical experts and the production engineers who are trying to understand the Toyota Production System. In addition, this is written from the perspective of practitioners who have implemented real *Kaizen* activities, which will hopefully further aid your understanding of TPS.

This book is set in the production workplace, but I have tried to limit use of technical jargon to help readers who are not familiar with production. There are many books based on the Toyota Production System being introduced widely to other industries, either directly or indirectly. The fundamental ideology of TPS is useful both in direct and indirect presentations. However, there are still a lot of unknown technical terms that may be challenging for novices who are just starting their study of the Toyota Production System.

So, the words used for referring to aspects of the Toyota Production System are described on occasion with various explanations. These variations in language are spreading in the world of TPS. These words are commonly used among TPS practitioners, but they can be incomprehensible to a novice of the Toyota Production System. I, the author and formerly an engineer, couldn't understand these terms at the beginning when thrown into the world of the Toyota Production System. I suspect this was the intent that by using jargon, TPS practitioners could prevent outsiders from developing a full understanding and therefore keep their knowledge of the process proprietary.

But still, the ideology behind the words is often important, so this book tries to present and explain them.

This book also weaves recent events into the story of the Toyota Production System, which so many books have not touched on. In addition, to deepen the readers' understanding, the original study of the Toyota Production System is described based on my understanding. My ideas may not always be the same as other TPS specialists, but I believe they are not far from the basic ideology. Please let me know your thoughts.

As mentioned, this book eschews systematic explanations. Technical figures and tables appear in the midst of some of the stories for those with a technical background. Those without such a background should skip them and any difficult parts that contain technical words and ideologies. However, reading the whole story will provide the framework of TPS. I'd like to write another book, if I have a chance, for those who would like to know more about the TPS methodology in detail.

This story mainly focuses on the workers. However I'm afraid readers might trivialize the Toyota Production System as a methodology that only looks at worker's improvements, because there is little description about equipment and overall processes in the factory. Therefore, I'd like to emphasize that the ideology of the Toyota Production System helps the management of the whole company in its entirety.

The Toyota Production System can be adjusted and made appropriate for any situation a company may face. It would be a shame if those studying TPS only achieve a simplistic understanding, perhaps of tools such as *Kanban*, as this will certainly result in chaos in the workplace. This is likely due to attention being paid only to those parts of the TPS process that are clearly visible and easy to understand. On the other hand, we should understand the Toyota Production System has an essential ideology: "We always have to be pursuing the ideal state."

Such ideologies in the Toyota Production System are said to be useful even in white-collar and other types of non-manufacturing industries. There are some methodologies which are different from the Toyota Production System, yet they transform business processes in pursuit of the ideal state as well. I expect this book will offer some clues to solving particular issues in your manufacturing situation, even if the ideas are simply from my own perspective.

Finally, I would like to express my deepest gratitude to friends, especially Mr. Jiro Taga, who helped in the actual writing of this book. Completion of The Toyota Production System Journey was also made possible thanks to the cooperation of my family: Hiroyo, Toshinori, Hidenori, Kaori, Misako, and Reiko.

About the Author

Noboru Takeuchi is Executive Consultant in a Japanese consulting firm for manufacturing called Process Design Co., Ltd. Japan, where he shares his knowledge and experiences of the Toyota Production System, known as TPS. He is Ex-Adjunct Professor at Aichi Gakuin University Graduate School, and the former Chief Adviser of the Production Engineering Management Meeting held by the Japan Management Association (JMA). He worked at an automotive company of the Toyota Group for *Genba* innovation based on the Toyota Production System, researching and developing the production process technology for the automotive elemental components, and leading the business administration flow process based on the concept of TPS. He has worked on cost reduction, the 5S, *Kaizen* of operations and logistics, the *Kanban* system, productivity enhancement, lead time shortening, and quality in the production workplace.

He completed his Bachelor of Engineering from the Nagoya Institute of Technology and a Master of Chemical Engineering from Osaka Prefecture University in Japan.

The original Japanese language edition of the content of this book was published serially in the Japanese magazine *Factory Management* from April 2013 to July 2014 through The Nikkan Kogyo Shimbun Co., Ltd. (The Daily Industrial News).

Publication in Japanese:

"*Seru Seisan* (Cell Production)," through JMA Management Center 2006 Japan. ISBN 4-8207-4393-7

Publication in Chinese:

Chinese language edition of the book "*Seru Seisan* (Cell Production)," through The Oriental Press 2014 China. ISBN 978-7-5060-7537-4

Chinese language edition of this book, "*The Toyota Production System Journey*," through The Oriental Press 2017 China. ISBN 978-7-5060-9791-8

E-mail: mail@jitps.co.jp

URL: http://www.jitps.co.jp

About the Translator

Takehito Kimura was born in Tokyo. As a graduate of the Sophia University's department of English Studies, his lifelong pursuit has been finding an ultimate cross-cultural communication. While being involved with some inbound businesses in Tokyo as a hire/limousine driver and a tour director after he ended his contract with the Waseda University as a multi-media contents developer regarding foreign language educational fields, he has also developed his career as an English-Japanese translator.

E-mail: kimoore@mac.com

The Characters

Journey One: Growth Journey

Sensei The main character of the story, Mr. Takeuchi, who is growing as an Instructor through his experiences using TPS to solve production issues.

Julie Bright Team Leader at a food company where about 200 people work.

Journey Two: Meditation Journey

Takeuchi The young main character who is an up-and-coming technical expert at the East Automotive Co., Ltd. He also serves as Assistant Project Manager in the R&D Division and Assistant Manager in the Production Engineering Development Division. He is 37 years old, has a wife, two sons, and one daughter, and is transferred to the factory with his newly invented product.

Sensei The imaginary TPS expert who is the future main character and has grown into an experienced and knowledgeable teacher. He appears suddenly to offer advice to the young main character about TPS.

Mr. Saitou A staff person in the TPS Secretariate in the Production Management Division.

Yoshitake T/L Team Leader at the factory who helps the main character.

Manager Matsui A manager who proclaims himself as anti-TPS as he opposes changing to such a system.

Journey Three: Implementation Journey

Manager Takeuchi The Manager in the Operations Management Consulting Division (OMCD), responsible for the instruction of TPS Activities at the main factory.

Sensei See the Journey Two description.

Manager Yamanaka A colleague in the Production Engineering Development Division.

Taga, Masanori An expert of IE. A senior staff person in the OMCD, responsible for education and general affairs.

Journey Four: Deepening Journey

G.M. Takeuchi The General Manager at OMCD, responsible for the instruction of TPS Activities to suppliers and global sister companies.

Sensei See the Journey Two description.

Mr. Kamiyama General Manager at the West Automotive Co., Ltd. He is a peer in *Jishuken*.

Mr. Chen A person in charge of TPS Activities in the East Asian Plant.

Mr. John A person in charge of TPS Activities in the European Plant.

Journey One

Growth Journey

WHENEVER I LOOK AROUND, IT'S ALWAYS RAINING

– Pursuing the soul of Manufacturing –

In this journey, several aspects of the Toyota Production System (TPS) will be introduced.

First of all, the business philosophy of *Kaizen* (continuous improvement) is described as key for implementing TPS. The TPS activity of the main character is shown from the perspective of an apprentice. A female team leader at a food company conveys how she is going to teach TPS and guide the workers. She grows into a good *Kaizen* leader at the manufacturing site. This story shows the importance of training workers and implementing TPS company-wide.

As a result of the main character's experiences at the workplace, one might perceive him as a hero who was able to finally realize some important work principles. He believes that keeping an eye on every aspect of the job, valuing the employees, and proper training of human resources at all phases of operation globally are what it takes for Manufacturing to be reliable and efficient.

DOI: 10.4324/9781003323310-1

Part I

The Team Leader Grows as a Production Supervisor

1

Team Leader Julie Looks Back at Her Notes

Her name is Julie.

She has been working at a food company that has 200 employees. Her company has developed her into a good *Kaizen* leader at the production workplaces under the guidance of an excellent mentor. This story which is based on Julie's notes starts from her younger years.

"Bright?" Ms. Watabe, one of the team members, calls to the Team Leader.

Ms. Watabe joined the company recently. She tends to call Team Leader Julie with names like "Bright" or "Pretty" without using the obligatory "Miss." She may think of Julie as her own daughter, though Julie is her boss, the Team Leader.

Ms. Watabe calls out to Julie just as she is hurriedly on her way to meet with her boss, the Assistant Manager, who has been waiting in the break room next to the production line, which seems to establish that Ms. Watabe's question is not urgent enough.

Julie says to her, "Please wait. My boss wants to see me immediately."

Even though the Assistant Manager was expecting her, Julie's no. 1 priority is always supposed to be making sure the production line is operating smoothly. She has to always be willing to take the time to listen to what her team members have to say.

When someone on the production line presses an emergency button, the signal is sent directly to the Team Leader's desk. It's a warning system using an electronic message board called an *Andon*. This time, Ms. Watabe does not notify Team Leader Julie through the *Andon*.

DOI: 10.4324/9781003323310-3

She has been taught that a Team Leader is essentially a Production Supervisor. The names "Supervisor" and "Team-Leader" are used interchangeably for the same position. It is said that the role of a Production Supervisor is the same as of a Chief Executive Officer (CEO) in a small or medium enterprise (SME).

A Team Leader has the responsibility of managing all of the workers on a production line. There are even times when the Team Leader must substitute for an absent worker on the production line.

Another main duty of a Team Leader is attendance management. The Team Leader is even expected to encourage members of the team to take paid holidays systematically in order to not to make disruption to production.

This entails making sure workers actively try to use up all of their holidays by the end of the fiscal year. However, there are cases where workers try to take more holidays than they are actually allowed. One of the biggest headaches for a Team Leader is the sudden absence of a worker, often due to illness. If there is a sudden shortage of crew on the production line, she may have to ask other teams for their help, of course after consulting with the Assistant Manager.

Her full name is "Julie Bright."

Julie works for a food company called "A Food," which consists of around 200 workers and is located in a town near a big city with a castle as a landmark.

Her joining the company was the result of a chance encounter, one particular evening in the past.

That night, Julie, still in high school and after finishing her club's activity, reached the bus stop near her school. However, it was late and the bus had already left. It was also raining, and she realized that she was without an umbrella.

It began raining harder, and her school uniform was already soaking wet. She was at a loss as to what to do when a car stopped beside her.

It was a company car belonging to the A Food Company. The car was on its way back to the office when it came across this high-school girl standing in the rain.

"Do you need a ride? Please don't hesitate," said a woman from the passenger seat. The man who was driving the car was actually the CEO of the company.

This encounter led to Julie being offered an interview and then eventually a position with the company after she graduated from high school.

In January of the year prior to her being promoted to the Team Leader position, the company had already scheduled for there to be personnel changes, which paved the way for Julie's eventual promotion. However, the promotion did not come as much of a surprise as eight years had passed since her graduation and hiring at the company, as well as over two years as a sub-Team Leader.

Female Team Leaders are not rare any more these days. What does remain constant is the huge amount of responsibility the position entails.

Her performance was efficient, and it was due in no small part to the support she received from her Manager and Assistant Manager.

Her friends and the Assistant Manager call her "Julie" or "Juli," while her team members are content with calling her "Bright." Why "Bright?" Because she always says to her team members, "Make the workplace shine bright." Or maybe because part of her family name includes a character with a similar meaning. She's actually not quite sure how her name came about. When asked about her nickname, she often take the liberty of flattering herself saying it is because she is bright and cute.

Julie commutes to work in a car she recently bought, and which she absolutely adores.

One particular morning at work seemed like any other morning. As usual, Julie arrived at the office early, and attended the morning meeting after she was done preparing the information talk she was to give to the team members. Her team consists of 15 members – all female – who comprise three in-line production lines and another three production points off the line.

When everyone gathers together after the morning warm-up exercises, Julie starts her speech.

"Good morning. First I would like to announce that we're expecting a guest today. You can behave as usual. However, everyone please don't forget to greet the guest respectfully.

About possible issues of the quality of our products, we had no complaints from our customers yesterday.

As for the Master Production Schedule, we are a little behind. Let's work hard to make up for the delay.

As soon as the meeting is finished, everyone please go to your assigned position and start today's work."

In the morning especially, Julie pays close attention to her team members' health conditions to ensure operations proceed smoothly.

This particular morning, however, no sooner has work started that she is summoned by her Assistant Manager. She rushes to his office with another Team Leader, who heads the team next to hers.

At a section of the factory called the "hot corner," where there are tables and chairs for the workers to take breaks, the CEO of A Food is sitting together with a man no one has seen before. Sitting beside them are the Manager and Assistant Manager.

After everyone takes a seat, the CEO starts talking.

"Let me introduce Mr. Takeuchi, who is going to be our coach, our *Sensei*," the CEO says.

And then, with a stern look in his face, he says something even more unexpected.

"As business at this company has been steadily increasing, it may be about time to overhaul the manufacturing process to prepare for future growth.

To kick off this restructuring process, we're going to have a company-wide meeting. That is why we now have *Sensei* coming all the way here to see our factory first hand."

Julie did know there was going to be a guest, but what surprised her was that the guest was a part of a grand scheme to restructure the company's manufacturing. It seemed his specialization was in imparting his knowledge of the Japanese business concept of *Kaizen*.

The CEO then proceeds to give *Sensei* a guided tour of the factory.

When they would stop at each production line, each of the line's Team Leader would explain how they go about their tasks. On this day, *Sensei* was merely listening to what was being described to him by everyone he talked to. He continued this right up until it was time for him to leave.

During *Sensei*'s visit, the CEO was informed of some matters that seemed to be secretive, but which required attention.

Later on, Julie and other Team Leaders were informed of the following from *Sensei*:

"The most important thing is that the person in the highest position take the lead and the necessary action. In overseas companies, we often find CEOs who don't even visit their production workplace.

I believe such situations seldom occur in Japanese companies. As well, it is really important for the person at the top, as a leader, to adopt major innovations.

This requires that the head of the organization be highly motivated and a risk-taker.

This time, it'll work out alright because the CEO has recognized that we are at a critical stage of our growth, but there are looming issues that need to be dealt with. That is why we need to take the action necessary to avert these problems and ensure that operations are maintained at an optimal state.

The person at the top is supposed to guide workers. Therefore, I'm here for you, to provide assistance to you, if needed.

However, I won't come here every day. Usually, you carry out your daily tasks somewhat autonomously, implementing your own methods for dealing with situations as they arise."

These words indicated to Julie and her colleagues that their CEO would begin to come to visit the factory more frequently than he had previously.

The Manufacturing Renovation of A Food thus began. It's going to have an official start with a special kick-off event this morning.

It is being held at the company's dining room, and attendance by all of the employees is required.

At the kick-off, the CEO begins with a speech, saying that sales have picked up well, though a drop in profits has caused him to worry about the future. Following the CEO, *Sensei* greeted the assembly and opened with some words of encouragement. He then proceeded to give the gathering a brief introduction to *Kaizen*, as well as an explanation of the coaching style underlying the concept.

"When I talk to the technical professionals, if I have imparted some advice or explanation, I try not to repeat it. Among real professionals, it really depends on each person whether or not they can put what I imparted to good use. Trust in the workers' own abilities is what I believe will result in success. I guide them more directly only when it is certain that some gross error is about to be made.

Nonetheless, you may notice that my style of coaching *Kaizen* is something you are not entirely accustomed to. I tend to keep a 'coaching record,' in which I make meticulous notes of every step of when and how I taught something.

In the process of trying to instill the *Kaizen* concept at this company, I'll try to explain the important matters step by step and repeatedly so you improve your *Kaizen* skills.

Even if some of what I say seems similar or the same as what you may have heard previously, how much you will eventually understand will be much more than what is now.

By applying what you learn in the actual work area, your *Kaizen* skills should improve gradually. In order for you to truly understand *Kaizen* under the TPS, for example, you will hear me emphasize two particular concepts: 'Just-in-time' and 'Jidoka (autonomation).' I'll keep explaining them again and again, and try to use simple expressions to help you understand."

Sensei speaks quickly, so Julie and her colleagues are focused intently on following what he is saying. He finishes up his speech by saying the following: "I want to be called by my name, not '*Sensei*'."

Next, the manager of the Production Department, who has also been assigned to help instill *Kaizen*, gave a speech.

One day before the *Kaizen* campaign got underway, all of the group leaders in the Production Department gathered to receive instructions regarding the project. The Production Department has two divisions consisting of five groups. There are two additional groups, from the Production Control Department and the Engineering Department, which brings the total number of work groups in the operation to seven.

Each department is assigned a particular *Kaizen* theme which is as follows:

- The Production Department: *Kaizen* of each work area.
- The Production Control Department: *Kaizen* of planning, receiving, and shipping.
- The Engineering Department: *Kaizen* of equipment and *Kaizen* of quality inspection tasks.

At the event, each group leader was introduced, and each presented a speech announcing their resolution to everyone.

Julie, who, after two years as a group leader, never imagined she would be asked to speak at such an event, simply said "I'll do my best." Another group leader in the same section as Julie's seemed relaxed and confident when she spoke, likely because of similar experiences she had at her former company.

This is how the Manufacturing Renovation restructuring process had begun.

Julie keeps an "Activity Notebook," in which she takes memos of points she notices or has been told. She makes it a habit to review this notebook often.

-KEEPING EVERYTHING IN ORDER, *SEIRI-SEITON*

Today, I walked around the factory with Mr. Takeuchi (*Sensei*). He was kind enough to give me some direct advice as we inspected each site together. Our CEO was also with us the whole time. And he always seems to be listening intently to what *Sensei* says.

Mr. Takeuchi asks, "How do you want to change this working environment?"

After seeing she is at a loss as to how to answer, he rephrases the question:

"What kind of things are happening at the workplace?"

It seems he's hoping to pinpoint problems in our workplace, thought Julie.

"What I'm getting at is: How do you envision this workplace moving toward the ideal state?" he clarifies again.

He knows perceiving "the ideal state" is difficult for many, so he suggests that we form a vision that can be attained within six months from now. "However, judging this from the current condition of the workplace, determining how to proceed is still unclear. We should strive to achieve 2S: *Seiri-Seiton*," he says.

Julie insists, "I always keep cleaning, telling my members to keep their workplace tidy and shining bright."

"What is the meaning of '2S' to you?" Mr. Takeuchi asks.

"It means *Seiri-Seiton*."

"OK, then what does *Seiri* mean? And *Seiton*?" he asks again.

"*Seiri* means clearly distinguishing what we need from what we don't, and discarding anything unnecessary. *Seiton* means placing the work items we need in an order and in positions that are easy for everyone to find and use," Julie answered.

Mr. Takeuchi then asks, "What is this for?" As Julie seems stumped as to how to answer this question, *Sensei* proceeds to provide his explanation, in a polite tone.

"It's been said that achieving *Kaizen* starts with 2S.

We become convinced that by applying *Seiri-Seiton* alone, our work will become more efficient and effective. Because it really makes the processes of daily work more effective, some companies are adopting a '5S' concept, which includes 2S, into their *Kaizen* activities.

For example, if time is wasted by looking for certain tools, then it automatically makes the production process less effective. By following the 2S concept, we should first remove any unnecessary items in the work area. We should then place commonly used tools in a place where they are easy to find and easily accessible. Just following these steps immediately results in improved efficiency and less wasted time.

Now let's also consider the following concept of 3S: *Seiso* (Sweeping and Washing), *Seiketsu* (Spick-and-Span), and *Shitsuke* (Discipline) – all steps necessary to ensure a clean work environment. 3S is applicable to all types of production. For example, here at this company, we're producing food, but at every step of the production process, there is the possibility of contamination from foreign substances. To maintain hygiene and guarantee the safety of our products, 3S is especially important.

That said, in order of priority, 2S should come first and foremost.

It's essential in the *Kaizen* process that we be aware of what's going on in every facet of the operation, and we can ensure rules are being followed. This awareness will enable you to easily pinpoint an abnormality in an otherwise normal work system."

Upon hearing this, Julie asks,

"So, telling normal from abnormal is the key to *Kaizen*, right?

What sorts of abnormalities should we especially be wary of?"

Sensei answers,

"When we look at 5S, each S has a fundamental rule which should be standardized at your workplace.

You should encourage all the members of your team to follow these rules until they become the corporate culture. You said that you constantly remind your workers to 'keep the office clean and shining bright.' My advice is to keep at it, but try to also explain why it's important to maintain cleanliness and order at the workplace. It is important for you to explain to your members politely that cleaning up contributes to the company's future progress. Cleaning up is not done just for the sake of being clean but because efficient operations depend on this," he emphasizes.

According to Mr. Takeuchi, in many foreign countries, it is common for companies to outsource cleaning of the workplace to a third party instead of having their employees do it. However, 5S, though thought to be a very Japanese concept, has been gaining popularity overseas.

Sensei also emphasized the distinction between "clear up" and "clean up": "Clear up" means *Seiri-Seiton*, while "clean up" means cleanliness as well as *Seiri-Seiton*.

Maintaining fastidious cleanliness is a desire among many Japanese that perhaps comes from their experiences growing up in small houses. Often, these homes have only one room that functions as a living, dining, and bedroom, and so this room is where those residing there spend the majority of their time when inside. That is why the area is kept meticulously clean, and why shoes are removed before entering this area.

As for achieving *Kaizen* under TPS, the seven steps in the procedure below are considered fundamental:

- Procedure 0: First, maintain 2S so that it is easy to see what's going on in the workplace.
- Procedure 1: Have a clear understanding of the current state of the workplace.
- Procedure 2: Sketch an image of the ideal state of the workplace – an image of how the workplace should ultimately be.
- Procedure 3: Sketch your image of the target state that should be established by the target date.
- Procedure 4: Pinpoint the gaps between the current state of the workplace and the target state.
- Procedure 5: Schedule in detail each step which must be taken to change a particular aspect of the workplace.
- Procedure 6: Implement the targeted change to move closer toward the ideal state. Then go back to step 1 to clarify the result of changes, and then plan another change that will help you move closer to reaching the ideal state.

Whatever the changes, it should be implemented by starting 2S, and they should work toward reaching the ideal state. Thus, *Kaizen* repeats as a cycle of never-ending improvements, where "*Kaizen* After" replaces "*Kaizen* Before" at the same time.

-*KAIZEN* IN OPERATION

Today, there was a lecture on workers' actual performance of duties.

"Anything you ask of employees that is related to instilling *Kaizen* has to be related to something that can benefit the company. Otherwise, it cannot last. Here in this department, that means productivity improvement," *Sensei* says.

Then he explains the difference between the work and the motions of a worker.

"Work is any motion that produces value.

Motion that doesn't produce value is nothing but waste. Through activities that keep with the *Kaizen* philosophy, we expect there to be less wasted effort."

He advises Julie to observe her team members, and pinpoint anything that could be considered a wasteful action.

He tells her that the ultimate goal is to enable the team members to perform their duties not only more efficiently but also more easily.

As an example, at the workplace, if a worker often moves between point A and point B, then the time it takes for that worker to walk the distance between the two points should be reduced as much as possible. Waste is determined by how long the workers walk between two points and move their hands.

Supposedly, it takes somewhere between 0.5 and 1 second for each step while walking. If the number of steps could somehow be reduced, perhaps by moving points A and B closer, then precious seconds could be saved. Similarly, moving our hands 10 cm supposedly takes 0.1 second each time. Therefore, reducing the distance workers' hands have to move can make production more efficient. Saving seconds or even tenths of seconds all add up to less wasted action in the workplace.

Sensei knows many people are not fans of this system of speeding up operations down to seconds. The image of a Team Leader with a stop watch telling workers "move more quickly" can be unnerving.

He cannot deny that it seems something like discipline, or training. However, less wasteful motions in the operation will result in a smooth production process. To outsiders looking in, these motions should seem swift and effortless. While some may have studied the standardized work *Kaizen* in theory, the achievement of *Kaizen* in operations starts with this focus on less wasteful motions. By establishing the standardized work *Kaizen* in the actual workplace, productivity increases, which leads to increased profits.

In addition, this standardized work is essential to ensuring the quality of our products as well as the safety and productivity. Mr. Takeuchi says that standardized work and quality/safety/productivity are basically the relationship of cause and effect. He emphasizes that safety especially is the result of our own activity, but we rarely realize the relationship between safety and standardized work. Julie is informed that Mr. Takeuchi leads what's referred to as a "production day" once a month. The company's three departments, Quality, Safety, and Production Control, hold a company-wide meeting and collaboratively look at the related issues.

So she has decided to accompany Mr. Takeuchi on his rounds observing the operations so perhaps she can become aware of things that she otherwise would not have noticed.

After their first go around, he asks Julie, "Have you found any points to be improved?"

"The box of items which the operator is always reaching for should be placed closer to her hands," she answers.

"Good point. You noticed the wasteful motions of her hands," he says praisingly.

"*Kaizen* is applicable even regarding actions as simple as picking a necessary item out of a container. For instance, if the container is full of other items, you may have a hard time grabbing an item you need with one swift motion. Granted, some items are just difficult to be picked up easily. It depends on the items, but basically, as much as possible, you should come up with a way in which workers can grab them easily, almost without looking. It's actually a very effective way to lower their stress levels.

You may think it's a really small step, but when it becomes part of their routine, it sure makes a big difference."

"What's the next step in fostering *Kaizen* here?" Julie asks.

Sensei then lists the following:

1. Create an operations manual.
2. Politely explain to the operators the specifics of the manual.

3. Provide demonstrations of key points from the manual.
4. Let the operators try to perform the recommended tasks by themselves.

He explains,

"Creating this manual requires input from the workers themselves, who can give you insights beyond what you are only capable of observing. Ultimately, you'll have a manual that will run into less resistance among your workers when trying to implement its policies and procedures. The manual is also supposed to be an educational reference for newcomers to ease their transition into this company. Of course, keep it updated as more things about the operations become apparent."

Mr. Takeuchi, who has had experience both as a production worker and as a supervisor, states this opinion on *Kaizen* in operation:

> Some people think efficiency is only about profits, but the Japanese don't realize or have lost sight of the fact that a company that emphasizes efficiency is being virtuous by keeping their employees' comfort in mind. Though I don't quite follow this rationalization that cutting costs may not be the primary reason behind prioritizing efficiency, I have written in my work diary that I contribute to the happiness of the nation through working in the manufacturing industry.

He continued, "When I used to work on a production line, I was never aware nor made aware of wasteful actions.

I couldn't help but question if previous production methods, technology, and my former supervisor's handling of operations were really sound. I'm pretty sure the experiences there have made me who I am. I am certainly a product of my own experiences. As a supervisor, I realize that it is my job to weed out wasteful methods in the production operation. The important thing is for workers to realize that efficiency in motion is not just about the motion but the contributions it makes to operations as a whole. In turn, supervisors feel more confident about the state of operations. With these effects in mind, my goal is to create a workplace where all the workers can be proud of what they do.

It's preferable that each worker feels what he or she is doing is a major contribution to the team and the company as a whole. We sometimes see the overseas workers are forced to work under severe conditions where every motion becomes a burden. It only makes sense that the focus be on weeding out inefficiency rather than cost cutting."

-MANUFACTURING THE AMOUNT THAT HAS BEEN SOLD

Today, I hear a lecture on how to decide the appropriate amount of production.

"How do you decide production for the day?" Mr. Takeuchi asks.

"Every evening, the section manager tells us the items and their quantities to produce the next day. Based on the information, I set about producing the desired amount," Julie says.

"I can imagine that is quite hard for the section manager. How would you handle a sudden change of quantity or an unexpected order?" Mr. Takeuchi asks.

"In that case, we would have to work overtime," Julie answers.

"I can see that the production rate tends to fluctuate vastly every day. I've also noticed that the products of this company are relatively durable. So, I advise a specific system where a certain amount of stock items is kept on hand, which would not be wasteful as these items are durable," says Mr. Takeuchi.

Ultimately, the goal is to keep enough of the products in stock so that sudden changes or surges in orders will be much less disruptive when trying to reach daily production goals. Less fluctuation in production quantity means more steady operations. It's basically based on the *Heijyunka* concept in TPS.

Until now, the whole process of deciding production goals has been done by the section manager, but such decisions require the manager to factor in the amount of stock available. Therefore, production should focus more on maintaining a certain amount of stock rather than just fulfilling particular orders as they come in. Basically, his suggestion is for operations to shift toward what's known as **Fill-up System of Production**.

Then he introduces an outline of how to execute this system:

- First, have a certain amount of stock in the Store/Shop warehouse. It is essential to keep **FIFO (First In First Out)** for this system.
- The maximum amount of stock to keep should be enough to meet demand, even if there should be a sudden spike in orders.

- Instead of the clients, assume that inventory control at the Store/Shop was your customer, where you take the parts that will be shipped from the shop as "sold," and the number of the parts becomes part of the feedback data to the production site. Tagging a *Kanban* on every item is necessary. After each item is shipped, each *Kanban* is detached and is returned to the production workplace.
- This method will help keep production steady: *Heijyunka* production. Information is the key to ensuring that the Production Department's operations remain steady. The production section should convey clearly the quantity produced each day.
- Stocked products should also be categorized and separated accordingly. For example, which products are sold daily and which are less so? Also, which items are sold in bulk amounts, and which are sold more individually?

Ultimately, the goal is to manufacture only the amount necessary to replenish stock of an item – to replace what has been sold. Mr. Takeuchi says,

"Though we use *Kanban* as a tool, it is preferable that we understand it as a means to achieve *Kaizen*. However, managing it properly is very important. Manufacturing only the needed amount to replenish stock ensures that customers receive their order swiftly and that the production of their order is of high quality, because they are receiving product that is already in stock. This is why we should cooperate to see that this particular production philosophy is followed. As this is a rather new system, I certainly understand that we're likely to encounter difficulties in the beginning, but let us not be deterred in giving it our all."

⏀ -AS A PRODUCTION SUPERVISOR

Mr. Takeuchi's period of service finished after six months, and it was capped off with a final presentation.

During his tenure, we were able to fully integrate the Fill-up System of Production in our operations.

As a result, the total amount of overtime hours had been reduced, while the inventory at the shipping site was maintained at a reasonable level, which reduced the total stock. Yet, there are still a lot of things left to do for *Kaizen* to be truly implemented.

After Mr. Takeuchi's final presentation, the CEO took the reins of A Food Company's production restructuring efforts. It seems from time to time, he gets in touch with Mr. Takeuchi for consultation.

In addition, an employee feedback system, which in its prior incarnation had never been fully implemented, was resurrected. Though the system has its drawbacks, it is now an integral component of the continuous effort to improve operations by enabling management to become aware of their employee's grievances.

Mr. Takeuchi used to say, "*Monodzukuri* (Manufacturing) is training individuals themselves.

Actually, at the end of seminars or talk-shows on business, lecturers tend to tell audiences that fostering the skills of the employees is the most important aspect of running a company, implying that the other factors they have taught are not really important at all," he said half-jokingly.

"Overseas, it is more common for employees to change jobs often, so spending the time and energy to train them can be a liability. But in Japan, that's less of an issue, where investing in your employees pays off in the long run. Admittedly, the lifetime employment system in Japan has been steadily disappearing, but we still try to think with a long-term view regarding our employees. Assessment of our efforts is based on how well we can implement TPS, which means prioritizing human resource investment and employee incentives," he says.

From when she was younger, Julie had always had the feeling since childhood that working at a production workplace would be more suitable for her than being an office worker.

She had actually loved baking sweets and had always dreamed of being a fully fledged pâtissier.

However, during high school, she worked part time at an apparel shop.

Her boss there appreciated her performance so much that he offered her a position in their office, but she declined.

The Assistant Manager, upon hearing that, informed the boss that Julie would probably prefer working at a production site.

Thus, instead of making pastries at a confectionery company, her career path led her to making products at a company.

Soon after beginning her job in production, she started living by herself in an apartment. However, her work hours were so long that after a while, she found that her day consisted solely of work and commuting between her apartment and the company. By the time she got home, she was exhausted. Everyday seemed monotonous. Though she wanted to change the situation, she didn't know how. She obsessed over questions she couldn't answer, and this raised her anxiety.

Back at A Food Company, a year had passed since the start of the restructuring campaign, and the CEO pays a visit to Julie at the production line.

"We are seeking presenters for an upcoming event to be attended by representatives from some major companies." To Julie's surprise, he asks, "Will you be one of the presenters?"

As the representative of a company, presenting to an audience consisting of reps from other larger companies is hard and comes with high risk. The CEO hopes that the outcome of her presentation is increased motivation among the employees at A Food Company. Of course, he assures her that everyone, including the section chief, will support her however they can.

There are two options being considered for the topic of the presentation. One is on quality control. The other is on the so-called "*Genba* Management Conference & Award."

Based on the activity of A Food, it seems it will be more suitable for the presentations to be on the "*Genba* Management Conference & Award." This is for front-line supervisors, but they say they are still wondering if it is appropriate to have a presentation competing with the other presenters from the larger companies.

Presentations by Production Supervisors are usually by each person presenting practical cases of how he or she approached certain matters, like managing and training team members.

A front-line supervisor is the leader of the production workplace.

Revolving around the theme of "Growing with the team members in implementing *Kaizen*," two titles being considered for A Food Company's presentation are as follows:

- How has Julie progressed as a leader in instilling *Kaizen* in every member of her team?
- The growth of the production team functioning as one unit through *Kaizen*.

Julie understands how tough of a task it would be to be a presenter of either of these topics, yet at the same time, she relishes the opportunity. She's still debating.

Later, she receives a follow-up letter from Mr. Takeuchi, who wrote the following:

"Some believe that TPS doesn't apply to some companies under the assumption that the system is originally for the auto and affiliated industries, or that the way of implementing, practicing, and maintaining the system effectively requires an unrealistically high level of diligence. Adopting a tool-typed system, if needed, sometimes runs the danger of becoming unstable if anyone in the operations were to misunderstand its goals.

However, the idea of TPS will work for almost any industry if all you are trying to do is pursue the ideal state – a rational production system.

I visited south Asia recently, and I noticed that the number of companies that want to adopt TPS is increasing.

However, I told them that trying to adopt the system just because it's a business trend may ultimately result in failure. My concern is that on the surface, it may seem a company has successfully implemented TPS, but in reality, this system they've implemented lacks soul or vision.

Only a surface-level imitation of TPS without the proper understanding and attention to its underlying motivations will more than likely, at the very least, result in little or no improvement in operations. We cannot expect success in such cases.

However, what leaders who follow TPS should try to obtain seems to be, I say a bit hesitatingly, not a particular skill but a personal principal. This principal is something that those tasked with implementing TPS should realize or develop on their own individually. What principal drives their efforts depends on each leader. What is certain is that for TPS to be effective, leaders must individually take charge of where they are assigned by strictly observing the operations and swiftly addressing any problems that may arise."

Part II

Overview of the Purpose of the Toyota Production System

2

Trigger

Mr. Takeuchi works at an automobile components maker.

He was chosen as one of TPS apprentices at a manager tier. He had experienced a sad situation when a big flood disaster occurred, and he will remember this situation repeatedly in the future.

It's raining like a waterfall. There is no other way to describe it.

Usually, it takes no longer than 20 minutes to the main factory by car. However, he is driving carefully due to the weather. There have recently been many occasions of going to the outside of his company using car. Though he is foremost a technical expert, he sometimes thinks of himself as a salesman visiting his clients. That is because he has been going in and outside the company frequently as a *Kaizen* instructor for the factory.

Takeuchi belongs to the Operations Management Consulting Division (OMCD) at the East Automotive Co. Ltd. A few years have passed since he became a manager.

Today, he has some companies to visit.

"Thanks, Mr. Takeuchi," he said as he got in the back-seat. He soon begins to casually mention, "Believe it or not, I owe some money."

In the passenger seat, sits a slender woman slightly over 20.

Among his old friends, some have children who are of the woman's age, Mr. Takeuchi thought. In his own case, his child is still in elementary school.

Since a few days ago, many houses in his hometown were badly flooded.

In the main factory he belongs to, there was an in-house announcement to encourage employees to go home early because the rain was getting stronger as evening approached, yet Mr. Takeuchi had one document he needed to submit by tomorrow. After working overtime and completing what he needs to do, he heads to the parking lot, where only

DOI: 10.4324/9781003323310-5

a few cars remained. The flooding has risen up to the bottom of the door of his car. The car is actually floating a little. Upon opening the door, it settled back down for a moment, making a sound similar to air leaking from a tire. The water level is highest around the exit of the parking lot. He floors it to propel the car through the exit. He luckily finds a detour that allow him to make it home, but upon arriving, he finds out his house is flooded as well.

The next day, scenes of flooding around his hometown are broadcast nation-wide.

"Last night, the Shinkawa River, which runs through A city, overflowed its banks!"

According to news reports, this is heavy rains that happen only once in a hundred years.

Then a phone call comes from the company's contact network.

"What? The whole operation is down?" replies Mr. Takeuchi.

Due to this deluge, one of our factories has been flooded, and that has shut down operations there. The main factory, however, has largely escaped unscathed. The production information system computer along with production machinery have been seriously damaged at the crippled factory. The factories of a cooperative company nearby have also been flooded.

The East Automotive Co. is a subsidiary of a major automotive company, a so-called *keiretsu*, or "series."

Therefore, the halting of the *keiretsu* company's operation directly affects the production line of their main parent company. Under the *Kanban* System, no issue with assembly line parts should ever cause a disruption in production.

Pundits on TV are saying that shortages in the supply of stock are one of the major drawbacks of the *Kanban* System, seizing the recent events as an opportunity to point this out. This kind of criticism has become inevitable and commonplace whenever disruptive natural disasters occur.

Originally, the *Kanban* System was designed to be able to ensure minimal disruptions in the event of a disaster. However, there are few who understand this aspect of the system. Suppose you had a fire in a warehouse with a full inventory of assembly parts, the loss would be huge.

Yet, the division of OMCD, which Mr. Takeuchi belongs to, has to be the first responder to problems, and this means promptly going to the *Genba* (the production workplace) when disasters strike. As it is such a rare occurrence, very few can truly grasp how formidable of a task it is to mitigate disasters until experiencing one.

Mr. Takeuchi has been assigned just such a task at the factory of a company in the cooperative, and to which 50 workers belong. As representatives of the parent company tasked with leading the recovery efforts, he and a colleague head directly to the factory. If they are lucky, they may be able to go home by evening.

He is constantly exiting and entering the two-story factory, while taking a never-ending flow of phone calls. There is no time to take a lunch break.

At last, a rare lull in the day may provide him a fleeting opportunity to dig into the lunch box prepared by a CEO's wife, who suggested he eat it before it gets too cold.

His day often does not end until after midnight. And so dinners at 3 am are not at all unusual, nor are trips back to the factory after only a few hours of sleep.

This cycle, as extreme as it can be, has become the day-to-day routine in his life.

As this work stoppage was caused by a rare emergency, the labor managers are in the process of implementing special measures to cope.

Every worker at the factory, including manager, is expected to cooperate fully under the temporary policies.

Yet, the factory manager of the cooperating company has been lazy in taking any positive actions himself, and arrogantly says that it's natural a parent company helps its own subsidiary company. As the representative of headquarters assigned to support this disaster-stricken facility, Takeuchi doesn't respond. This is Takeuchi's way of mitigating the effect of a situation such as this.

A technical specialist sent from headquarters manages to repair the machinery. However, they have to make up for the lost time in production.

Adding to the pressure, the Assistant Manager in the Procurement Section from one of the client companies visits the factory every day and reports back to his headquarters the status of their order's production.

He is full of energy with an outgoing attitude, as is expected from those who come from Procurement.

After the Assistant Manager returns from the countermeasures meeting held at the main factory, he suddenly kicks one of the office chairs with all of his strength, yelling at Mr. Takeuchi.

"It was reported at the meeting that the factory didn't have any problems. No staff there have come here to report the situation. However, just looking at this report, how can you say there are no problems?" he asks, showing a report from the factory.

The meeting consists of the president of the East Automotive Co. as well as major staff members. A board member of the client company, who is the Assistant Manager's boss, also took part in the meeting.

The Assistant Manager becomes irritated, telling Mr. Takeuchi that one shouldn't be able to present a report at the meeting without observing the site at all.

Mr. Takeuchi loses control of his emotions and for the first time in his life, tears wells up in his eyes. He just cannot understand how anyone can think production issues could be resolved through a simple document without even going to see the *Genba* (production workplace).

The person who issued the report in the meeting is in a managerial position belonging to one division of the East Automotive Co. Previously in the parent company, only a handful of workers were under his age, and his position garnered little respect.

It seems the report was based solely on a phone conversation with the cooperating factory chief. Mr. Takeuchi himself was never asked for input.

It was only through catching wind from the client company's representative that Mr. Takeuchi become aware of all that was reported. He wasn't even given the chance to offer his perspective on the problems anyway.

Upon realizing that the report made claims far from what was actually going on, he supposes that he is perceived as a person struggling with managing the situation at the *Genba* (production workplace), and so the meeting members assembles for what is called "An Imperial Conference."

It seems the CEO's verdict was also judgment of his competency in handling the factory situation. In fact, his instructions are precise and clear.

It's been said that many organizations when faced with disaster suffer from a lack of leadership. However, this time, the company is lucky to have someone skilled and experienced at the top to limit the damage caused by the flooding. It was just recently that he had come from the parent company.

What makes Mr. Takeuchi extremely annoyed are the board members who had been brought up by our company.

For instance, suppose Mr. Takeuchi had explained the problems politely to the board members because they were told by their CEO to investigate the extent of the damage and delays. Upon realizing that the reporting process would be very tiring, they would say to Mr. Takeuchi,

"Well, regarding the reporting of these matters to the CEO, we'll leave it to you."

His frustration comes to the fore as he wonders, "What on earth did they come here for?"

They seem to be all talk and no action. These days, most of the executive officers do is just put their stamp or signature on documents.

These executive officers, often in manufacturing, have been sitting at the top and collecting high salaries for so long that they wind up becoming incapable of innovating or coping with problems as they arise.

Any persons lacking in a particular "belief" in their own work principles wouldn't be able to cope with emerging situations that require a swift response.

Normally, this "management style" of stamping approval and doling out meritless advice would be allowed to continue without a raised eyebrow from anyone. In fact, "Major-scaled" companies would tolerate those types of managers and even regard each of them as "a manager who has strong leadership ability."

Yet, the type of people who are most capable of dealing with emergent situations should actually be highly capable of doing anything asked of them, at least those with a strong conviction toward ensuring the integrity of the manufacturing process.

From the moment the flooding shut down the cooperative company's factory, Mr. Takeuchi, who became the most important person at the site, has been trying to cope with a wide number of issues in attempting to get the factory back to normal.

He himself thinks his duties liken him to a soldier who's been forced to stand and do battle at the frontline.

Before anything, making up for the production delay is necessary.

Firstly comes the scheduling of the employees, determined by the workers' individual employment status within the company, which can be either regular or temporary. In the 24-hour operating schedule, regular employees are given preferential treatment, and therefore the preferred daytime operating shift. Temporary employees are left taking turns staffing the nighttime and overnight shifts.

It's another rainy night. We hadn't had any rainy days since the downpour that caused the flooding. As the night becomes deeper, the rain becomes heavier. An evacuation order is issued in the factory. There is no choice but to call off the scheduled nightshift production, by way of an executive order from headquarters.

When Mr. Takeuchi tries to go home, he notices the silhouette of some workers standing about. He finds out that they are young workers from the temp staffing agency.

Basically, staffing agencies are responsible for their own staff's work shifts.

"We were told to go to the main factory of the East Automotive Co. by taxi," the eldest of the workers says.

It's obvious that no taxi would make it through the flooding, especially so deep into the night.

The staffing company is being nonsensical issuing such an order to their employees. Mr. Takeuchi has no choice but to give them a ride, though their destination is in the opposite direction to his home.

For the first few minutes of the ride, he tries to engage them in conversation. However, they gradually become silent, perhaps due to the mood brought on by the heavy rain.

"You know what? I was in debt for a few million yen," the man, who was the leader of the team, says while seated in the back.

He is telling the man sitting next to him in the backseat that an unfortunate event had caused him to incur this debt. It is not the kind of topic one should be speaking so proudly of. However, he insists that he is succeeding in reducing his debt thanks to the salary from the staffing company, which he claims is a fair amount.

He blathers on and on. The voices sound like they are coming from afar because of the competing patter of the heavy rain.

There is a female staff member in this temp group. She sits in the passenger seat and keeps her silence.

She seems to be a shade over 20 years old, pretty with long flowing hair, yet whose disposition hints at a level of gloominess or frailty. One might even wonder if her body's shell was composed of nothing but glass.

It's already past midnight.

Mr. Takeuchi's driving is deliberate as the car plunges through the heavy rain.

The young woman, gazing at the darkness outside, seems uninterested in the conversations in the car.

Then suddenly,

"My father has left me," she murmured.

That was why she had to find a job. Though girls of her age normally would go to school dressed in neat clothes, she is now in a car heading to a factory she has never before seen, and at midnight.

Although these days, it is not uncommon for female workers to work the midnight shift, Mr. Takeuchi, being old-school, prefers that this temp worker not do so.

Females working the nightshift is becoming more accepted as competition from foreign markets forces many companies to find any willing body to staff shifts that will keep factories churning 24 × 7.

When Mr. Takeuchi first started working at his company, the number of workplaces that were open to hiring females at all was very limited. That kind of production workplace was mainly for assembly work, and the women who worked there were mostly of post-child rearing age. Since then, the number of production workplaces with nightshifts has gradually become larger, as competition among companies within Japan has become more intense.

Now, due to the stoppage at their original factory, these temporary workers have been forced to move to the main factory to work. The temp staffing agency has contracts with the East Automotive Co. so the temporary workers were sent to work in their several factories.

The availability of a labor force to work at all hours enables the companies to keep running uninterrupted.

In manufacturing especially, under the specter of increasingly intense global competition, such workers have become even more crucial.

One wonders: Are we on earth creating a society that is kind to workers?

While having such thoughts in his mind, Mr. Takeuchi pulls the car up to the main factory.

Mr. Takeuchi says good-bye to them, somewhat hesitatingly.

It has been a while since the last time he visited here.

He pays a visit to the assembly of officials charged with deciding the countermeasures to the disaster. They occupy an area sectioned off in one corner of the factory floor. There is a simple-designed conference table and a number of folding chairs scattered in the makeshift area. The factory floor itself only has a few people.

"Long time no see, Mr. Takeuchi," the chief, one of Mr. Takeuchi's colleagues, says. The chief is positioned on the main factory as a staff to support the OMCD members at the other factories whose operations have been disrupted by the disaster.

On several free-standing bulletin boards are notices regarding the current situation and the countermeasure schedules.

With all of the countermeasures decided, it can be argued that the hardest part of countering the disaster has been achieved.

The current issue now is exactly when all of the operations will return to normal.

An initial assessment of the effects of the countermeasures seems to indicate a recovery quicker than what would normally and reasonably be expected, perhaps owing to the flexible support from the clients.

The CEO's skillful decision-making abilities seems to have contributed greatly to the success of getting factory operations back on track.

On the other hand, it should be noted that among all parties involved, some carried their weight, while others did not.

Certain parties did absolutely nothing, instead simply waiting for the passing of time.

There were also people who offered guidance that was neither helpful nor practical.

After all, how is one able to assess the situation of a factory beset by disaster without so much as setting foot in the factory? We should adhere to the principle of *Genchi-Gembutsu* taught by TPS.

Mr. Takeuchi strongly doubts it is possible, after himself struggling to get operations back online as a frontline member of OMCD.

3

Purpose

Mr. Takeuchi is devoting himself to the TPS activity as a general manager.

He travels around the world as a person in charge of the global TPS division in order to raise the global sister companies.

Sometime around New Years, Mr. Takeuchi arrives at a hotel, one apparently of historical significance, in a foreign country.

The ground floor restaurant is packed at dinner, with even more customers waiting near the entrance. Placing an order would take ages to make.

As well, he is an absolute stranger here, so he goes back to his room to enjoy some biscuits he purchased earlier with his favorite tea.

After breakfast, he is picked up by a member of his company's staff, an expat, to be escorted to a factory in the suburbs.

"It's been a while, Mr. Takeuchi," the staff member says.

Before he was transferred to this foreign land, this staff member used to belong to the same department as Mr. Takeuchi's. He seems to have adjusted well, though his current position and need to stay in contact with headquarters in Japan force him to pull overnighters because of the time difference.

Upon arriving at the factory, Mr. Takeuchi realizes that the place is not functioning as a "factory" at all.

The building looks grand with some accoutrements many would consider luxuries, but Mr. Takeuchi is not there to admire the facilities.

He was sent there because he was told the factory needs a complete restructuring due to problems with management.

A staff concerned in the factory, upon hearing Mr. Takeuchi was planning to be in the neighboring country, expressly asked that he visit the site – a visit scheduled to span a couple of days.

His mission is to improve operations in the Production Division.

DOI: 10.4324/9781003323310-6

The Japanese staff working at the site understand the severity of the situation, yet they are at a loss as to how to deal with it.

Mr. Takeuchi hopes to craft an effective plan after his tour and observation of the *Genba*.

His two days at the *Genba* will be spent observing with his own eyes and hearing from the staff about the state of operations.

Though he has made it clear that he will only be an observer this time, he guesses that the local staff expect him to do more. They expect to receive advice that will enable them to eventually right this ship.

Yet if it was a matter that could be corrected immediately with some simple advice, the staff wouldn't be struggling like this.

It often happens that though the situation observed is the same, the perception of what is happening depends on who is doing the observing. This leads to recommendations that vary depending on the person doing the observing.

At a dinner meeting with the resident staff, Mr. Takeuchi tries to patiently listen to their opinions.

His task upon his return to Japan is to devise a plan that factors all of what he saw and heard into a plan of action.

He is then expected to oversee the task of implementing his plan, estimated to take approximately two years.

The hotel where he is staying reveals its age with the floor sloping a little, yet the atmosphere and the structure are tranquil.

Tomorrow night, he will leave for the region where he had originally planned to spend time.

It is already midnight, but he is still awake lying on his bed. Perhaps it's jetlag.

Under the dim lights in his room, he's been gazing at the pictures which adorn the worn wallpaper.

Twenty years have passed since Mr. Takeuchi started working for the East Automotive Co.

His thoughts now drift back to when he was a graduate student.

It was a harsh, cold era for students job-hunting.

Without much thought, he accepted an offer from the East Automotive Co., giving up university as a result to begin his employment there early.

He once thought of staying in university and devoting his life to academia, as was suggested to him by one of his professors. However, he opted to start working in the hopes of eventually becoming an entrepreneur and contributing to society.

The mission he set for himself was that one day he will design and surely release products that will be useful to many people.

His industriousness was evident in university as he held part-time jobs which enabled him to pay for his tuition and living expenses on his own. He even managed to build some savings as a result. He studied hard in university partly to show his commitment and gratitude to his parents for allowing him to go to university, despite his family's lack of finances. He was also fortunate to get accepted to a graduate school in a big city, albeit far away, and was luckily allowed to receive a national student loan. His savings and the student loan enabled him to rent an apartment for two years while in graduate school.

"I see you're not well-off financially. If you go to a doctoral course in the U.S., you should try to get another scholarship there," the professor advised upon suggesting that he continue his studies. However, his family's financial situation eventually proved to be too difficult to overcome, thereby forcing him to abandon any thoughts of continuing his education. Further academic studies were out of the question.

That was why he was eternally grateful to his country for the financial support that enabled him to study until he completed graduate school.

After starting working, his income was high enough where it was possible for him to repay his student loan earlier than planned, but he opted to stretch out his repayment schedule.

"Because I want to repay with my gratitude every year," he used to say to his wife.

He realized that even though he was raised in a poor family, he was very lucky to have been able to continue his studies at university.

He owes his chance to work at his company to that opportunity.

From very early in his tenure, Takeuchi has been assigned important duties at his workplace.

However, his will to contribute to society has remained steadfast throughout.

Ever eager to meet his company's demands when carrying out his duties, he focuses on practical methods that can bear immediate fruit and stays away from matters that one might deem "academic."

As in every company, the East Automotive Co. as well has some employees who lack the drive to work hard. In fact, their actions are so counterproductive that they often become a drag on overall productivity.

To generously put it, what they were doing at work had very little meaning.

During his early days working at his company, Mr. Takeuchi had numerous opportunities to finish out his university. He was only one thesis short of graduating. His former professor from university was willing to assist him with it.

Yet, Mr. Takeuchi decided not to pursue it any further, as he decided to focus his energy on the mission he had set for himself when entering his company. Also, given his immediate tasks, it was hardly possible for him to do otherwise. As part of the company's efforts to shake up personnel and improve productivity, he volunteered to be assigned to work at the factory.

When he started working for the company, he had a strong desire to one day be the person to lead the company forward. Surely, no enterprise can survive and thrive without starting new ventures and updating its offerings.

Mr. Takeuchi, asked to be an Assistant Manager at the factory, also became one of the workers there.

That experience gave him insight into the inner workings on the production side of his company, where he has remained focused.

Being a worker at the factory also allowed him to gain a perspective from a technician's point of view, and it was through this he started noticing that some steps in the production process were not ideal. At first glance, one could easily fault the workers. However, it turned out that the blame laid in the facility and production process themselves.

Mr. Takeuchi kept on working diligently at the factory without complaining, all in the interest of reconnaissance.

The East Automotive Co. has adopted a production method called "the East Production System." Per the client company's instructions, the East Automotive Co. has officially studied and been practicing the Toyota Production System.

To "truly" understand the goal and the ideal of TPS is no small feat.

Toyota's methods have been heavily criticized for being applicable only to big companies.

There are certainly times Mr. Takeuchi thought these criticisms were on point. Indeed, TPS is still an evolving process. However, the key to accepting TPS lies in understanding such concepts as "Respect for People." So what is behind the criticism then?

TPS' origin can be traced back to a looming machine. The founder of Toyota, Sakichi Toyoda, designed a new looming machine to help reduce his own mother's workload. He was also driven by his desire to lift his family out of poverty, a state they had been in throughout the Meiji Period more than 100 years ago.

Mr. Takeuchi cannot help but think that criticisms of TPS are borne from misunderstandings of its underlying principles. Unsurprisingly, people instead tend to notice the impact of TPS on their everyday work life, rather than the trickle-down effect of TPS on operations as a whole.

The term *Haken-Giri* literally means slashing temporary workers, and it has become an issue. In one case, a TPS instructor said that he unsuccessfully tried to dissuade managers at certain jobsites from cutting their temporary labor force, who seemed to think *Haken-Giri* was a means to improve productivity.

Instead of staff cutting, however, TPS emphasizes reallocating resources to improve efficiency. This means that prior to letting temp staff go, attempts should be made to reassign them to areas where they may add value to overall operations.

Human resources are never to be regarded simply as manpower, or a cost that can be easily cut.

In reality, though, this is how many companies regard their staffing.

Perhaps under pressure, managers take the easy way out by simply reducing staff rather than exercise due diligence to see if what they are doing is really in the best interests of their company.

This tendency is especially indicative of companies that have little or no respect toward their workers, especially those on the frontlines of production.

This way of thinking is surely a major problem. The result is actions taken by managers that wind up doing more harm than good, where low-waged temporary workers are just used and discarded.

In today's globally competitive market, human resources have been treated like a "throw-away camera."

Suddenly, one image pops into Mr. Takeuchi's mind: the young female worker he gave a ride to that one evening in the rain.

Nowadays in Japan, one out of three women live in poverty.

Surely, the main reason is because of the current economic slow-down, which makes job-hunting difficult for the younger generation. However, it can also partly be attributed to the trend of replacing human resources more easily.

Compared to back when most of the Japanese were extremely poor, one might say the current situation is much better. But comparisons to the past should best be avoided for the time being when analyzing current conditions.

One only needs to look at the handful of people who are unimaginably rich and wealthy.

The world today is full of examples of people who are well-off as a result of hard work and perseverance.

If that wasn't the case, the world can be justifiably deemed as unfair.

Such a complex world we live in. Nevertheless, Takeuchi still is in search of the "better way."

He lies awake in his hotel room, with a stream of thoughts circling like a merry-go-round in his head.

Gradually, these thoughts and images blend with a picture of flowers hanging on the wall. The room is shaded in a red glow, and his thoughts become a chaotic mess.

4

Consideration

Mr. Takeuchi has been continuing to teach and learn the TPS ideology as a freelance consultant.

"Mr. Takeuchi, we were really shocked to hear about the earthquake." The person speaking to Mr. Takeuchi is referring to the great earthquake that hit East Japan in 2011.

"Thank you for your concern, and also for calling us at that time," Mr. Takeuchi says.

Here, in this developing country, he is shown the room of the factory's CEO.

On his hearing the news, the CEO had called Japan to tell Takeuchi that he thought the Japanese people were surely unbreakable and would overcome this disaster.

He was brought up to become a CEO by the same company. It was extremely uncommon for anyone in his country to continue working at the same company and reach an upper management position if they had graduated from university. The fact the CEO did just that was a testament to his hard work and ambition. Yet here, continuing at the same company seems to be a very rare case indeed, even if the CEO, who has a degree from a famous and highly-ranked university, seems to have been happy working at several of the top enterprises.

The company manufactures car engines, thanks to the technological support provided by headquarters in Japan. That experience taught the CEO about just how hard Japanese people work.

Seeking to implement the Manufacturing Renovation system at the production site, he has decided to ask a Japanese consultant for a guidance. As one of the leaders in this developing country, he exhibits a high degree of exuberance.

DOI: 10.4324/9781003323310-7

Something needed to be done to connect the dots, so calling on Mr. Takeuchi for his assistance was the answer.

Six months have passed since he was assigned to this factory.

The memory of that night in the heavy rain seems like a long time ago.

After the flooding disaster, he had a chance to visit this developing country. There, he began to wonder if he could somehow use his knowledge and experience in Japan to not only help with their manufacturing, but in doing so, to contribute in some way in their fight against poverty. This was the impetus behind his quitting the East Automotive Co. and becoming a freelance consultant.

Now, he is lunching with the factory's CEO.

From their conversation, Takeuchi can glean that the CEO is rather humble.

"Mr. Takeuchi, what has been the current state of manufacturing in Japan?"

"The word *Monodzukuri*, making things, is an oft-used term in Japan. When translated, it means 'manufacturing,' but in Japan, it is more than that. It perhaps means manufacturing with the Japanese soul, and whereby pride in this may call for the translation to be 'Manufacturing' with a capital 'M.' When we hear the word *Monodzukuri* in Japan, we feel how Japanese tradition and craftsmanship are able to powerfully influence the world of mass production.

You may have heard that the population, especially the working-age population, has been decreasing in Japan. And Japan is a country that cannot thrive without exporting its products and services due to the scarcity of natural resources," Takeuchi finished up his answer.

"I imagine that the flood disaster 6 months ago left a big scar, right?"

"The disaster not only exposed the supply chain problems but also issues with the manufacturing process itself. Even before the disaster, those in the manufacturing industry had already been debating the future of Manufacturing in Japan. Specifically, they wondered: How should Japan shape Manufacturing in the midst of global competition."

"You mean Manufacturing in the global environment, right?" the CEO asks.

"Right. The manufacturing companies of Japan, the EU, and the U.S. have moved operations to developing countries, to be more competitive.

You may have heard the phrase 'locally produced and consumed' (*Chisan-Chisho*). I wondered at first why we had to open local factories in foreign countries.

However, gradually I came to think that having foreign factories offered many benefits.

For example, it could produce jobs for local people paying fair salaries, but with the labor cost still much lower than if produced in Japan. This enables customers to buy their products at reasonable prices, and in turn, the Japanese enterprises earn substantial profits. So far, nothing should be wrong.

Unfortunately, Japan and other developed countries have seen a 'hollowing out' of numerous industries where manufacturing has been shipped abroad, all for the sake of staying globally competitive.

As a result, it has become increasingly difficult for these developed countries to maintain the actual number of jobs in the homeland.

The harsh reality is it's always the end workers who pay the price. The company's size doesn't matter. It's the same fate that befalls workers in all types of companies in developed countries.

Thus, manufacturing has shifted drastically to global production, to remain competitive in the global marketplace. Whether one likes it or not, the Manufacturing process itself seems to be undergoing an irreversible change. As well, the production method of many models in small quantities is in more demand now than the conventional mass production methods of larger quantities popular in the past.

Therefore, it's been determined in developed countries that this should be the method of manufacturing."

"What do you mean by that?" the CEO asks.

"Well, I guess the simplest analogy is sports, whereby manufacturing can be divided into two major parts: an 'offense' and a 'defense.'

An 'offense' means to create something 'new.'

This includes all kinds of new creations from industries – finished products being the culmination of lots of research and development (R&D).

On the other hand, a 'defense' means trying to make the existing Manufacturing process increasingly better.

It's an ongoing process to find ways to provide better products at reasonable prices to consumers. In short, the goal is always to be 'more efficient.' For manufacturing to progress, safety and quality are paramount. Nothing else should take precedence. Making sacrifices shouldn't be an option, although these days, manufacturing seems to be following a different philosophy.

Only when both the offense and defense work in unison can we say that *Monodzukuri* (Manufacturing) in Japan is in a position to affect business the world over," Takeuchi said.

"How has TPS been perceived in the *Monodzukuri* (Manufacturing) industry?"

"I'm not in a position to be able to say that TPS, at least in its current state, is the Manufacturing ideal. Moreover, forcing workers to abide by the rules and philosophy of TPS, especially with a raised voice or intimidation, is counter-productive, and simply wrong.

We have seen the emergence of many methods of manufacturing throughout history, and none more revolutionary than Ford's system of mass production.

More recent analysis of manufacturing shows that the Toyota Production System is at its core a quest for efficiency.

Yet, I think that there still might be better methods of *Monodzukuri* (Manufacturing).

However, I have searched for this better way, and so far, nothing yet rivals TPS.

The antithesis of TPS is a production workplace whose issues are rooted in its pursuit of cost-cutting at all costs, even of its human resources.

So for starters, a proper understanding of TPS is needed.

It is necessary to understand its basic concept, which starts with a willingness and ability to thoroughly investigate any problems at the actual production workplace.

Although it may seem the only goal of TPS is efficiency, there are other elements, such as respecting your workforce, and pursuing ideals.

All of these elements, working in unison, help create a better work environment overall – one that above all, shows consideration for people, which is the true foundation of '*Kaizen*'.

In reality, and regretfully, mostly people try to practice it without fully understanding what truly makes it successful," Takeuchi explains.

"What do you mean by 'practice it without fully understanding it'?"

"For example, even in big enterprises that have officially implemented TPS as their guiding principle, I have seen TPS 'instructors' whose words and actions betray a complete misunderstanding of TPS principles.

Luckily, they have managed to keep things running due to many years of getting by using an already established mode of operations. I wonder if any person in that organization has any understanding of TPS' principles.

The same can be said not only of TPS, but of other aspects regarding *Monodzukuri* (Manufacturing)," says Takeuchi.

"I guess the issue is personnel training," the CEO says.

"The important thing is whether TPS practitioners are truly understood or not. They do try to execute it to some extent when instructed to do so. However, it becomes apparent that they actually do not understand what it is they are being instructed to do, and this belies a proper understanding of TPS. Sometimes, their actions run counter to the TPS ideals.

Goals should be made clear. And there should always be the belief that today should be better than yesterday. For these purposes, every practitioner needs to be educated properly.

With proper execution of TPS, and by tasting the fruits of resulting success and realizing its potential, one can gain clarity in the next steps to take.

This sequence is possible only if TPS is properly taught from the beginning.

For instance, when confronted with 'excess inventory,' some leaders fail to realize the extent to which this is just *Muda* (Waste), while others simply shrug their shoulders and think having a large stock of items in inventory is natural. In either case, efficiency of operations is jeopardized, as often, chaos befalls manufacturers even in the absence of something seemingly as simple as deciding an appropriate level of inventory of materials based on projected need.

It is apparent that in either case, the leader is in need of training or re-training on what TPS really is."

"I can see that you are really bothered over companies seemingly not being humane, or showing a lack of respect towards their workforce," the CEO surmised.

"That is correct. It is the essence of the goal of TPS.

Yet, I still feel that for many companies, reaching that goal is still elusive, and could be why it is often criticized.

It is important to realize that TPS is an ongoing process, and companies who implement it must be ready to accept that.

And, in order to reach the ideals of quality and safety, etc., it is essential to remember the concept of the 'Standardized Work'.

When seen in action, Standardized Work is about efficient production through repetition. Its original intent is to lower the workload of each worker, by having them do certain tasks repetitively until it can be done easily and almost instinctually. However, managers sometimes force the workers to perform actions that are inefficient and even unnecessary, but saying they still must be performed as decreed by the company.

Due to their lack of knowledge of *Kaizen*, companies become obsessed only with efficiency, and in their attempts to strengthen the skills of their labor force, they neglect to reduce the workers' workload – a potentially costly error.

Yet, the burden of responsibility falls on the workers to make the system work.

The prevailing attitude in production nowadays is that the human workforce is simply part of the machinery in factories. Many of these companies forget that production success is often achieved due to the flexibility of humans.

This attitude can lead to production breakdowns company-wide.

Perhaps the simplest way for management to realize the value of their workforce is to ask: Would you really do the same thing towards your own children?"

"I have heard the terminology: 'deepening the Toyota Production System.'"

"That is correct. Typically, it is called either the 'evolution' or 'deepening' of *Monodzukuri* (Manufacturing).

It means that although its form will change gradually in continued pursuit of the ideal process, the philosophy of TPS should stay the same."

"Could you give me some ideas on how the people who are involved with Manufacturing should learn TPS," the CEO asks.

"It is better to learn from practical experience.

Of course, gaining the proper knowledge is very important.

However, the knowledge by itself is still not enough to realize the true ability of TPS to transform the workplace. Only through first-hand experiences will it become apparent.

I myself am still continuously developing my knowledge and abilities in pursuit of constant improvement of Manufacturing.

In reality, so many problems have been piling up at many factories.

Solving these problems requires a sense of urgency.

For the ideal to be reached, it is necessary to be at the *Genba* (production workplace) and to show consideration for the people working there.

Pursuit of flexible means of Manufacturing that are widely applicable and sustainable, even when operations are in other cultures, should also be sought.

We should also be conscious of what our elders have already established regarding Manufacturing.

And to those who are just beginning their training in TPS, support should be provided by everyone around the workplace.

The belief that Manufacturing is very important to all of world should be held by all involved.

Together, with a common will and vision, we can move forward.

As I am still learning TPS, however, the attitude of 'Now or Never' propels me to be a 'communicator' or 'interpreter' of the ways and means of Manufacturing and TPS." Takeuchi concludes.

Mr. Takeuchi speaks with conviction, inspiration, and commitment, which come from his strong reverence for the pioneers and elders who for many, many years worked tirelessly to build Manufacturing to where it is so revered in the country.

Journey Two

Meditation Journey

LEARNING THE TPS IDEOLOGY BY TRIAL AND ERROR

– Weaving the Toyota Production System into the R&D stage –

In this journey, the story progresses with *Kanban*, which is one of the tools of factory management, so that readers can easily understand the outline of the ideology in the Toyota Production System, known as TPS.

The main character invents a new component, and afterwards he begins to struggle with the Toyota Production System in order to successfully launch its mass production. He is struggling with the question, "What is TPS?" and he continues to have on uneasy feeling.

He learns that TPS is not only useful in the "follow-up" activity as the means of continuous improvement in the production workplace, but also TPS should be woven into the activity "in advance" at upstream stages like R&D or production preparation. He knows TPS' underlying pursuit is to reach the pinnacle of ideal manufacturing, whereby a manufacturer can provide a product whenever requested by the customer.

DOI: 10.4324/9781003323310-8

Part III

Encountering the Toyota Production System

5

Prologue

The East Automotive Co. is a tier-one supplier of a leading automaker.

Here, Takeuchi has several positions. In addition to being an up-and-coming technical expert, he doubles as Assistant Project Manager in the R&D Division and Assistant Manager in the Production Engineering Development Division.

He just turned 37 years old, and has a wife, two sons, and one daughter. Recently, he's been so focused on his work that he once bluntly responded to his wife about his lack of assistance with child-rearing tasks, "Just consider me dead."

One morning deep, in autumn, Takeuchi, sitting at his desk, leaned back in his chair and let out a big sigh.

The day before, he visited the person in charge of the Production Management Division to ask a favor, and it didn't go over well. The department is said to be a special division of the company's original production system.

The R&D group which Takeuchi leads has developed a particularly unique finished product after a few years of R&D. The product was highly praised at its unveiling – an event attended by many clients and other guests. The product was displayed on a rotating platform so onlookers could gain a clear understanding of its features. Takeuchi gave a presentation to the attendees that was polite and detailed, but he also quipped, "Behold the future of displays."

As the event was coming to a close, Takeuchi finished up his presentation, at which point the Managing Director of R&D approached him.

He asked Takeuchi to start planning the product's assembly line, even though no orders had yet been formally received.

DOI: 10.4324/9781003323310-10

This was not unusual, as Takeuchi submitted a business plan for a different product the year prior. There was actually a time in this company's history when "creating a business plan" did not exist. The year before when Takeuchi submitted his plan, the Managing Director said simply, "I saw many educational elements in this. Well done." And then he promptly returned the pages of the plan to Takeuchi. Perhaps it was his first time to see such a thing. Anyway, that was his professional way of saying, "Thanks, but no thanks."

Before this period of devising production plans, it was not unusual for the company's automotive products to be manufactured with malfunctions. One such malfunction resulted in reducing drivers' visibility – a seemingly simple yet critical necessity. What Takeuchi developed in his plan was a way to address the inconsistencies in the production process that often led to malfunctions. This included dealing with issues in the process prior to the product being produced on the assembly line.

It was not easy to get the products to a point where they could be considered suitable for sale, much less usable, out in the market. At the unveiling, the product was just at the point where it was ready for assembly line production, this after some new manufacturing techniques were developed. Several necessary machines had been developed by working with machine builders.

The result was a product that looked a little awkward, and so it became the target of criticism. This seems only natural considering the laboratory-like environment of that product's unveiling, in which attendees came ready to scrutinize what they were examining. More or less at the beginning, every product, including liquid crystal panel displays and semiconductor equipment, had glaring imperfections – a point Takeuchi realized and aimed to fix.

His new business plan required a huge commitment and investment by his company, but it was ultimately approved at their board meeting. Takeuchi and his group then went about creating a production process – and ultimately, a product – the likes of which had never before been seen.

6

Encountering the Toyota Production System

When Takeuchi was still fledgling in the R&D Division, a book called *"TOYOTA PRODUCTION SYSTEM"* had been distributed to each staff person in the division. Written by Mr. Taiichi Ohno, it is a remarkable masterpiece that many in manufacturing and business still regard as a "Bible." This was also when the company had just started adopting the *"Kanban* System."

Initially, TPS was just a vague acronym to Takeuchi, who thought it was perhaps related to some matter regarding employees' lives. Quite simply, he didn't understand it upon his initial and cursory read. Who could blame him, as the book is notorious for pushing its readers to think deeply, and to make new discoveries with each subsequent reading.

On one sunny autumn day, Takeuchi was meeting Mr. Saitou in person, the latter regarded as an expert in production management. Some matters regarding the manufacturing of the new product had already been decided, but in deciding the actual machinery and facility to use, Takeuchi consulted a TPS expert for advice.

"Mr. Saitou, could you tell me how this project could be carried out under the TPS?"

"With TPS, eventually, you should be able to find an appropriate method somehow," Mr. Saitou answered. Takeuchi was taken aback, as it was a rather simple and unexpected response.

Upon hearing it, Takeuchi realized figuring out TPS was not going to be an easy task.

He replayed Mr. Saitou's words in his head: "Eventually, you should be able to find an appropriate method somehow." At the same time, a wave

DOI: 10.4324/9781003323310-11

of discouragement came over Takeuchi as he thought, "If there is no clear answer, then what should I do?" Little did he realize that he stood on the cusp of what would be a long journey toward understanding TPS.

These were to be processes and machinery which were wholly unfamiliar to the company prior. Takeuchi was able to surmise that Mr. Saitou was being sage by saying "Eventually, you should be able to find an appropriate method somehow."

Yet, Takeuchi was still disappointed and discouraged at the thought that there is no concrete way to apply TPS at his company. That was the irony in the company's decision to adopt the Toyota Production System: No one was able to lay out a clear path to properly implement it.

With this, the reality that there were no practical steps beyond the conceptual, that no user's manual was or was going to be available, that there was not going to be any hand-holding by expert practitioners, Takeuchi went about setting the wheels in motion on his own. It became apparent later that TPS instructors (*Sensei*) were mainly in the position of *Genba Kaizen* in existing production lines. Therefore, few were available to guide newcomers to the system.

Takeuchi would sometimes drift off into a deep state of thought – daydreaming. Once while in one of those states, out of nowhere, *Sensei* appeared, and proceeded to offer Takeuchi the enlightenment he had been seeking and needed.

-THE TERM "TPS"

"*Sensei*, in the first place, why is it called TPS?" Takeuchi asks.

"TPS stands for Toyota Production System. People call it 'TPS' affectionately."

"Well then, *Sensei*, it would seem that Toyota has a registered trademark on TPS, right?"

"In fact, it was some time in 1978 or thereabouts when a company first coined the term 'TPS.' As it turned out, the company's initials also started with the letter 'T.' At another company whose initials started with the letter 'N,' the employees there declared, 'Our production system is NPS.' For every company, there seemed to be an accompanying acronym for their production process: NPS for 'N' company, IPS for 'I' company, DPS for 'D' company, and so forth. That was the time Toyota's Production System started gaining popularity, which was due to Toyota's strength and resilience as an enterprise, this despite the oil shock of the 70s."

"Yes, that's right, *Sensei*. I often see articles in production magazines mentioning what you just described. Each company adopts an acronym to represent its own processes. In some cases, their systems appear to be different from Toyota's – a result of the situation and products unique to those companies," Takeuchi said.

"They were still based off of the Toyota Production System described by Mr. Ohno, the author of '*TOYOTA PRODUCTION SYSTEM.*' So now, if you hear the acronym TPS, it undoubtedly refers to 'Toyota Production System,' which has become standard in manufacturing at production sites all over. Alternatively, in management lingo, it is also referred to as 'PW': Production Way.

TPS itself is still evolving. Those involved in its evolution reason that it is not so much 'changing' as it is 'deepening.' The concept of TPS has layers of depth just waiting to be unearthed," *Sensei* said.

 ## -COMMITMENT TO THE TERM

"But *Sensei*, I noticed that the author of '*TOYOTA PRODUCTION SYSTEM,*' Mr. Taiichi Ohno, never actually used the term TPS in the book. He politely uses the term '*TOYOTA SEISAN HOSHIKI* (Toyota Production System),' and thereupon describes it," Takeuchi said. Please note that the original Japanese terminology "*TOYOTA SEISAN HOSHIKI*" had evolved to change to TPS as an acronym.

"That the term TPS has become so widely used is a testament to the scope of its impact.

After the Second World War, Toyota was surprised by the huge productivity of automotive manufacturing in the U.S. Toyota then committed themselves to becoming competitive, but at the same time they had to take great care not to let the trade secrets of the Toyota Production System become public prior to the enterprise becoming a manufacturing powerhouse. This required the creation of code words to cloak aspects of TPS and keep them a secret from competitors.

The word '*Kanban*' is a good example.

It means papers, the size of currency bills, to be used for giving directions and guidance regarding creating and picking up products. It is different from the widely-used meaning of *Kanban* in Japanese: Signboard. I will explain this in more detail later.

I can see that there are many terms which are a play on words. When I just started associating with TPS practitioners, I had trouble with the terms they were using, so it took me a long time to fully understand them. There are always terms that appear mysterious and call for a tacit understanding to have meaning. Such jargon exists in any field.

In this case, it is 'TPS terminology.' There is a glossary in the appendix of Taiichi Ohno's '*TOYOTA PRODUCTION SYSTEM*' that is a 'basics of the basics.' In this field, we're are urged to use unique terms and language that are different from ones used in usual situations. So please don't hesitate to ask me when you have questions. The important thing is to understand the essence of the particular terminologies," *Sensei* concluded.

7

Getting Through the R&D

Takeuchi used to be in charge of product design and development early in his career at the East Automotive Co. His ultimate dream was to make a new product that could be sold to the public. Each airplane consists of several hundreds of thousands of parts, while each car has several tens of thousands. Both are complex and influential products.

The East Automotive Co., the supplier of the leading car manufacturer, develops and produces automotive components. Therefore, in Takeuchi's company, automotive components are the finished products.

Takeuchi, doubling as Assistant Project Manager in the R&D Division and as Assistant Manager in the Production Engineering Development Division, was in charge of one particular product's R&D. As he delved deeper into the R&D, he gradually came to feel that developing and patenting the various elemental components of the product would be essential to surpassing competitors in the industry. For example, the liquid crystal panel is a key elemental component of liquid crystal TVs and such.

Though the situation has changed somewhat since 2000, when globalization began accelerating rapidly, the product Takeuchi was developing was about to ready to be manufactured, with its elemental component patent-protected.

As a result of the division's diligent R&D, Takeuchi and his team succeeded in obtaining a foreign patent on a particular technological innovation in the product. However, there remained uncertainty in how to mass produce the product itself. Breaking down the production process, two particular problems became apparent:

- How would the proto-type machinery developed for R&D need to be altered so that it could be mass-produced easily?

DOI: 10.4324/9781003323310-12

- And also, each unit in the production depends on batch-type machines working in unison, so how could they be configured to ensure materials flowed smoothly? In short, how could the production schedule and procedure be arranged under the "Job Shop Manufacturing System?"

It was then that Takeuchi visited Mr. Saitou. While a number of problems were to be expected regarding mass production, Takeuchi and his team members were struggling to make even a little headway in cracking the code that would reveal the secrets behind successful adoption of the Toyota Production System.

8

Setting Up a Production Line

Takeuchi has been involved in R&D right from his first day in the company. Though he had been in charge of various R&D departments, there was a physical distance between where he was and the actual production workplace, which meant he was also distant from the production line and related machinery at the site. This also meant there was still much to learn about the management at the production site. Still, Takeuchi and his crew were obliged to move forward with the mass production planning, and do so without fully grasping the ins and outs of the production workplace nor fully understanding the concepts behind the Toyota Production System.

The machine that was to be used in the mass production process had already been decided and assembled, and it was configured for optimal performance, at least as best as they could determine was necessary. They also ultimately determined how the facility was to be laid out and how the production process was to be executed to ensure maximum flow efficiency of workers in the cleanroom. On the surface, all seemed ready, with what is referred to as "a batch-typed" facility set up. But even with the facility poised to start production, there seemed to be something amiss – a lack of knowledge or experience behind the setup.

Oh, and, by the way, no explanation on the details of the finished product had yet been provided to the staff in the facility. What was produced here was a kind of elemental component that would be a uniquely designed part of a larger finished product. The products originally came from a big plate like a sheet on which several types of icon designs were printed, which was then cut into individual shapes by a press machine.

DOI: 10.4324/9781003323310-13

Clean room; Class10,000, Thermostatic and Humidistatic

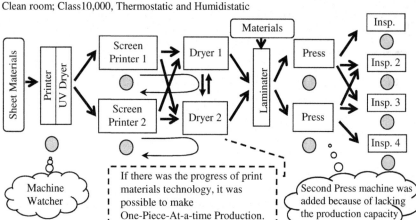

FIGURE 8.1

Process at the start of the mass production. (Translated from Takeuchi, Noboru, "*Seru Seisan*," JMA Management Center, 2006, P.222.)

-FIRSTLY, A REVIEW OF THE MASS PRODUCTION PROCESS

"*Sensei*, from the viewpoint of a TPS expert, could you give us your impression of our setup of the mass production of our products?"

"OK. This has become for you an initial case study that is worth examining. Let's evaluate each part of your setup through a TPS lens. It might be difficult to grasp at first, so for now, I recommend you just keep what you have learned so far about TPS somewhere in the back of your mind."

"Would you be so kind as to spare even a clue, as I am determined to know as much as I can," Takeuchi said, his face flushed with seriousness and sincerity (Figure 8.1).

-IF SEEN FROM *THE GOAL*, THIS IS "THE PUSH"

"Intuitively, this case's process reflects ideas presented in '*THE GOAL*,'" as *Sensei* starts on a topic which, at first, seems to not be related to TPS.

"What do you mean by '*THE GOAL*'?" Takeuchi asks.

"I'd like to introduce you to one book: '*THE GOAL*' by Eliyahu Moshe Goldratt (The North River Press Publishing Corporation 1992). This book explains TOC (the theory of Constraints), and it is a best-seller. It presents the story of the rebuilding of a company against all odds and despite opposition from certain opposing parties. The solution was clearing up the bottlenecking in production that perennially put the factory in danger of shutting down operations."

"What ideas are presented in TOC?" Takeuchi asks.

"The author says that the theory does not aim simply for partial improvement (sub-optimization, or best in part) to overcome problems, but rather it strives for overall optimization (or whole of the best) of operations. Simply put, 'The level throughput is dependent on the pace of the slowest person (process) in production – the source of the bottleneck.' Therefore, focusing on freeing up the bottleneck can have a huge impact on overall operations, and it can be done with relatively minimal effort."

"*Sensei*, do you have any thoughts on how to apply TOC to this case?"

"First of all, it is preferable to have inventory-in-process on the ready to use as a buffer to stave off potential bottlenecks.

In short, the TOC theory promotes the idea of 'Push-type Production,' which needs a prerequisite condition that is essentially ensuring the smooth flow of operations by discovering or anticipating defects in the system. Therefore, when problems or a slow-down emerges, there's a strong possibility it is due to some kind of *Muda* regarding workers' productivity. Also in such cases, managing and adjusting the whole manufacturing schedule would be necessary, especially because there are so many different parts flowing on the production line."

-FROM THE PERSPECTIVE OF TPS, THIS IS "THE PULL"

"I will certainly heed your advice. Therefore, *Sensei*, how do you see this case, from the perspective of a TPS expert?" Takeuchi asks.

"TPS has 'Pull-type Production' system as its foundation. The Pull System is one of the fundamental principles of TPS. More succinctly, TPS' method is the 'Pull-type Production Instruction.'

To break it down, the latter process (Downstream) only takes the number of products necessary to fill an order, which results in the former process

(Upstream) production of only the amount of the taken products to refill stock. With every process executed this way, one systematic chain of production will have been established. In a TPS environment, *Kanban* is used to execute Production Instruction as the means of transferring information on how much product to take.

Looking at your charts now, it is not clear whether your system is a 'Pull-type' or a 'Push-type,' as it only includes the general 'Goods Flow.' On the chart, you should have indicated the method of Production Instruction.

However, based on what you have explained, it seems you have started the mass production under the 'Push-type' system. Even though the 'Pull System' is standard in TPS, your system may still be alright, as long as each machine and process in the entire operation can be synchronized with each other, and if the manufacturing from the very beginning is based on information about the customer's needs," *Sensei* said.

"*Sensei*, that is exactly what I was thinking. Since the start of mass production, I have been experimenting with different ways of passing Production Instructions from the first process to the latter. However, I was still never able to achieve absolute synchronization due to the machinery not being able to work in unison due to their differences."

"OK. Let's see if we can pinpoint some of the problems when looked at through a TPS lens:

1. First, I have already guessed that your manufacturing was a 'Push-type.'
2. Thus, the 'Goods Flow' overlaps with each other between the machineries, and this is called 'Turbulent Flow.' That said, what is preferable is 'Straitening' or 'Laminar Flow' – in other words, no overlapping. Perhaps you are already aware that 'Turbulent Flow' and 'Straitening' or 'Laminar Flow' are technical terms used in the field of Fluid Mechanics.
3. Under the system, it seems that a 'One-Piece-At-a-time' production is not possible. Only lot production, or batch production, is possible.
4. Also, some workers seem to be 'Machine watchers,' which makes it difficult for them to be assigned 'Multi-Machine Handling' duties. Taking workers' efficiency and productivity into consideration, I have to say that there are many problems. There is a work system

called a 'Flexible Manpower Line,' and it seems your current system doesn't allow for that, so that makes it hard to achieve what's known as 'Manpower Saving.'

5. It seems yours is a 'Job Shop Manufacturing System,' which is a combination of each individual batch-type machine. From the looks of it, when asked to manufacture many kinds of finished products, setting up and arranging these machines to fit each situation will be rather challenging. Also, based on what schedule and procedures are you going to manufacture products?"

"*Sensei*, I have realized that I should have taken into consideration the improvement of the machinery and what procedures to employ."

"Yes. In general, what you're going to study with me are the following:

1. The TPS activities coming from the Development Stage.
2. Developing new machinery in line with the TPS concept."

"What is the major difference between Pull-type and Push-type?" Takeuchi wonders.

"Again, in principle, TPS emphasizes 'Pull-type production,' which follows a rule of the Pull System: every time latter processes run out of any items to be processed, further items out of their former processes are to be pulled. On the other hand, in Push-type production, it is from the former processes to the latter ones that items flow.

These two processes seemingly look similar in terms of Goods Flow, as they are much less vulnerable to typical emergency situations, such as machine stoppage, allowing for the general smooth flow of the manufacturing process. In most theoretical cases, with the TPS' Pull System, processes have more stocks of 'inventory-in-process' because there are 'stores' (storage places) where a certain amount of goods are kept at any given time. In a well-functioning Push-type system, the whole operation winds up with no 'inventory-in-process,' which is called *Ikki-tsukan*, in proceeding from the first process to the end without stoppage. However, in reality, due to issues such as defects or emergencies, a lot of 'inventory-in-process' may result. As a result, this compromises the efficiency of the production line as there ends up being a considerable amount of *Muda* (waste) in the operation. This is not so uncommon."

Responding to what *Sensei* has explained, Takeuchi says,

"That is absolutely right. In fact, my production line as well had to have a 'store' in the middle of all the lines soon after its 'line off (SOP: start of mass production).' Under the Pull System of Production method produced by *Kanban*, we had to deal with maintaining processing ability while handling issues with the machinery."

9

Transfer to the Production Workplace. How Should the Factory Be Managed?

Every day, Takeuchi had been focusing on the preparations for the start of mass production next year, even with his limited understanding of the conversation with *Sensei* he had in his obscure dream.

When the business plan was being made, he figured that the most important element to guarantee the smooth startup of mass production was the human resources at the actual production workplace. At first, the business plan was written for the "E" business department, which had quarantined clean rooms for hybrid IC and the sort. Besides, they provided electronic parts to the other product departments within the company as well as assembled various electronic products themselves. Due to the E business department's essential role in providing the electronic parts for each factory of the product departments and each factory of the suppliers, Takeuchi thought it to be natural that the business plan be written for his new product with primary consideration of the E business department's role.

The business plan, compiled and written with those ideas as its basis, had been approved by the company's board, with one correction. The department for which the development plan was to be considered was changed from the E department to the A product department. Some political motivations by the top leaders were behind this decision.

This perplexed Takeuchi to where he was consumed with questions by the decision. Takeuchi's original plan was specifically for the E department, even to where employee assignments at its factory had already been decided. However, human resources at the A department were unsuitable and short of the manpower at its factory needed for the operation.

DOI: 10.4324/9781003323310-14

There were also issues with the technical staff room as well as its product department, and no matter how hard Takeuchi tried to look for ways to compensate, he found it was not possible. In particular, the scarcity of suitable candidates to be Assistant Managers and Team Leaders became obvious. Under these circumstances, starting up mass production smoothly was in serious jeopardy.

It was the summer time, one year before the scheduled completion of the mass production preparation, and Takeuchi went over to a Director who was in charge of the factory at A department. He was also Takeuchi's former boss. Upon Takeuchi telling him about his worries, he simply said,

"From next spring, you're going to belong to the production department. It's been decided by me with the Senior Managing Director in charge of R&D."

Although it was more than six months before the official announcements of new assignments, Takeuchi was now expecting that soon after overseeing the starting up of the mass production system, he would be re-assigned to R&D, where he had originally belonged.

Thus begun the preparations. At the factory, it started with the clean room's construction. Then with each new and necessary machinery set up one by one, the factory came that much closer to the planned state for mass production. Yet, he still had concerns about the factory management, for that aspect of operations was quite new to him, unlike the technical matters he had to deal with while he was at R&D.

-DEVELOPING ONESELF THROUGH PERSONNEL TRAINING; THE TOYOTA PRODUCTION SYSTEM IS PERSONNEL TRAINING

"*Sensei*, after all, as it seemed there was no one else that was considered but me, I ended up being moved out from the R&D division to the factory as if it was by my own will. I still don't know if my performance was good or not. I was even told that such a personnel change was quite rare among the group of leading car makers. One of my mentors at the R&D division saw me off by saying I was going to have bigger projects awaiting when I returned to the department, and he was certain I would return.

As it turned out, I never did return to R&D, at least not within the timeframe he had in mind. All of what I've done so far in production was because I didn't want to see my invention be stalled, but admittedly, I've wondered what would have happened had I not left R&D. Could I have invented more items? Could I have contributed to the division more?" Takeuchi confided.

"Mr. Takeuchi, we will never know if you could have come up with more inventions had you stayed at the R&D Division.

When asked a seemingly basic question like 'What is the purpose of each company,' though people answer in many ways, the correct answer should be 'maximization of each company's value.' Because each company is called *ho-jin* (a Japanese legal entity), each company is regarded as its own life form, expected to be perennially evolving.

In such an environment, each employee of a company has various ways of contributing to his or her workplace. What is important is how each employee acts under a given condition. Anyway, what of value did you obtain from the job in the factory?" *Sensei* asks.

"Well, first of all, the ideology of the Toyota Production System," Takeuchi answers.

"And, the book '*TOYOTA PRODUCTION SYSTEM*' by the author Taiichi Ohno. The fact that I was able to immerse myself into 'the world of TPS' was definitely a blessing."

"In fact, when I joined the company after graduating from university, I dared to challenge myself to answer questions such as 'What exactly is a company?' or 'What exactly is a manufacturer?'

As I continued furthering my understanding of TPS, I realized one crucial element that needed to be understood, and that is IE (Industrial Engineering).

I was in awe after only reading the preface of the book '*The basics of IE, New Edition*' by Akihisa Fujita (Kenpakusha 1978).

Through what was said in the book, which was published long before I started working, I really thought I had found a perfect answer to 'What exactly is a manufacturer?'

Of course, maybe I reached the answer because I was gaining practical experience in company life."

"So, if you can think that all of what has happened to you has given you a great opportunity to grow on your own steadily, you should be very grateful in a sense.

By the way, every time I go to a seminar or a conference, almost always at the closing, the speaker says, 'Proper personnel training is quite necessary for success in any operation.' I find this common understanding very interesting. And I myself follow this philosophy all the time when I talk to somebody about this topic.

Especially in TPS, I feel the most important thing is each participant's mind and attitude are undergoing growth at the workplace.

Otherwise, it would be impossible to understand TPS deeply, leaving only a surface knowledge of the concept," as *Sensei* explained, trying to further emphasize the importance of personnel training to Takeuchi.

10

Encountering Kanban at the Start of Mass Production

It was right at the start of the new year when personnel transfers were implemented. Takeuchi was moved to the factory, which seemed to make the manager and other staff there unhappy, thinking that some of the R&D Division's activities had caused the factory some problems.

Takeuchi did not encounter anyone with the desire to help get new ideas and systems off the ground, and none of the previous managers there wanted to have anything to do with such projects. Thus, Takeuchi himself, as an Assistant Manager in the Production Section, had started the process of preparing for the Start of Mass Production (SOP) by the summer.

However, unlike the other colleagues, the Team Leader, Yoshitake, from the other Production Division, and though a quiet person himself, was more supportive, going about his various tasks with diligence and committed focus. Since the start of the personnel shifts in January, Takeuchi has kept on producing the proto-type products of the mass production trial, all while educating Team Leader Yoshitake. There were many things that had to be dealt with. Details of the manufacturing condition of the equipment needed to be clarified. With the assistance of Team Leader Yoshitake, Takeuchi produced each Operation Standards Chart one at a time. Mr. Yoshitake eventually came to understand all the operation processes well enough that he was placed in charge of the education of new operators.

Soon after the summer break, a customer company was to start assembling cars by using parts from Takeuchi's factory. The East Automotive Co., as a tier-one supplier, is supposed to deliver ordered items synchronized to the date of SOP. However, the subsidiary company, being the tier-one supplier of the East Automotive Co. and also

DOI: 10.4324/9781003323310-15

FIGURE 10.1
Kanban example which is inserted into a plastic bag (size of approximately 20 cm × 10 cm).

being the tier-two supplier of the customer at the same time, is asked to help with assembling finished products and delivering them. In supplying the parts to the factory, various problems occurred to where staff were panicking. They had actually asked for more parts than Takeuchi expected and was ready to produce.

The East Automotive Co. gets *Kanban* information requesting the amount of new parts, which is to equal what the supplier factory had used (Figure 10.1).

The parts written on the *Kanban* are delivered to the subsidiary company. A *Kanban* is tagged on a container which holds some items at set numbers. This type of *Kanban* is made of a paper inserted into a plastic bag, because they go back and forth frequently between factories and must be protected. There is another disposable paper *Kanban* used only once. One rule which must be strictly followed is that *Kanban* requests must be fulfilled within a certain time frame.

Individual items also have a fixed number of *Kanban* which can be issued. Another rule is that each item (container) and *Kanban* is to be managed together as one. However, the supplier factory had violated this rule one season when they intentionally detached the *Kanban* from of each container, causing consternation in the company.

One maxim on issuing *Kanban* is "Do not bother the former process with the big fluctuation of the number of *Kanban*." It is a rule born out of the concept of *Heijunka*. Yet, such management terms do not resonate with suppliers bearing poor work attitudes. It seemed that however many parts Takeuchi produced, it was never enough, as the supplier would remove each *Kanban* tag soon after the container of parts arrived from the East Automotive Co.

Unaware this was happening, Takeuchi's group was forced to keep producing parts for the supplier with no holidays for two months. Takeuchi was strictly following the rules, while the supplier factory was not. Only after a lengthy investigation this fact was revealed, and a huge amount of excess inventory was found. The parts leftover were equal to a one-month supply. Obviously, supplier part production was halted for the time being.

Yet, such an occurrence was not without precedence, as it is referred to "Parts Withdrawal *Kanban*."

On the other hand, at the production line, Mr. Yoshitake, the Team Leader, had assembled "Production Instruction *Kanban*" for each process. Team Leader Yoshitake had determined the "number of issued *Kanban*," which is calculated based on the production lot size of each machinery. Owing to the new system of producing items only in amounts sufficient to fulfill what is requested by the *Kanban*, it became easy to decide the production sequence.

From that experience, Takeuchi had learned from Team Leader Yoshitake that in producing parts for "many kinds" of finished products simultaneously, *Kanban* was very effective, which made him truly grateful for the system.

Kanban is the means to produce only what is really necessary. Its basic principle was "Pull-type Production," and in following the rule of the "Pull System (of Production)," gradually the initial mess was resolved.

-WHAT IS THE MEANING OF *KANBAN*? BEING ABLE TO USE *KANBAN* AS A TOOL OF *KAIZEN*

"*Sensei*, surely '*Kanban*' is a very interesting system and effective. If used properly, I am sure the management process will become pretty smooth. So, what is '*Kanban*' exactly?"

"Well, it is often said that '*Kanban*' functions like money, or bills. So, in situations where the total order issued on the *Kanban* is higher than what is necessary, it is called 'Inflation *Kanban*.' The term of 'issuing' is used in the same way as it is for money. The important thing is to issue '*Kanban*' according to the ability of each production line. I used to be told by my boss angrily, 'Do you handle money that badly?,' when looking at '*Kanban*' orders left on the machinery or a desk."

"Generally, when hearing the term '*Kanban*,' one imagines a sign board or a notice at the entrance of a shop. Why is the paper sheet called '*Kanban*' here?" Takeuchi asks.

"Well, because, it started with the 'Standing board plate (Japanese: *Kanban*).' I myself don't know the answer to that in detail. My knowledge stretches only as far back as what I've been told about its background. It was a 'Sign-board Display,' like the placard found at stockyards for parts. If stock of the item at the standing board's area has run out, that particular area's items only are supposed to be produced in the specified number on the signboard. So the 'Sign-board Stand' started being used as a tool for keeping the quantity of inventory-in-process as low as possible. Then, out of fear that this unique 'Fill-up system' would be copied overseas, it started to be called '*Kanban*'; at least, that is what I heard. That is why hiragana is used when writing '*Kanban*,' not katakana, which is supposed to be used when writing words borrowed from overseas."

"Now the story is clearer. Then *Sensei*, adopting '*Kanban*' results in having less inventory, which should be a great benefit, right?"

"The best thing is that '*Kanban*' is a useful tool in practicing *Kaizen*. However, there is some possibility of it failing in its implementation, especially at production workplaces with poor management. In fact, once, after the oil-shock that occurred in the Showa Era, and the Toyota Production System was booming in popularity, a certain number of enterprises failed when trying to adopt the '*Kanban*' system because it was done rather blindly.

What we have to realize is the following: adopting '*Kanban*' without understanding its true meaning and essence is not recommended. The result will be nothing but chaos if used in an environment where rules are not strictly followed.

'*Kanban*' is simply 'the means' in adopting and implementing TPS. Nothing more and nothing less. One should keep in mind that just simply adopting '*Kanban*' does not directly lead to actual practice of TPS. The best thing is for each company to find ways that consider their own unique situations when pursuing the TPS ideal.

In spite of these admonitions, once used, it should be generally felt that '*Kanban*' is extremely convenient and effective.

In the future, '*Kanban*' should be gradually changing its form as IT continues to evolve. In fact, e-*Kanban* already exists. Also, it will be inevitably affected by huge global systems. When that time comes, understanding the true essence of '*Kanban*' will be all the more necessary."

-WHAT IS THE BASIC KNOWLEDGE NECESSARY TO USE *KANBAN*?

Here, *Sensei* gives Takeuchi a brief lecture summing-up *Kanban*.

1. Basic kinds of *Kanban* (Figure 10.2)

   Under the classification in application, *Kanban* is generally divided into "Ordinary *Kanban*" and "Temporary *Kanban*." Moreover, "Ordinary *Kanban*" has two types. One is "Production Instruction *Kanban*," and the other is "Parts Withdrawal *Kanban*." In addition, "e-*Kanban*," the form-evolved version of *Kanban*, and other specific names of variations of *Kanban* are used to fit individual situations and purposes.

2. The contents of information included in each *Kanban*

   (1) Part Number and Name, (2) Packaging Specification, (3) Quantity, (4) Storage Location, (5) The title of the following process and production line (Downstream Process), (6) The title of the former production line (Upstream Process), and (7) The *Kanban* order quantity issued and the serial number (#).

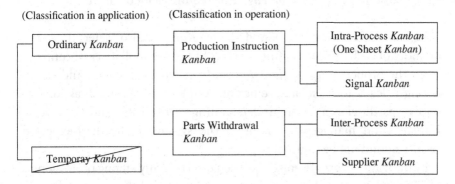

FIGURE 10.2

Classification of *Kanban*. (Translated from Takeuchi, Noboru, "*Seru Seisan,*" JMA Management Center, 2006, P.149.)

3. *Kanban* rules

Toyota Production System by The Japan Society for Production Management (The Nikkan Kogyo Shimbun, 1996, P.213) is a recommended reference.

a. Defective products: not to be accepted, nor produced, nor sent.

b. Strictly follow the quantity of each *Kanban*.

c. Always pull necessary items for the following process from the previous process.

d. No producing items more than what the *Kanban* specifies.

e. No pulling more items than what the *Kanban* specifies.

f. Produce the quantities of the *Kanban* according to the order specified by the timeline. Produce higher quantity amount items firstly.

g. Tag a *Kanban* on each actual item produced.

h. Each *Kanban* must show a number that is identical to what appears on the actual item.

i. A whole production line needs to be under *Heijunka*.

j. Adopt a stable Sequential Parts Withdrawal.

k. Adjust *Kanban* if necessary, according to each Time, Place, and Occasion.

l. In cases of any unplanned productions, arrangements must be made after contacting all departments concerned in advance.

m. Systematize and stabilize the whole process.

4. Drawbacks of *Kanban*

Adopting *Kanban* doesn't guarantee positive results. In short, maintaining the "*Kanban* System" requires a lot of effort.

Kanban determines the Goods-Flow. *Kanban* also determines the quantity of each inventory. *Kanban* is nothing but a tool of visual controls. With the proper usage of *Kanban*, *Muda* becomes apparent, and eliminating it leads to a "strong," efficient production line. Thus, as long as one keeps developing their understanding of the rules and the role of *Kanban*, and manages to maintain the system, better-than-expected results should not be unusual.

By the way, the term "strong" has been used casually among professionals of TPS, and it is often found in this book – for example, "strong production line," "strong constitution," and "the strong Manufacturing workplace."

These are somewhat relative, literary expressions. It would be appreciated if you, the reader, can understand its meaning as reflecting an ability to flexibly adapt to market fluctuations or any changes to the work environment.

-WHICH BOOK SHOULD WE START WITH TO STUDY THE TOYOTA PRODUCTION SYSTEM?

"*Sensei*, recently I have seen many books on TPS, but which one should I start with? I have already picked up a few of these books, but understanding their content has hardly been easy. Could you recommend an appropriate one for me as a starter?"

"Yes, I know there are a number of production system-related books. Let me offer a bit of clarity regarding them. Out of all the books I currently own, if I were to name the ones related to Toyota, they should be categorized as follows:

1. Toyota Production System, Toyota System, Toyota Way, Productivity in the Toyota Way, etc. – all derived from Mr. Taiichi Ohno's original idea.
2. Just-In-Time Production System – Experts' perceptions of TPS from different points of view.
3. Synchronized Manufacturing System – Basically similar to TPS, though its designers tried to be unique with their own information transferring method.
4. The Toyota Way – Ideologies based on concepts developed by Toyota Corp.
5. All other categorizations: 'Toyota Style,' 'Toyota Language,' or Toyota in general.

When looking at these books by executing positioning analysis, they are largely divided up into two core bases (Figure 10.3).

Either they are professional, or they are basic.

Or rather, they are a technical-terms-oriented approach, or more like storytelling.

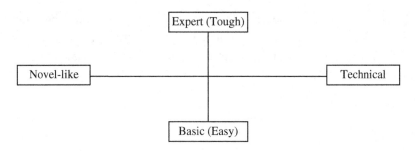

FIGURE 10.3
Positioning analysis for the literature of the Toyota Production System.

With such varied viewpoints, one should choose the most appropriate literature based on one's purpose."

> *Sensei*, that would force me to study a wide variety of books. And besides, it seems impossible to tell which are most helpful, even after careful studying. If *Sensei* would be so kind, could you name your recommendations?

"If I dare to name a few, at least ones which can directly lead to efficient production, the following are recommended. They are all educational and practical, though there are likely other books as good as these," *Sensei* said. He then recommended the following to Takeuchi:

- "*TOYOTA PRODUCTION SYSTEM* (English version)," by Taiichi Ohno (Productivity Press 1988) – The "bible" written by the pioneer of TPS. Anyone involved in this field is likely to have to go through this book at some point. It's a must-read book.
- "*Jikiden Toyota Hoshiki* (Direct teaching the Toyota System)," by Kiyotaka Nakayama (DIAMOND, Inc. 2005) – The author is an ex-Toyota Motor General Manager in the Operations Management Consulting Division. The content seems to be for experts and professionals.
- "*Kangaeru Toyota No Genba* (The *Genba* of Toyota that Thinks)," by Masatomo Tanaka (Business-sha Inc. 2005) – The author, also an ex-Toyota Motor General Manager in the Operations Management Consulting Division, reveals his own methodology.
- "*Nyumon Toyota Seisan Houshiki* (An Introduction to the Toyota Production System)," by Masamitsu Ishii (Chukei Publishing-KADOKAWA 2005) – The author is an ex-Vice President of the

Toyota Taiwan factory, and the information presented is helpful as an introduction to the system.

- "*Seru Seisan* (Cell Production)," by Noboru Takeuchi (JMA Management Center 2006) – If at the level of understanding where one might utter, "OK, now I know what it is. Then how should I proceed?," then this book would be the next step. It presents the overall basic elements of the production workplace under TPS. Each chapter, each heading, and each sub-heading is ordered logically so that study can be done sequentially. It also functions as a reliable reference of unfamiliar TPS words or ideas – like a dictionary.

"Then *Sensei*, according to the Toyota Production System categories you listed, it is preferable for each reader to think about the position of the authors in their respective books."

"Even the word '*Kanban*,' where it may be said that TPS is synonymous with the *Kanban System*, is still just a means. Such distinctions have to be studied to be clear. Sometimes, some authors remember and record a particular fragment of their memory related to their experiences at Toyota, which causes them to write how they perceived it and what they experienced in particular noteworthy moments. As a result, their writing reflects an obsession with some irrational 'spiritualism' or trivialized understanding of '*Kaizen* items' as the true essence of TPS. As well, as each reader has their own purposes in mind, it becomes hard for them when trying to apply these principles to his or her own situation."

Part IV

Production by Way of *Kanban*

11

Machine-Based: The Machine-Based Workplace Managed via Kanban

Thus, the production line that has been created for the mass production operation is regarded as a **machine-based workplace**. It may be a little complicated to explain, but in such operations, machinery should be regarded as the most important as well as the highest expense, as the total amount invested in the machinery was likely huge.

On the other hand, the facility with the production line where workers assemble the products is called the **manpower workplace**, which regards manpower as the most important expense.

More concretely, both the "machine-based workplace" and the "manpower workplace" have "machine" and "manpower," respectively as their most important expenses, and so management must be sure to prioritize maintaining both.

From the point of view of the management, "Rate of Operation" of equipment or the "equipment operation rate" in general is seen as an important factor in measuring efficiency of the production line. The Toyota Production System deems "Operational Availability," not "Rate of Operation," as the more appropriate terminology.

The "Rate of Operation" is the ratio of the quota number to be produced for the following process relative to the production capacity based on a certain time frame. Therefore, the number varies according to the following process' quota. Basically, the operation rate fluctuates based on calculations of production quantities for each production run.

On the other hand, the "Operating Availability" shows the ratio (expressed in a percentage) at which machines or equipment can run under normal conditions when they are called into operation. Certainly,

DOI: 10.4324/9781003323310-17

the ideal ratio is always 100%. Operating Availability corresponds to the reliability of the machines resulting from the quality and maintenance of the machines.

In practicing TPS, the most important thing in the machine-based workplace is that machines operate smoothly. Absolutely, the speed of each machine should be the priority. However, machine malfunctions or other issues also need to be dealt with swiftly. Issues with the machinery, like "Big-Stop" or "Frequent-Stop," would not only decelerate productivity, but they would cause disruptions in the other sections that comprise the TPS operations. Therefore, a requisite for management in practicing TPS is maintenance of the machinery to ensure, among other things, its efficiency and safety.

It is worth noting that regarding the *Kaizen* methods in both the "machine-based workplace" and the "manpower workplace," though both are based on TPS, approaches tend to differ from each other in many cases due to the actual differences of workers' movements at each facility type.

The actual machine adopted for the workplace is a professionally customized apparatus, or Special-Purpose Machine (SPM). Two new processes had been added to help produce the elemental parts developed by Takeuchi. From the very beginning, these processes were achieved by the machine's use of Low-Cost Automation (LCA), helping it churn out parts that gave the appearance of being "hand-made."

The new product invention would never have hit the market if these two new processes had not been incorporated smoothly into the mass production-based machine. In that sense, the whole development was a success, though some problems still remain to be solved. That was also the reason why Takeuchi accepted the transfer to the factory during his company's personnel change cycle.

The first mass production-based machine they used was for the purpose of printing. For that machinery, workers had to attach and detach sheet material one at a time. Thereafter, a new machine was brought in, and it was equipped with a special mechanism that could automatically feed sheet material one by one, but this proved to be very problematic. Essentially, its auto-sheet-feed function did not function well because the sheet material was so unique.

After sensing the limitations of the machine's manufacturer, Takeuchi's group had decided to thoroughly inspect the machinery and, if needed, to fix any of the issues that had come up thus far. To aid the start of the mass production operation, Takeuchi, as a worker at the factory, examined every step in the process, both fine-tuning and fixing the machines. He was essentially determined to solve the problems of the mass production machines with his own hands, and as the person in charge of R&D.

The second machine in the operation was a punching machine. The machine had its own issues, and delay of its delivery made the situation more chaotic.

Fortunately, these machines were stabilized in the early stages of the operation after the start of mass production, which is a feat considering their unique specifications. They were different from existing machines at the company and also very rare models not commonly available in the open market. In a sense, Takeuchi often felt, "I am here basically as a 'machine-sitter.'" Though there were no Big-Stop incidents, there were many Frequent-Stops.

Since the start of mass production and with production able to sufficiently replenish the required inventory, no major problems have happened.

Yet, reaching the ideal state of TPS still seemed to be a long way off. The reasons were:

- The whole system followed specifications for a large lot-size production.
- Each process had a different production lot size from the other.
- Due to the many Frequent-Stops, workers in charge looked more like guards of the machines than operators.

Overall, in this facility's operation, there were issues with each machine. It was then that Takeuchi understood that the **Kanban System** was truly effective. The 'Kanban System,' which Team Leader Yoshitake proceeded to implement based on his experience at the other workplace, worked exceptionally well for the management at this new workplace. With intense clarity, Takeuchi felt he was finally getting a real taste of the *Kanban*, which until then he had only observed from the fringes since his entry into the company.

We utilize and manage *Kanban* in order to produce only what is necessary in the following process.

⊕ -WHY IS THE TERM "FREQUENT-STOP" APPROPRIATE? PM OF KEEPING THE MACHINERY FUNCTIONING PROPERLY IS ONE PREREQUISITE IN TPS

"*Sensei*, the apparatuses we adopted have many issues. I always feel like I'm here as a repairer.

By the way, in the realm of TPS, what does PM (Preventive Maintenance) or TPM (Total Preventive Maintenance) actually mean?" Takeuchi asked.

"In short, PM is supposed to be one of the elements of TPS, or a precondition for maintaining TPS. I've seen an example of an operation which assumed and adopted the *Kaizen* technique assuming it was TPS, but comparing it to actual TPS, it's clear the two are fundamentally distinct.

If considering the shape or character of each company – for example, the material device industry – a *Kaizen* activity as part of TPM may sometimes be appropriate.

On the other hand, in TPS, there is a precondition that PM in a narrow sense and QC (Quality Control) should always be a priority. Without going on too much about it, in TPS, producing 'zero' defects is a prerequisite. In reality, **zero defects** is hardly possible, but the mindset of trying to achieve it should be in all of the workers and the actions they take."

"So then *Sensei*, in TPS, how exactly should the facility be perceived?"

"In TPS, the Operational Availability ideal is 100%. It goes without saying that any sort of machine stoppage is nothing short of a catastrophe.

It is not only contrary to the idea of *Jidoka*, but it also jeopardizes the ability to meet the requirement of Just-In-Time, which you will study in the Two-Pillars of TPS later. It is crucial that there be a system on standby to guarantee that any sudden problems with the machinery can be fixed immediately.

Certainly, to avert any mechanical problems during operations, machines should be made that can operate smoothly with little chance of issues arising."

"I've noticed the term 'Small-Stop' widely used and often repeated when describing mechanical issues. What exactly does it mean?"

"Yes it has been used a lot. Currently, the term '**Frequent-Stop**' is more appropriate for certain problems. Why '*Choco* (Small)'? I have no idea. Is it because when there are '*Choco Choco*' stops (frequent small stops), each time, the machines are able to function normally again in '*Chocotto*' (a short amount of time)?

That said, 'With *Choco* (Small) stops, it is strange that they occur many times throughout the day.

It looks like it happens so often that we simply get used to it, just letting things work themselves out without intervening. Let's consider the term again,' the suggestion was made. Thus, after considering what were a few thousand suggestions for a more appropriate term from various people, the term 'Frequent-Stop' was adopted.

Nowadays, the term 'Small-Stop' has become inappropriate with respect to ensuring the efficient functioning of *Kaizen*. Terms tend to be swapped like this, reflecting the times. Nonetheless, the measures to deal with 'Frequent-Stop' are regarded as crucial in TPS as part of the overall production line's *Kaizen* Activity."

Sensei continued, "Now, let's go through each term related to issues with machine stoppages.

First, '**Big-Stop**.' It is the most serious of the machine stoppages.

Second, '**machine trouble**.'

It could be defined as such: 'The state that a machine loses its ability to function, thereby needing 5 minutes or more to repair it.' Actually, with this definition, one can easily say 'It's a Big-Stop,' which then makes the meaning of 'Big-Stop' vaguer.

Finally, 'Small-Stop' or 'Frequent-Stop' can be defined as the type of stoppage that is due to some relatively minor issue, and so can be fixed in anywhere from 2 to 3 seconds to as much as 5 minutes with some simple tweaking.

This type of mechanical trouble can either be fixed immediately, perhaps by removing some stuck item or making small adjustments, or operations can proceed without immediate intervention, though it may result in a slightly longer Machine Cycle Time.

Also, stoppages could be due to defects in individual machine parts or materials used for the machine. This surely is a Quality Control problem as well.

In addition, from the point of machine efficiency, it is necessary to focus on 'down time' caused by set-up.

The role of PM is critical for achieving the ideal whereby 'the machine is always in a state of ready for operating.'"

12

Manual-Based: Working on the Assembly Line

One year had passed since his arrival at the factory.

At both meetings before and after the personnel change, it was decided that Takeuchi was to go back to the R&D Division once the mass production operations had been set up. However, perhaps out of convenience for the company, Takeuchi was never asked to go back to the R&D Division, and seemingly his dream to create new inventions for the company was dashed. Yet, when he looks back on the experiences he has gained thus far at the company, he can only feel fortunate that all of his encounters and discoveries with TPS were beyond what he could ever have imagined.

Under directions from a new CEO, Takeuchi was even able to experience "the assembly line" as well. Then, as an Assistant Manager, he was placed in charge of the assembly line in addition to the machine-based line. The assembly line is also called "The manpower jobsite." There, it's the workers who are the major contributors in producing the finished products.

It can be categorized as a type of cellular production line operated by the Process Division Method, which is mentioned in the book "*Seru Seisan*" from JMA Management Center, 2006, P.45 (Figure 12.1).

It consists of one sub-assembly production line and three assembly production lines, with about 50 workers at peak times. On the customer's end, two production lines for A automobiles and one production line for B automobiles are in operation. Actually, there is not that much difference between the look of the products provided by the customers and the ones finished by Takeuchi's team.

Takeuchi's new boss, Mr. Matsui, was promoted to become a Manager in the Production Division, out of convenience for the company this year.

DOI: 10.4324/9781003323310-18

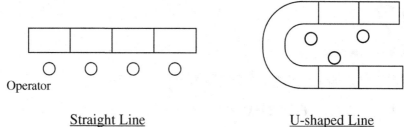

Straight Line   U-shaped Line

FIGURE 12.1
Cellular production line by way of the process division method. (Translated from Takeuchi, Noboru, "*Seru Seisan,*" JMA Management Center, 2006, P.45.)

Although much of his time at the company was to undertake production preparation, production itself was not something with which he was familiar. Thus, he spent the bulk of his time at work attached to his desk, which was situated at a corner of the production jobsite, and he would occasionally say boastfully, "I am good at filling out papers." At any rate, for Mr. Matsui, overseeing operations at the *Genba* seemed to be the last thing he wanted to do.

13

An Anti-TPS Force?

Often, when one starts something new, some entity opposing this change materializes. As it turned out, the opposition came in the form of the General Manager (GM). The old GM was notorious for doing very little if anything during his tenure. However, the new Manager was making his opposition to TPS apparent by relentlessly hounding Takeuchi about his work, even going so far as to try to get rid of him, although they were on the same team and supposedly working toward the same goal.

The new manager brought nothing but grief for Takeuchi, not only because of his poor understanding of the production jobsite, but also because of his personal opposition or lack of open-mindedness to adapt and learn new things. He was prone to tantrums, and would yell at his team members, "What the hell is going on!?"

Neither Takeuchi's former division nor the factory heads cared about concerns over one Assistant Manager. He was often simply advised, "Just ignore the stupid Manager." However, being in Takeuchi's position required enduring the pall on the workplace cast single-handedly by the manager. In fact, it seemed the Manager had managed to construct a barrier that was effective in preventing Takeuchi or any of his colleagues from airing their grievances to the Senior Manager or Chief of the factory, thereby confining their problems to within the walls of the production site. Further isolating Takeuchi's group was the fact that the whole company was at a major turning-point in an overall transition.

Still, with the whole company operating on a top-down management stream, Takeuchi's situation was perceived to be one he should consider bearable. The alternative is to try to rally as much support as possible from colleagues before making any attempt to resolve matters.

DOI: 10.4324/9781003323310-19

With that, Takeuchi seemed to have the understanding and support of Team Leader Yoshitake as well as the Manager of the neighboring division.

During these times, Takeuchi felt it important that he focus intensely on furthering his knowledge of TPS.

There is a term called "Anti-TPS." It is a somewhat "hidden" byproduct of TPS. In particular, people regarded as "technical experts" tend to use this term.

And among these people, there are two types. One type is those who on the surface publicly proclaim "I am anti-TPS," but they actually behave themselves as people who believe TPS to be of significant value. These type of people are not a problem. Despite how they appear on the surface, they are guided by a firm vision and conviction to achieve their goals. As a result, their actions show adherence to the ideals of TPS because they reflect the ideal features of those in the system. However, the other type of people are true "Anti-TPS," and they are the ones who bring about the most problems. Their actions do not reflect TPS ideals, rather instead becoming obstacles to reaching those ideals.

Implementation of any Innovation Activity, including the Toyota Production System, should also be accompanied by counter-measures for "How to deal with the anti-TPS groups?"

When a company executes any plan that may be regarded as revolutionary, it is of utmost importance to ensure all of those at the company understand the reasoning behind this change, or at least there should be agreement among the top brass of its value. It is also often the case that such a plan gets a kick-start via remarks by one of those at the top. The important thing is to firmly establish a leader acknowledged companywide as the person who will spear-head efforts.

When analyzing companies who have successfully enacted wholescale changes, the common element seems to have been having a leader who is able to get everyone at the company – division to division, from top to bottom – to move almost in unison. It stands to reason then that in a well-functioning corporate culture, the leaders themselves should understand the essential elements behind their success.

Therefore, where any missteps occur should be acknowledged by the leaders of that division to be their responsibility. The workers who made the mistake should also accept responsibility for their misunderstanding. It should also be noted that Innovation Activities are very difficult to implement when done so in an environment heavily scrutinized by many observers and visitors.

-*GENBA* (PRODUCTION WORKPLACE) ORIENTED POLICY; GO AND SEE FOR YOURSELF

"*Sensei*, it is often said that the production jobsite is the most important place at any manufacturing company. However, I cannot help but feel like those companies sometimes just go about their operations with little awareness of what is actually going on at the production jobsites."

"For example, while project designers may think the project is practically complete once their operation blueprints are submitted to the next stage, arrangers may also feel similarly once they have made all of the arrangements to obtain all of the items necessary for production to begin.

I call it 'The 'not my problem' attitude – where even if one's factory is letting polluted water flow out, one's job is done when one's job is done.' There is another major TPS principle that applies to any factory production operation: 'Don't bother those at the next stage of the process.' However, some at a certain stage may simply not be aware of problems from their end, and when carried over to those at the next stage may require them to fix and even cover up those mistakes for the good of the entire operation. There is also a high likelihood that those at the next stage won't take any action to rectify a problem that came from some mistake committed in the prior stage, and may instead just grumble over the carelessness of their colleagues in the prior stage.

In such a case, I would guess the company still has some flexibility and capacity to leave those problems be. Those at the site may be unaware if or how much '*Muda*' has permeated their environment as a result of their actions. It can be thought of as '*Muda*' of 'Structure.'

By the way, you should know that '*Shikumi* (Structure)' is an often used term. Often among those who use it, the meaning is rather ambiguous or broad. Dictionaries will say *Shikumi* stands for ways of building objects or other matter. Is that right?"

"I also hear the term '*Ji-Kotei-Kanketsu* (JKK, Self-Process Completing)' – taking responsibility upon oneself to complete a task thoroughly and satisfactorily."

"That is right. Yet, especially in manufacturing companies, it is critically important to know well what is going on at each production jobsite where shipment and inspection are done. When observing the *Genba*, there are ample chances to make aspects of the operation 'visible.'

There is the term '***Genchi-Gembutsu***.' It means being at the scene and witnessing first hand where problems exist. When reporting apparent problems to one's boss, the boss often asks, 'Have you actually seen it yourself?' Often, the boss has already seen it.

To some extent in non-Japanese speaking countries, just saying in Japanese, '*Genchi-Gembutsu*,' can help workers better understand the related situation. In fact, I have seen the term explained similarly in Europe in an alternative way but similar in intent: 'Go and study, and see what a team can achieve.'"

"Simply, it means 'GO, SEE, ACT,' right? One of my favorite phrases, by the way. Whatever may be underlying an issue or situation, first of all go to the site, then make your own assessment, then take appropriate action," Takeuchi said.

"Of course, for proper practice of '*Genchi-Gembutsu*' properly, just going to the site and observing is not enough. The ability to sense what the root causes of a situation are is also necessary. Without developing the ability to see right through problems to the core issues, one will simply only notice what is happening on the surface. But yes, mastering the art of '*Genchi-Gembutsu*' starts with, simply, '**Go to the *Genba* first**.'"

14

Kanban *as Part of the Daily Management Routine*

Kanban is one of the most important tools in the Toyota Production System. It becomes very useful when practicing one of the core idea of TPS: the "Pull System (of Production)." Of course, before anything, it is essential that a certain environment be established to enable proper execution of the *Kanban* system. Simply adopting *Kanban* without the proper setup jeopardizes the whole operation.

In the production line, Takeuchi is in charge of the management of the assembly of the parts received from the supplier and shipping them out as finished products to the customer – "Our Customers." The production line in the Production Division is responsible for all matters related to manufacturing at the site, while the Shipment Engineering Division is responsible for anything shipment-related. Based on the information in the "Parts Withdrawal *Kanban*" from the customer, the necessary items are assembled in the production line, and then finished items are shipped out.

Kanban works well as the tool of Production Instruction. When the line is flowing smoothly, the Production Division can just instruct its production line to focus on producing the necessary items according to the information on the "Parts Withdrawal *Kanban*" issued by the Production Control Division, which deals with shipments. Often in actual cases, each received "Parts Withdrawal *Kanban*" is exchanged to a "Production Instruction" *Kanban* in the Production Division. At such times, the Production Division sometimes changes "the Instruction of Production Sequence" and the lot sizes.

For the whole Production Division, punctuality is of the utmost importance as all items are supposed to be finished according to the scheduled withdrawal time of the Production Control Division. The idea is known as "Just-In-Time."

Therefore, the Logistics Division comes to pick up the finished products at the scheduled time they are to be shipped by trucks.

This basic idea applies to all facets of production, from assembling automobile parts to any source products and parts. The production process has to keep pace with the demands of "Our Customers" in the next step of the process. That type of production formation can be seen in the so-called "Conveyer line," or "Cell Production." Essential basis of "Pull System (of Production)" is to produce and hand over items only in the amount that "Our Customers" need.

The production method based on the *Kanban* information in the production line can be explained as follows:

At this site, operation is eight hours, with delivery to be every two hours. It means there are four trucks a day, which depart every two hours on time.

In its production line, approximately 800 finished items are produced per day, which makes each truck's total shipping load approximately 200 items. So each truck has a mostly identical load. Also, the contents of each truck's shipment is of similar kinds and quantities. Such is the standardization of each shipment.

For example,

1st Truck (10:00 departure): A Product – 100 pcs, B Product – 60 pcs, C Product – 40 pcs

Total = 200 pcs

2nd Truck (13:00 departure): A Product – 90 pcs, B Product – 60 pcs, C Product – 40 pcs

Total = 190 pcs

3rd Truck (15:00 departure): A Product – 100 pcs, B Product – 60 pcs, C Product – 50 pcs

Total = 210 pcs

4th Truck (17:00 departure): A Product – 110 pcs, B Product – 50 pcs, C Product – 40 pcs

Total = 200 pcs

The production and shipment of items is synchronized with the production capacity of finished products by the customer.

Finished items are shipped, packed in "to/from boxes, Tote Boxes." Ten finished items are in one box. So with 200 items, 20 boxes are needed. On each box is attached one *Kanban* tag, so 20 boxes make 20 *Kanbans*.

Each "Tote Box" comes back empty, after being handed to and removed by the customer. Likewise, each *Kanban* comes back to the Production Control Division with the truck driver. Eventually, only the *Kanban* attached boxes used by the customer come back. Judging from the number of returned *Kanban*, one can know the amount the customer used and how many items should be produced and shipped again. This is the "Pull System (of Production)."

Written on each *Kanban* are certain details.

Basically,

1. Item ID, item name
2. Packing type
3. Quantity
4. Location address
5. Following process production line name
6. Prior process production line name
7. Quantity issued, reference number, and anything else considered essential

These *Kanban* are made of paper and almost identical to paper currency.

It almost seems as if the customer at the following process pays for the received items with money bills, and hence the term "Buying with *Kanban*" is sometimes used. Based on what is written for the first detail on the *Kanban* – "1. Item ID and name," the item the customer "buys" vary. Each time, the amount of items produced is determined by the quantity specified on the number of *Kanban*.

For example, there may be instructions to produce 20 *Kanbans*: ten of product A, six of product B, and four of product C. The production deadline is 10:00 – the scheduled departure of the 1st shipment. Thus, with this Pull System (of Production), each product is produced at a pace that can meet a particular shipment time, which again, can be four times a day.

To emphasize again, the *Kanban* system is effective when the whole production line flows systematically and smoothly. Production and shipment based on the information of each *Kanban* should be able to be done literally without thinking.

If this can be achieved, then it frees up space in the worker's minds enabling them to focus on and process other "more immediate" tasks. *Kanban* is the tool. The tool is to enable "visual-control" of the production process. With wise use of *Kanban*, what is *Muda* and what is not will become obvious, resulting in a more efficient production line.

Team Leader Yoshitake has run to Takeuchi at the Assistant Manager's desk, which is a room in front of the clean room.

"Sir, Assistant Manager, we have a serious problem. We are about to drop '*Kanban*,'" Mr. Yoshitake said in a grave tone.

To say "drop *Kanban*" is something that other companies don't dare say. It is a kind of dialect in this company that is used when failing to produce what was specified on the *Kanban*.

Kanban is likened to paper currency. It is supposed to be handled with good care. Suppose if you dropped all your money somewhere, you would be in a bit of a bind. Surely, it is a worry that Takeuchi and his group deal with daily when handling *Kanban*. Stopping the customer's line production due to some failure of delivering a scheduled supply order can be grave indeed to Takeuchi and his group.

> "We see that the particular item we're expecting to get hasn't arrived yet, sir."
> Issues with parts from the supplier have been a chronic problem for years.
> Of course, with the supplier as well, an ordering system whereby "Supplier *Kanban*" is issued has been adopted.

One common misunderstanding in this field is that "adopting *Kanban* leads to bullying sub-tier suppliers." When *Kanban* is practiced at the tier-one supplier level, operating between a leading manufacturer and its tier-two supplier, this sort of misunderstanding often comes up, especially in cases where the production is in a less-than-ideal state. *Kanban* is essentially a useful and simple system which eases the process of each supplier to prevent disruptions caused by delays at some prior stage. Problems arise when there is a fluctuation of issues in each *Kanban*, with perhaps orders getting larger or changing frequently.

The phrase "Bull whip" is used to describe cases where inconsistencies in each stage prior cause *Kanban* numbers to fluctuate, thereby affecting later stages of the process. The production quantity fluctuations by the suppliers tend to become wilder at each subsequent stage of the process.

This tendency is compared to a "Bull whip," named such because when cracking a whip, the tail end of the whip has a much wider fluctuation than where the whip begins at the handle. Issues in a next stage of the production process, where the number of *Kanban* issued is also affected, can cause problems in the former stage of the process. Therefore, an expected production quantity – the amount issued on the *Kanban* – has to be stabilized, as fluctuations are certain to affect the performance of the supplier the *Kanban* is sent to.

Takeuchi and Team Leader Yoshitake had decided to look into the inventory and the production situation of the finished products once again. During this period of overtime, it was supposedly time for a break. Yet, both men continued their checking of items stocked at the production line.

They were so focused on their work that they didn't notice an unannounced visit by the Manager, Mr. Matsui, who rarely came to the production line. From behind, he suddenly yelled at them, "What on earth are you doing!?"

Though they had mentioned to the manager, "We are short on stock of the finished products for the next shipment," in the hopes of receiving advice, they also knew that Manager Matsui was more likely to ask, "So, what are you going to do about it?" Hence, they began trying to find the cause of their shortfall prior to reporting anything to the manager. Nevertheless, he began yelling at them, saying he was unable to submit a document because of the situation, which to the Division Manager did not seem like a matter urgent enough to warrant a scolding. He insisted that though the Division Manager was about to go home, Takeuchi and the Team Leader Yoshitake have yet to bring a document that they were supposed to submit soon. Team Leader Yoshitake answered, "We're working on it, sir."

Takeuchi had experience being yelled at by a superior – twice – yet this time around, he was so shocked by the Manager's reaction that his heart couldn't stop racing, even 30 minutes after the yelling stopped.

Eventually, delivery failure with *Kanban* was averted thanks to the efforts of Team Leader Yoshitake. However, there was still a problem which needed to be solved.

It was related to the production line side of operations. The inventory of a particular stock at the production line side was not well managed. In particular, the stock item's supplier factory was located far from where they were held in inventory. Usually, the flow of *Kanban* remains steady if initial number settings are unchanged. However, in the case of the supplier, eventually it turned out that the number issued on the *Kanban* needed to be set larger. This allowed for there to be a proper amount of inventory at the production line side to be kept.

Thus, it is necessary to set each *Kanban* to where supplier's competence or capacity is considered – a matter that requires awareness and adjustments.

Kanban makes daily routine work very easy, as long as general rules and principles are adhered to properly. This also allows for any *Muda* to be swiftly identified and dealt with, which leads to a production line that is well-functioning.

This is why *Kanban* is said to be the essential tool for *Kaizen*, as it is the tool for "Visual Control." Therefore, for the *Kaizen* Activity to work, the initial setting of *Kanban* is critical. Understanding the rule and role of *Kanban* properly, and linking this knowledge with the actual practice of *Kaizen* is what a manufacturing operation should strive to achieve.

On the other hand, it cannot be considered sufficient for *Kanban* to be adopted rather blindly and simply assuming all will work itself out. Sometimes, examples at actual sites can be seen where *Kanban* has been adopted only in name but not in principle. Its only function, more or less, is as an "item tag."

It is important to keep in mind that *Kanban*'s essential role is as **the tool for the Pull System (of Production)**. And *Kanban* gradually changes its form as time passes. Instead of paper-based "Returnable *Kanban*," "Electronic *Kanban*" is being used nowadays, and this technique is spreading in popularity thanks to the Internet.

In the future, it may become commonplace for *Kanban* figures to change according to certain situations. A more vast range of accepted methods may be developed.

Still, the principles behind the original paper *Kanban* exchanges, and which serve as the basis of the *Manufacturing*, will never become obsolete.

Thus, at first, the most important thing is not only just adopting the "*Kanban* System," but how to fully develop the ideal Manufacturing jobsite based on the idea of the Toyota Production System,

It is worth noting that research into discussions on "Lean Manufacturing" overseas indicates that it was established after studying TPS, and in many cases shows an obsession with the technique.

One reason is when the Toyota Production System was first being implemented at actual production sites in the U.S., the number one priority was catching up with Japanese counterparts by doing the same things that Japanese factories did. So, they started off by studying the technique, at least how it appeared on the surface. Then eventually, it seemed they were able to reach a stage where they could have essential discussions about the fundamental ideology of the Toyota Production System.

-THE TERM "SEE": BEING ABLE TO DO A STANDING OBSERVATION BY FOLLOWING *GENBA* (PRODUCTION WORKPLACE) ORIENTED POLICY

"As *Sensei* also mentioned before, practicing '*Genchi-Gembutsu*' would need some specific abilities, right?" Takeuchi said, still feeling a sense of powerlessness.

"Obtaining the ability to understand what is really going on behind the scenes, and the ability to see through the problems, are indeed, I believe, indispensable," *Sensei* said.

"How can I develop those abilities?"

"OK. But before that, I'd like to lay out a few scenarios for you a bit. One day, to address a problem at the *Genba*, Mr. Taiichi Ohno, who first taught me TPS, ordered the chief at the factory to stay standing inside a circle that he drew on the ground with some chalk. Initial perceptions by those witnessing this unfold were that Mr. Ohno was dishing out some form of extreme punishment on the chief. However, Mr. Ohno, as a matter of course, was simply demonstrating his idea of how tasks should be prioritized. Then it became clear that Mr. Ohno, in an act of kindness rather, was giving the chief a symbolic space at the *Genba* where he could concentrate on essential matters and not let non-essential matters interrupt this process.

This action by Mr. Ohno taught us the importance of observing at each *Genba* astutely and conscientiously."

Sensei also said, "Oh, speaking of 'extreme.' I heard a story from the actual chief about something else Mr. Ohno had done, a case that involved a molding machine that seemed to be working less than optimally and so whose full potential was not being realized.

The problem had remained for a long time.

In response to the machine's performance, Mr. Ohno stepped in and roped off the molding machine so it could not be used. It was a strict execution of '*Yosedome*,' as we call it today, which literally means consolidation and stopping of malfunctioned machines.

'Everyone was at a loss as to what to do,' the person who was at the site said to me. They were extremely upset because it was necessary that the machine be operational to meet the next scheduled shipment. So, what did they do? Well, they decided to wait until Mr. Ohno went home in the evening, un-rope the machine, and operate it.

Somehow, Mr. Ohno knew what they were doing. But what could be understood about the workers was that everyone made some effort to solve the problem. It seems a bit extreme, but the story reminds us of the term 'oft-repeated flaw,' and warns us of the consequences of leaving a situation in a state of sub-optimal performance."

This episode was one memory of *Sensei*'s he had heard in his younger days.

"That person, who was originally a Production Engineer, retired from another factory's position as the chief, and then he became my consultant. He told me that he should have studied TPS more. I had no idea why he said that," *Sensei* said, as if he was mentally staring off into the distance.

"In the old days, TPS instructors were often disliked because they were using such extreme methods to teach TPS principles.

My mentor used to say, 'In that particular era, it may have been necessary to teach by showing extreme examples first, and then letting each worker apply what they learned practically, and this was done despite being rather hated for such instructional methods. Workers could not really understand and appreciate the full benefits of something until practical application allowed for such, and so it was important this kind of learning be fostered by the instructors.'

At that time, leaders needed to be seemingly extreme. These days, there is no need for that, which signals we have reached the next phase of TPS enlightenment. Now that the Toyota Production System has become more well-known and wide-spread, lessons are taught by mentors more politely and carefully, unlike the old days.

Old-school instructors can still be seen, often at organizations on the fringe who top off TPS lessons by proclaiming loudly, 'This is the TPS's way!' I would say that this method of instruction is just for show, that they are simply trying to appear on the surface to adhere to tradition.

Even though TPS is highly regarded, practicing it requires clear and logical explanations. In overseas operations especially, this need is even more apparent. That may be why foreign companies tend to become rather fixated on technique."

"Let's go back to the story of the factory chief 'standing' inside the drawn circle. I admit it to be a way of thinking professionally as a *Kaizen* practitioner, and it has some relationship with the term '**Standing Observation**.' I feel a need to explain it, as I feel it to be one of the primitive concepts of '*Genchi-Gembutsu*.'

On the *Kaizen*-technical-skills-check-sheet for the TPS *Kaizen* practitioner, there is one particular item: 'Can practice Standing Observation.' When I first noticed it, I was taken aback and wondered, 'What on earth is this?'

The definition and purpose of the 'Standing Observation' is as follows: 'Standing where the production line is clearly visible so that any problems with machines or Frequent-Stops can not only be detected quickly, but also any underlying issues at the *Genchi-Gembutsu* can be almost immediately understood, and in so doing *Kaizen* is properly followed.'

'Standing Observation' is applicable to all facets of an operation: human resources (Man), facilities (Machine), items (Material), and the quality of the products.

The different mindsets for practicing it are:

1. Perseverance and the fortitude to keep standing until one knows the root cause of any problems.
2. Actively and thoroughly observing operations from start to finish.
3. Taking actions guided by *Kaizen*.

Here, even simply regarding the term '*miru*' of four Japanese homonym: '**See**,' '**Look**,' '**Observe**,' and '**Taking care**' in English, there exist some particular ways of thinking in TPS. They are:

'See,' as in simply seeing scenery during a trip or other adventure.
'Look,' as in looking at actual sites, as in the case of factory visits

'Observe,' as in watching carefully while monitoring a plant's operations.
'Taking care,' as nurses would when taking care of patients

Those various kinds of 'miru: See etc.' exist, and in the case of the 'Standing Observation,' the attitude of 'Taking care' is particularly important.

A true *Kaizen* practitioner takes measures to ensure that problems are not repeated, and this is a result of looking for the root causes, after questioning 'why' five times by oneself, 'why, why, why, why, why,' while performing a 'Standing Observation.'"

⬛ -INVESTIGATING THE ROOT CAUSE USING "VISUAL CONTROL" AND THE "FIVE WHYS"

"I have noticed many 'play on words' exist in TPS. That would cause beginners to think it to be difficult to learn," Takeuchi says, perplexed.

"I see. In foreign countries, like this '*miru*: See etc.' example, there are many words that are hard to explain outside of the Japanese language. That is why it is crucial that they be explained patiently and thoroughly. Depending on the situation, sometimes explaining it requires some explanation of the Japanese language. For example, I explain that 'the Japanese writing system uses three kinds of character, kanji, hiragana and katakana, blah.' In some cases, a Japanese term is used as is and has become a worldwide adopted word," *Sensei* says, based on his own overseas experiences.

Then, he explains "Visual Control" in detail as the following:

"The reason why people have a hard time understanding the content when they start reading '*TOYOTA PRODUCTION SYSTEM*' by Mr. Taiichi Ohno is perhaps Japanese meanings are not conveyed clearly enough for readers. In addition to its technical contents, it is full of useful expressions and phrases with special meanings, which still cause readers to make new discoveries, even 40 years after its initial publication. Therefore, this book, keeping to its solid foundation of focusing on nurturing human resources as the priority, might be hard to grasp at first. Yet those who wish to master TPS must read it at some point in their journey.

OK, let me offer up further explanations of '*miru*: See etc.' and see if it might lend a bit of clarity.

There exist two terms. One is 'Visual Control,' and the other is 'Visualization.'

Mr. Ohno describes '**Visual Control** (Management by Sight)' in '*TOYOTA PRODUCTION SYSTEM* (Productivity Press, 1988, P.129)' as following:

Autonomation means stopping the production line or the machine whenever an abnormal situation arises. This clarifies what is normal and what is abnormal. In terms of quality, any defective products are forced to surface because the actual progress of work in comparison to daily production plans is always clearly visible. This idea applies to machines and the line as well as to the arrangement of goods and tools, inventory, circulation of *Kanban*, standard work procedures, and so on. In production lines using the Toyota Production System, visual control, or management by sight, is enforced.

In this original quotation, the term 'autonomation' is used instead of the Japanese term '*Jidoka*,' which I always use. I'll explain the meaning of *Jidoka* in detail later.

In many cases recently, we see 'Visualization' based on TPS being introduced into the workplace. I sometimes feel these introductions are a bit off point.

In these situations, what is missing is the crucial concept of 'Visual Control' – 'to specify what is normal and what is not' – and it is important that there be proper understanding of this concept.

The original purpose of 'Visualization' based on 'Visual Control' is to enable smooth operations at the jobsite, where people can easily find any defects or abnormal states, and fix them instantly.

Without 'Visual Control,' 'Visualization' merely becomes an exercise that serves little purpose except to proclaim that it is being done, akin to 'Management for Management's sake,' or as a way to demonstrate to and convince one's boss that one is working hard and on top of their duties. As a result, it runs counter to the goal of trying to create a more efficient jobsite, instead resulting in much wasted energy and time.

So, if the jobsite is made so that one can practice 'Visual Control' easily, what can one expect will result? It should allow workers to find any abnormalities or inefficiencies more easily, right? In such an environment, becoming a true *Kaizen* practitioner who can perform the kind of 'Standing Observation' I explained before will become easier to achieve.

Mr. Ohno presents in his book, at the beginning of his explanation of the 'Standing Observation,' that repeating 'Why' 5 times (the 5 WHYs) should be done when presented with a problem. By doing so, you will realize the root cause and understand how to deal with it.

Also, the priority should be on finding the 'root cause' rather than just the immediately obvious 'cause,' because behind any apparent 'cause,' there must be a 'root cause' waiting to be discovered. He also emphasizes that it would be nearly impossible for anyone to take any effective countermeasure to a problem without asking the '5 Whys' to dig up the 'root cause.'

As such, in just trying to pursue the meaning of the word *'miru*: See etc.' in *Genba*-oriented policy, I cannot help but feel that there are yet deeper concepts that exist at the core of TPS.

Henceforth, through the understanding and practice of the 'Standing Observation,' it is my sincere hope that you will develop into an independently capable *Kaizen* practitioner of TPS, and as an instructor, you will become well knowledgeable about the *Genba*."

With that, *Sensei* concluded his epic story. And with that, Takeuchi became even more determined to try to understand every *Kaizen* term's true meaning and essence so that implementation of TPS can be done on a practical level with confidence that success can be achieved.

Part V

Standing Still and Observing the Jobsite by Means of *Genchi-Gembutsu*

15

Observing the Production Workplace Closely Using Standing Observation; How Worthless Management That Exists Only on Paper Is!

Takeuchi was asked to oversee both the machine-based jobsite for parts-modifications and the assembly jobsite for finished products at the same time, which was very unusual for someone in an Assistant Manager's position at the East Automotive Co. Ltd.

The major challenge in assuming both roles is certainly trying to juggle shifts and maintain productivity among the members of his teams. Takeuchi himself usually spends half his day on a production line as one of the workers because of the difficulty in maintaining the proper number of workers for each shift at both of the jobsites he manages.

The Manager, Mr. Matsui, is of no help as he intervenes and questions every move of Takeuchi. The Manager has a rather unfavorable reputation among those at other jobsites. Rather than being seen as a source of guidance, he is regarded as a nuisance who seems to go out of his way to become a behind-the-scenes distraction among the workers.

The clean room at the machine-based jobsite is where over ten workers are surrounded by transparent walls of glass. Standing behind this glass, Takeuchi stands observing every move of the workers on the assembly line. Takeuchi, in his spare moments, tries to practice "Standing Observation," where from a particular vantage he can easily observe both inside and outside of the clean room.

At that moment, he would contemplate the place where he conducted his "Standing Observation" and half-jokingly say, "That spot one meter

DOI: 10.4324/9781003323310-22

in diameter has absorbed a fair amount of my sweat and tears." It was a sequel to the story about how he would later be transferred to another department in the midst of the company's periodic shifting of personnel.

By practicing Standing Observation and formally evaluating the performance of his workers, various problems and potential improvements become apparent. Also, it makes the practitioner think about many things.

One of the first things that Takeuchi noticed was that the production preparation process was not particularly well-structured. It is a major handicap of the company in that it makes each successive process inefficient because of the absence of concrete ideas and directions. Further complicating this is the company's unwillingness to heed the opinions of someone like Takeuchi, despite him having a technical background. The whole system is not conditioned for improvement of even a slight defect in the facility or process, until, that is, some major issue regarding the quality of the products surfaces.

Takeuchi strongly feels it necessary to adopt the "TPS protocol in the planning phase."

Though he is sure improvements can be made incrementally, attempting so seems futile in the Production Division and so long as he is just the Assistant Manager. Resistance to change is endemic company-wide, and it is upon this realization that Takeuchi makes it his mission to find a way to restructure the system.

Takeuchi has even kept a log of what he has observed and has aptly titled his notes "System-wide problems in the launch of a new product," from the product R&D Stage to the Mass Production Stage. Before the personnel change that sent Takeuchi to the Production Division, the previous Senior Managing Director had assured him: "Like at S company, I fully expect you to be returned half a year to the R&D Division as an Inventor after gaining enough experience and learning as much as you can in the factory." This is why he makes it a point to share updates of his experiences in the factory with the Senior Managing Director, as he plans to apply what he has learned in his future R&D role.

As is often the case in many companies, although the company's work process operates as one big flow, and though each department is optimized for this (sub-optimization), it is not always the case that the company has reached an optimal level (overall optimization). Particularly problematic is when issues exist in a department, instead of solving them right then and there, the buck is passed down to the next department. This structure is referred to as "Interface," whereby a company's daily work flow and organization could be illustrated as a "node," such as here: "O – O – O." It has become obvious that *Muda* exists throughout this interface process. It is with this realization that Takeuchi notices the importance of smoothing out the workflow and stamping out these inefficiencies.

Even though in TPS, the primary focus is on *Genba Kaizen*, the situation often seen is one where each department and each step in the process practices *Kaizen* within their individual area, but it is done with little or no consideration of departments in the former or latter part of the process. "It is not 'overall optimized'" would be a fair criticism of this situation, yet this creates the opportunity for a capable person to "right the ship." Nevertheless, it is still necessary for all workers in each step of the process to learn to read the situation themselves and gain a broader picture of what is going on.

While Takeuchi is in position to conduct his "Standing Observation" of the production line, he is unable to block thoughts from entering his mind that occupy his attention away from the immediate task at hand.

Takeuchi cannot stop thinking about why such a Manager can be assigned to a production workplace, as he has proven to be someone who shows little care about whether daily productivity is done optimally or not. That Matsui was promoted to Manager of the production workplace indicates an internal issue at the company in terms of appointing the appropriate people for certain positions. However, that he can spend the entire year as a Manager without paying attention to *Genba* reflects a much deeper level of ignorance or incompetence. Another way of looking at it is to ask how production can continue daily among the workers without major problems, even in the presence of a disruptive Manager?

Although manufacturing companies in Japan have been increasingly adopting new methods to streamline paperwork, Manager Matsui spends his whole day at the jobsite physically cutting and even pasting them on the bulletin boards of each production line.

Then one day, Takeuchi realized: "Ah that's right. Without any managers, daily production can still continue." Simply put, Manager Matsui can be ignored, but production will be none the slower. Though it may seem like a resignation to one's fate, or perhaps it can be seen as a major flaw in the production side of the *Kanban System*, letting Matsui Manager continue as he usually does is a rather simple compromise for the sake of convenience.

In the East Automotive Co., almost all of the products are processed using the *Kanban* information system. The Forecast Information of products volume is estimated for production each month, and it is presented to the Production Control Division and the Production Division as guidance for their operations. With that information set, when a *Kanban* is returned showing the amount the customers have used, a daily production number that equals that amount is decided. In addition, *Heijunka* is applied to the *Kanban* info.

Here, in this context, *Heijunka* means "leveling the quantity and kind of each product." These numbers posted on the *Kanban* can fluctuate prior to or even at the start of mass production, but they tend to become stable as production continues.

Even for transactions with some customers who haven't adopted *Kanban* and are using-another information method, the Production Control Division still applies their daily orders into *Kanban* for the Production Division.

However, orders information from such customers can vary wildly, from three times the daily estimated number one day to much fewer than the estimated amount the next. In this case, the Production Control Division arranges the *Kanban* issued to the Production Division so that the numbers of *Kanban* each day are about the same. This system is derived from the concept of the pull system in TPS.

In the planning of mass production, variations in customer orders were factored into estimates so that daily production and shipments could be processed consistently without disruption. So whether practicing *Kanban* as the medium or the means, it is assured that daily production activities will become "routine."

With this, the presence of only the Team Leader directing operations on each production line should be adequate enough to ensure smooth production daily. No Assistant Manager is needed, unless there is an emergent situation. That could be said for any company, even without a *Kanban* system.

With the absence of a Manager, *Kanban* can be regarded as one of the best systems under the idea of Production Management in terms of convenience, certainty, and the ability to function autonomously.

Whatever the case, even with drops in *Kanban* amounts, failure to meet the product requirements due to issues on the production line of one's own company and the resulting stoppage of the customer's production line should never be allowed to happen.

No matter what the situation is, various countermeasures should be at the ready to prevent disruptions. Even one disruption can cause a chain reaction resulting in major problems, so it is crucial that countermeasures be in place. Takeuchi has already experienced a situation at the start of mass production at the machine-based jobsite and where he saw firsthand the effectiveness of having countermeasures to deal with it. In that situation, despite the absence of a manager, a potential crisis was averted due to the countermeasures taken by Takeuchi and the Team Leader.

The product assembled in Takeuchi's production line was the most crucial part of the kind of car being produced by the client company, who themselves were ambitiously trying to drastically change their method of car manufacturing, primarily in the interest of achieving high-quality.

Therefore, there should have been tasks that needed to be done in preparation for production. In turn, the Manager, Matsui, should have been leading these preparations. However, it seemed all Manager Matsui was interested in doing was hanging around his desk and accumulating piles of paper that were seemingly unrelated to the production line. Some of what he said and did betrayed his aloofness regarding the *Genba*, due in no small part to him not noticing what went on in the *Genba*. The paperwork he produced was for a virtual world existing beyond what was actually happening around him.

Team Leader Yoshitake has been very angry.

Data on every day's productivity results and rate of defects are compiled in a monthly reporting form and attached to a bulletin board near the production line. This report is original, not a copy. Inexplicably, Manager Matsui has told him to re-write the data.

The data is, of course, factual. Yet, in the interest of concealing unflattering data, he instructed Team Leader Yoshitake, and thereby bypassing Takeuchi, to re-draft the report to make it more flattering. Once this type of cover-up begins, there is almost certainly a need to continue covering the tracks of the original perpetrator. It becomes an endless process. The paperwork he produces and presents at company meetings could all be part of this cover-up process. Reporting is done once a week every week and every month. He insists to Yoshitake that no one notices any data modification because no one remembers any of the past results.

Takeuchi knows, or so he wants to believe, that such a cunning and deceptive Manager is rare when considering how many Managers there are around the world. What makes this case perplexing is that this

Manager can continue his charade and still maintain his current position in the company.

A few days later, Team Leader Yoshitake has still not come to the office in the morning. Sometime before the morning assembly, he calls for asking, "Please let me have the day off today."

The company wants workers to consume paid holidays as much as possible, so Team Leader Yoshitake is following this creed and encouraging his members to do so as well. Takeuchi, having known Yoshitake for more than a year, had never seen this kind of attitude from him. Yoshitake being absent for anything other than an illness was unprecedented, which is why Takeuchi has become worried.

"Assistant Manager Takeuchi," a deputy of the Team Leader, talks to Takeuchi (not related) after the morning assembly.

"To tell the truth, Team Leader Yoshitake said he quit, after coming back from an afternoon-long meeting with Manager Matsui," he says.

Takeuchi, away on a business trip all afternoon yesterday, hadn't been updated until now. Soon, he calls Yoshitake.

Takeuchi says to Team Leader Yoshitake, who still insists on quitting, "Anyways, today is today, but be sure to show up tomorrow."

For a half-day yesterday, Yoshitake was interrogated regarding the monthly productivity results report, printed on an A3-sized form. He was angrily asked over and over, "What on earth are these numbers? How are we going to deal with these?" There should be no matter that requires a Team Leader to be away too long from the *Genba*. A competent Manager must understand each Team Leader's role. Here, an unscrupulous Manager literally tore up this month's original monthly report – the version that should have been posted on the wall of the production line – and tossed it into a garbage can.

Takeuchi is very surprised to hear about all that happened, and he runs to the table near the Manager's desk. He finds small pieces of the report in the garbage. He collects what he can find and tries to piece them together, reassembling the report with tape on the back.

Soon, Takeuchi goes directly to the Division General Manager, a person he had not seen for a long time. The General Manager tells him that Manager Matsui is not the kind of person who would be capable of tearing up the original report made by Yoshitake. One fact to have come out after the meeting with the General Manager was that the Manager had kept all of the reports that the General Manager had asked Takeuchi to make, and he blamed Takeuchi for allowing this situation to occur.

The General Manager goes so far as to say that it is all Takeuchi's fault that Team Leader Yoshitake is quitting. Takeuchi cannot believe what he has just been accused of. Also later, he became aware that Manager Matsui had told the Human Resources Department personnel a series of lies. Someone notified Takeuchi that Manager Matsui was telling made-up stories about Takeuchi.

Manager Matsui, seemingly friendly with Takeuchi when face to face, at times affectionately referred to him as "Takeuchi-san (Mr. Takeuchi)." He superficially called Takeuchi's name using the suffix "-san," which implies affection but can also be regarded as condescension; otherwise, he often called one's name without using a suffix, which has its own implications. However, in fact, his plan was to eliminate Takeuchi. It left Takeuchi to wonder what else the Manager was doing behind his back.

A similar incident by Manager Matsui had happened in the neighboring department, which resulted in the sudden resignation of a promising Team Leader, and who had been asked to head the startup of a production site in the United States. Eventually and fortunately, Team Leader Yoshitake changed his mind, and the result was Takeuchi and Yoshitake working together from there on. In fact, Yoshitake is about to take over Takeuchi's position as Assistant Manager after Takeuchi's reassignment to another division.

Takeuchi cannot help thinking that originally, the management at the production workplace was there to make the state of the site better, focusing on its human resources. Yet Takeuchi's situation is far from the Manufacturing ideal, and it causes those at and associated with the company to needlessly suffer from delays.

⊕ -*KANBAN* WRITTEN IN *HIRAGANA*, AND HOW TO MAKE CHOICES REGARDING *MUDA* USING *KATAKANA* AND *HIRAGANA*

Here comes *Sensei*'s private lesson. Again, explaining a term is one way of thinking under TPS.

"Sometimes we see the kind of book which preaches, 'You can know all about TPS,' even though the true content is focused on particular individual techniques, right? For example, 'Elimination of *Muda*' is surely one crucial concept in practicing '*Kaizen*' of TPS, yet it is just a part of the picture. If that is believed to be 'everything' of TPS, it would be a misunderstanding, wouldn't it?

Regarding the term '*Muda*,' it could be written '無駄' in *kanji*, 'むだ' in *hiragana*, or 'ムダ' in *katakana*. In which of the three Japanese characters should it be written?

In TPS, there is one unspoken rule that any terms expressed in *hiragana* should be intangible, or, if I can go so far as to say, something like software. *Katakana* should be for tangible or hardware-like things.

For instance, '*Kanban*' is written in *hiragana*, not in *kanji* or *katakana*. And so if '*Andon*' is written in *hiragana*, it might seem like an error was made. Some people would say outright, 'It is wrong.'

However, if those terms were used in foreign countries, deciding how they should be written could become more difficult.

In a new factory in China, the usage of '*Kanban*' in English characters has been regulated, including the nuance of using *hiragana*. However, the older factories there which have adopted TPS still have many areas where '*Kanban*' is written in *kanji* that is the same as the Chinese characters. Yet, even though '*Kanban*' may be written in *kanji*, it may still be fine as long as the leaders and workers there have a firm understanding of what the concept truly means. That said, there have been times when I visited factories where *kanji* was used, but where I got the impression that their understanding was replete with misunderstandings regarding '*Kanban*.'

Now let's consider '*Andon*,' a 'Line-stop indicator board' that is hung above the production lines. There are several types of '*Andon*.' It also has some basic rules regarding its appearance, particularly related to color. The color green means everything is normal, while yellow means the schedule is delayed, and red means production should be stopped on the line. However, these tend to be mysterious to those from outside the company because they are often internal rules.

'*Andon*' itself is a hardware apparatus.

I remember once when I visited a factory to explain the overall TPS system to overseas members, one person from either a European country or the U.S. referred to the term 'eindon,' where the 'ei' was pronounced 'ay,' as in 'stay.' On hearing that, I couldn't realize immediately that the person meant '*Andon*.' At first, I thought the misunderstanding was due to my poor English ability. It turned out it was more so due to how I envision

'*Andon*' to be a kind of hardware device, used under the system to clearly indicate the state of the production line.

The type of '*Kanban*' I have mentioned so far is the type where information is written on a bill-sized piece of paper, which is inserted in a '*Kanban*' case: a 10 × 20 cm rectangular-shaped vinyl plastic bag with a zipper. Some '*Kanban*' are presented using the printed-out papers as they are, while other times, the paper is laminated.

'*Kanban*' explained here has to be written in *hiragana* because it has to be filled with information, like the way to process daily tasks, for practicing Visual Control. These are not the type of signboards which we would see at shop entrances and write '*Kanban*' in Japanese *kanji* characters.

Of course, the line between what can be considered hardware-like and software-like, tangible or intangible, is somewhat ambiguous.

In expressing these terms in written Japanese, during my TPS site observations, it is rare that I did see the term '仕組み, *shikumi* (system)' in *kanji* characters, which seems hardware-like. In other words, in most cases, the TPS *Kaizen* approach is done for the whole processing system, which is categorized into the software-like term 'しくみ, *shikumi* (system)' in *hiragana* characters. But in only a few cases can they be categorized as individual hardware-related tasks. Things that are software-like are mainly the foundation, and some particular hardware-like elements are scattered there. Thus, most of such activities wind up being expressed with 'しくみ, *shikumi* (system)' in *hiragana* characters.

So how about the term '*Muda*?' In TPS, '*Muda*' at the production workplace is categorized as follows:

1. *Muda* of overproduction
2. *Muda* of waiting
3. *Muda* in conveyance
4. *Muda* in processing
5. *Muda* of inventories
6. *Muda* of motion
7. *Muda* of making defects

In total, there are seven types of '*Muda*' in *katakana*. However, regarding software-like '*Muda*,' I have been taught they should be expressed in *hiragana*. For these seven types of hardware-like '*Muda*' in *katakana*, it may seem difficult to distinguish one from the others, despite the possibility of some software-like 'Muda' being written in *hiragana*.

Thus, though the line between when to use *hiragana* or *katakana* is blurry, we should attempt to make the distinction to demonstrate understanding of core concepts and its components.

At least, let's keep to the basic idea that 'Kanban' should be in *hiragana*, while 'Andon' should be in *katakana*."

16

Is It Easy to Manage in the Kanban's *World!?*; What Is the Role of the Manager?

Today also, Takeuchi is practicing the "Standing Observation."

He is standing at the center of the invisible one-meter-long-diameter circle, yet no part of his surroundings have come into view because he is so deep in his thoughts.

"How come such a Manager who has been so far removed from the *Genba* can be allowed to continue in his capacity in this company? With the situation as it currently is, no matter the efforts I make, any efforts to improve the actual situation of the *Genba* would be in vain," he thinks.

More or less, such managers tend to be in any company. Still, in search of some form of clarity, one must ask himself why such a manager is allowed to be in his position.

If I dare say, perhaps it is because workers are so appreciative working in the *Kanban* system that they paradoxically feel that having a poor-performing and also dare I say, strange manager is less problematic than one would think. This could be said not only for any of those in *Kanban*-practicing companies, but also for any of those in other highly-respected production systems.

In the East Automotive Co., the *Kanban* system has already been applied to the point where it functions stably. *Kanban* has become so entrenched in the company that it could be regarded as a matter of "common sense" that it be followed. It's the *Kanban*'s world! When applied as a method of evaluation, which will be further elaborated later in this book, the following categorization range should be applied to the company: "Level C" to "Level D."

DOI: 10.4324/9781003323310-23

In an attempt to avoid misunderstandings, let's look into the rest of the story that conveys what we call the *"Kanban* System" as a part of the Toyota Production System.

Also, for companies where *Kanban* is nothing more than just "Tags," they cannot be considered as having fully transformed to "the *Kanban*'s world." In such cases, they can only be said to have reached "Level B," which again, will be further detailed later on.

In the Production Division at Takeuchi's company, a whole system of "Production Management" has been implemented with *Kanban* at its center. It is said to be easy to set up that system, even when a new production line is launched. Of course, successful implementation of the *Kanban* system relies on the premise that its management is stable and reliable.

As daily production and shipping are processed based on the information provided via *Kanban*, how smoothly and naturally production flows is reliant on the condition that each worker follows the rules. This is where the concept of "routine work" becomes less about mundanity and more about being a critical cog in the *Kanban* machine.

In the East Automotive Co., any delay of delivery caused by issues would be unacceptable.

As a result, the company has molded itself into one where production is achieved without dropping any *Kanban*. To put it simply, success is when *Kanban* is operating smoothly. Of course, it is also important that in the process of smooth efficient production, the resulting products themselves are of high quality.

By regarding dropping any *Kanban* as more important than achieving productivity targets, companies often try to keep increasing manpower to an amount in excess of what was originally thought needed. As such, controlling costs becomes less important than meeting deadlines for delivering goods. However, it may also happen that no measures are taken even though it becomes apparent that some improvements are needed.

Surely *Kanban* is a useful tool. What all practitioners have to do is to ensure that everyone is doing what they are supposed to be doing daily to contribute to the *Kanban* flow. In that sense, management-wise, the presence of the Team Leader on each production line should be sufficient to ensure that everything is operating smoothly. It is surely one of the major strengths of production under *Kanban*. Thus, the Manager can simply hang out at his desk shuffling papers without ever seeing the production workplace.

One would think that there should be a lot to do as manager. Then, apart from "general" management, what should each manager's role in "the *Kanban* world" actually be?

Kanban should be regarded as the means by which one can maintain "Visual Control" of operations. By keeping tabs on the smooth flow of *Kanban*, one can be immediately aware of how well the whole production cycle is proceeding.

To ensure that such awareness is achieved, it is necessary that the entire *Kanban* system follow or be adjusted to follow certain core rules, such as that any unused *Kanban* be put in a *Kanban* Safe, or that each item is tagged with *Kanban*, or that *Kanban* is always handled appropriately according to regulations.

Of additional importance is that the management cycle "PDCA" (Plan-Do-Check-Act) be followed. With full adoption of the *Kanban* system, it becomes necessary to see and check daily if *Kanban* is being handled with appropriate care at the production workplace, and to take appropriate measures if there are any problems. This is called maintaining "Visual Control" within "The *Kanban* world," one of the major roles of each Manager.

Indeed, it is said *Kanban* is one of the most important tools for practicing *Kaizen*.

One major goal within *Kaizen* is to improve the jobsite by *Kanban*. It is not enough that *Kanban* is tagged on every product, but also that the jobsite as a whole functions more smoothly. Before, without such an idea, such a philosophy was previously ignored or not yet fully realized, thus causing many a company to implement the "*Kanban* System" unsuccessfully. Even for Takeuchi's company, where the concept of "the *Kanban's* world" has been widely implemented, it still takes time and consideration until *Kanban* is truly and fully practiced.

Professionally speaking, the type of manager who seems to offer no observation other than "We have too much stock in our inventory" is a manager who often lacks the ability to conceptualize how to effectively solve the problem.

It is similarly unconstructive if employees at the actual site take the defeatist attitude of "With the current situation at work, it cannot be helped." Without any constructive solutions within the *Kanban* system there is little chance that items stocked in inventory will ever be reduced. This would apply in "non-*Kanban*" systems as well.

At many Manufacturers today, as the management system has evolved and progressed, each manager is often asked to submit data that offers insight into the health of the manufacturing. This is why recently, managers at the production workplace have been under a great deal of stress and suffering from fatigue. Some issues are related to the actual physical structure of the manufacturing, which adds to the pressure managers are under.

With what is required of the managers, if they are the type who simply request the necessary data from their team and regurgitates it to their superiors at the company, there is little hope that actual improvements at the jobsite will be realized. In "the *Kanban*'s world," where the *Kanban* system and philosophy has thoroughly permeated, the fact that such incompetent managers can be allowed to exist shows one of the drawbacks of this system. It should be totally perplexing to have a boss like Manager Matsui who offers little but the words "Do it" or "How are you going to deal with it?"

When looking back, Takeuchi also recalled that he was far from aiming for a higher state of understanding, and that he simply wanted to use *Kanban* somehow.

Looking back, He should have considered the situation more carefully, when it had become obvious no essential improvements were possible without such consideration of the essence of *Kanban*. Or it was simply beyond his capacity at that time.

Upon reflection, he realized he had not been fully utilizing the *Kanban* function as a tool, a tool that could elevate the management of operations. It is clear that *Kanban* is an essential tool to make "Just-In-Time" possible, but before that, the attitude of trying to do one's best to contribute to an overall better jobsite should be a far higher priority.

-DRAWING THE SCHEMATIC DIAGRAM OF THE BASIC CONCEPT IN THE TOYOTA PRODUCTION SYSTEM

"*Sensei*, what is 'Just-In-Time'?" Takeuchi asks.

"I see our talking sessions have been based on the concept of '*Kanban*' so far.

I have already told you before that *Kanban* was the tool for practicing 'Just-In-Time.' Here, we need to go back a little bit, because

I have yet to explain one important idea in the Toyota Production System. That is the concept of 'Two Pillars,' consisting of 'Just-In-Time' and '*Jidoka*.'

The idea is sometimes mentioned in ordinary situations, and it is also found in a lot of existing books. Now, I'm going to explain briefly what 'Two Pillars' means in the field of the Toyota Production System.

In one of his books, '*Toyota Production System*' (Productivity Press, 1988, p. 4), Mr. Taiichi Ohno describes, 'The basis of the Toyota Production System is the absolute elimination of waste. The two pillars needed to support the system are:

1. Just-In-Time
2. *Jidoka*: autonomation, or automation with a human touch.'

With the idea of 'Just-In-Time,' the following process is supposed to be anticipated, and that determines the goal of the former process: the following production process withdraws the goods it needs, when it needs them, and in the exact needed amount, from the former process. The former process produces only the amount withdrawn.

Jidoka is the idea that when any abnormal event occurs, the machinery is forced to stop, or the operation of the production line is stopped.

For any manufacturing industry corporation to thrive continuously, it is like a supreme directive to practice 'Cost Reduction' with 'Thorough Elimination of *Muda*.'

TPS has been molded as an orthodoxy and a total production system through daily practices guided by the goal of 'thoroughly eliminating *Muda*,' making the most of each employee's ability to the fullest, elevating one's motivation, and utilizing the facility or its machinery to the fullest.

Soon after the book '*TOYOTA PRODUCTION SYSTEM*' by Taiichi Ohno had been published, one group, influenced by the basic idea of the TPS explained by Mr. Ohno, had created one schematic diagram shaped like a house, which was to aid their understanding of TPS.

This is the picture that shows how to achieve '**Cost Reduction**,' supported by the two major pillars of '**Just-In-Time**' and '*Jidoka*,' and with '**Thorough Elimination of *Muda***' at its core.

This picture presents the basic idea of TPS very well." (Figure 16.1.)

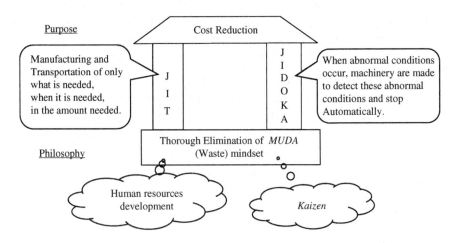

FIGURE 16.1

Cost reduction through thorough elimination of *Muda*. (Translated from Takeuchi, Noboru, "*Seru Seisan*," JMA Management Center, 2006, P.129.)

⟲ -THE TWO-PILLARS OF JUST-IN-TIME AND *JIDOKA*

"*Sensei*, I have to say that this picture, shaped like a house, helps us understand the core concept very easily," Takeuchi said to *Sensei*.

"That's right. And I see these days there have been some altered versions of this picture, based on various experiences with TPS. I have to admit that those altered diagrams seem to make it more difficult to understand the core meaning behind 'Just-In-Time' and '*Jidoka*,' where some items of the means and the technique depend on not 'Just-In-Time' or '*Jidoka*' individually, but both. And sometimes, some alien ideas in various levels are unified into these concepts. It's a matter of course that TPS will keep evolving and reach a deeper state, as will 'the means and the technique.' Yet, I suggest you simply start off first with understanding a basic form of TPS," *Sensei* said.

"*Sensei*, I have seen an instance where the 'Two Pillars' were transformed into a shape similar to a sports tournament bracket," said Takeuchi.

"Well, I see. Normally, I have many chances to offer some guidance activities on the Toyota Production System. For this Two-Pillars picture, I always say to my students at the beginning of a lecture, 'You tend to think you have understood all about what the picture means because it was the one that was explained to you initially, but for me, it was only after a few years before I was first introduced to this.'

Regardless of which of the various kinds of the TPS technique are explained, all ideas are basically supposed to follow the 'Two-Pillars' picture, with some wisdom about the *Genba* added.

As I mentioned before, '*Kanban*' is one management tool for practicing 'Just-In-Time,' right?"

"*Sensei*, could you tell me how those two ideas of 'Just-In-Time' and 'Jidoka' were constructed?"

"I see. Then it is time to focus on their history. First, '*Jidoka*' is not '自動化' (automation, the *kanji* '動' means 'movement') but '自働化' (autonomation, or automation with a human touch, which has the *kanji* '働' (*Ninben*), representing the element of humans working positively by themselves individually). At the Toyota Museum, the *Jido* weaving machine invented by Sakichi Toyoda, the founder of Toyota, is displayed. This machine has a structure to stop by itself when it detects any instances of threads being cut or running out. Unlike other 'automatic' machines that simply continue moving despite an abnormality, Toyoda's machine works with an element of human wisdom or instinct so as to reduce issues. That was how it started."

"Now I see how the idea of '*Jidoka*' cannot exist without the '*Ninben*' *kanji* character. The attribute of human will must be represented," Takeuchi said.

"The idea of 'Just-In-Time' was first proposed by Kiichiro Toyoda, the second founder of Toyota. When he came up with the idea, he was inspired by supermarkets in the U.S. He observed how the customers could get what they needed when needed, and in the desirable amounts they needed at the supermarkets. Kiichiro Toyoda, tried to add the '*Kanban*' system to it, which was for practicing the 'Pull-type Production System.'

The word 'Just' was added not only for being 'In time,' but also for not being too early, nor too late.

So, it should not exactly be 'On time' either.

In a movie I watched the other day, there was a scene where a bomb exploded. Right after the explosion, the actor said 'Just in time,' and its Japanese translation was 'The timing was right (that the bomb exploded).' So, in a factory situation, I guess it would be like 'OK, the timing was right that we're out of stock. The timing is right to start producing items to be passed on to our following process."

"*Sensei,* so efficient manufacturing under TPS is based on the ideas of 'Just-In-Time' and '*Jidoka,*' right?

From now, I am determined to study a lot more about this field, and I will be sure to consider its background or its core values, not only simply imitate it on the surface, sir."

17

The Role of the Assistant Manager in the Toyota Production System

Since Takeuchi started his career here, he has been taught that all actions taken by employees at the East Automotive Co. are supposed to be based on the Toyota Production System, though it would be somewhat hard for indirect staff outside of the hands-on operations to sense whether that principle is being followed.

That said, even the highest-ranking members of the Planning and R&D Division are to stay within the framework of the Toyota Production System, as everything from daily procedures to any ideas proposed are to be based upon its concept.

In Japan, most production workplaces, whether based on TPS or not, regard their workers (team members) as essential.

This Japanese virtue of regarding workers as central is carried over to overseas production sites of Japanese companies. Yet, it would be unrealistic to expect overseas operations to reach the level of efficiency and precision that have become standard in Japan. Besides, Japan has also been facing some crashes of the long-kept system due to changes in the surroundings (Figure 17.1).

Though the cost cutting competitions against overseas companies have been getting more intense, it would only be at the very moment of the collapse of the Japanese Manufacturing system established so far when each worker at the actual site will be regarded as less important.

There was one particular experience Takeuchi had more valuable than any prior: his transfer from R&D to the production workplace. Basically, Takeuchi used the term "the production workplace," since he hesitated to use the term *Genba* when considering the unique formation in production.

DOI: 10.4324/9781003323310-24

FIGURE 17.1
Human resources at the Cellular Production workplaces. (Translated from Takeuchi, Noboru, *"Seru Seisan,"* JMA Management Center, 2006, P.186–195.)

However, occasionally the term *Genba* is also used there, as *Genba* or *Gemba* is a widely known term and is universally used in the manufacturing industry. Other universal concepts are *Gogen-Shugi* (the five actuals) and *Genchi-Gembutsu*.

Takeuchi had to immerse himself in the Toyota Production System as a supervisor, and so a high sense of problem awareness was needed. Since it was his very first time to study the Toyota Production System first-hand in the actual *Genba*, his understanding of it was no better than any other beginners'.

Mr. Taiichi Ohno said that the supervisor of the *Genba* was to be the Production Foreman and equal to the manager of a Small and Medium Enterprise (SME). The Production Foreman here embodied the following:

- Someone with not only the ability to perform as a supervisor, but also as a manager.
- Someone who when functioning as a supervisor can direct each workflow.
- To fulfill these elements well, a basic understanding of IE would be necessary. Also, he devises standardized work for the team members to conduct, and he ensures the members obey it.

These were the conditions that Takeuchi was expected to fulfill.

Takeuchi in a self-evaluation of himself felt that his performance was not to a satisfactory standard in terms of fulfilling his obligations.

On the other hand, more abstractly, Takeuchi began to think that TPS' true benefits could become apparent if each team member performed to their utmost.

 -AS A TECHNICAL EXPERT OF R&D AND PRODUCTION ENGINEERING

Thus, after a few years of struggling in the Production Division, Takeuchi believed it impossible that he could be assigned back to a mere staff position.

However, he ended up being assigned to the Production Engineering Development Division, and was placed in charge of the development of environmentally-conscious material.

Upon his re-assignment, after an over four-year absence, Takeuchi consulted with *Sensei*.

"I remember, *Sensei*, you once told me that someone once confessed to you that his study of the Toyota Production System was not adequate, right?" Takeuchi asks.

"That gentleman was a Production Engineer who was relieved of his position as a factory chief. When I initially heard him, I did not understand what he really meant," *Sensei* begins his response to Takeuchi.

"His desk used to be right behind mine at the office when he was a technical advisor. Looking back at what he said to me, I guess I would have had to admit my lack of prowess in TPS.

I wish I could have more fully understood TPS as a technical engineer.

Basically, in retrospect, I wish I had tried to study and understand TPS more thoroughly, despite my young age. That would have enabled me to broaden the range of work I could cover. Also, in the area of design, TPS should be adopted, as it, of course, should in other job fields."

"Moreover," *Sensei* continued, "From the moment I started at the company, I had not actually understood what was truly meant when I was told that our company was based on TPS. Moreover, I had been under the belief that TPS was only applicable to the production workplaces.

After that period, and since I was placed in a position where I was to lead my members and therefore had to try very hard to gain a more thorough understanding of TPS, it took some time before I had gained some clarity on one particular point: that it was all about your 'way of thinking.'

First of all, it is very important to understand your 'way of thinking.'

At the same time, one may also have to learn the technique.

However, what is least preferable is to be Mr. Know-it-all without any practical skills.

On the one hand, this may somewhat contradict what I said earlier about how I should have studied TPS earlier. However, I am also sensing that absorbing the true elements of 'way of thinking in TPS' is harder to accomplish through actual implementation.

I had always dismissed the notion that 'it cannot be obtained through implementation,' whenever told to me. However, I now adhere to a similar notion.

No implementations, no gain.

I now feel that only the knowledge you obtain from practical experience, where your efforts cause you to sweat, can make you truly confident."

Part VI

Learning the Toyota Production System as a Technical Expert in Mid-Position

18

Learning the Toyota Production System Together with Young Technical Experts

B Electronics has the opportunity to gain TPS education, as technical experts of middle standing gather together there. The reason for this gathering is to educate its skilled technical experts more professionally over a certain period of time.

Mr. Takeuchi is here as a tutor. Up until yesterday, he had been teaching the general concept of TPS, and related professional case studies. Today, he is supposed to answer questions after talking about how one should deal with TPS as a technical expert.

-WHAT IS THE KNOWLEDGE THE STAFF SHOULD LEARN IN TPS?

"I am going to talk about the attitude towards TPS as a technical expert," Mr. Takeuchi begins his lecture.

"In recent years, people have gained a better understanding of *Kaizen* in the Toyota Production System.

In the old days, there was an image of a 'Pressure-type' person who was in charge of the instruction for the production workplace. It would be one never-ending activity to keep improving the production workplace once created, for making the workplace more efficient and productive.

However, only doing 'follow-up' under the *Kaizen Activity* on the production line once it was created would not be enough to say it's a true representation of TPS activity. It would be more preferable to try to build

DOI: 10.4324/9781003323310-26

up the ideal features of the Toyota Production System, by using 'The TPS activities coming from the Development Stage' or 'Developing new Machinery in line with TPS concepts.' 'Pre-stage phases' activities in the 'upper-stream' end are thought to be crucial.

When each corporation carries out TPS, it is simply classified into two major categories. One is 'In-advance TPS,' and 'Follow-up TPS' is the other. When explaining the features of TPS in Journey Four, 'Features of the initial workplace: An initial build-up of the features for the workplace' is the former, and 'Features of the improving workplace: The features for improvements after start-up' is the latter.

First, '**In-advance TPS.**'

Weaving the ideas of TPS into a start-up system at the planning phase. For example, by adopting the ideas of TPS at the product design phase, some innovative ideas can come about, which are different from the ways of the past. As a result, a new stream of innovation in the manufacturing processes can be expected. At least, there are some 'tricks,' like things that can become triggers that can make improvements to the production workplace easier.

Second, '**Follow-up TPS.**'

'Rationalizing, or increasing efficiency' through improvements (*Kaizen*). Compared to the previous way, competitiveness can increase due to Productivity thriving through the concept of 'making efficient.' This is a typical image of TPS that is widely known. In particular, the term has been called '*KAIZEN*,' mentioned by a number of books published so far.

Essentially, various know-hows which were improved and clarified in the previous lines had to be woven into a new production line from the start-up period. However, actually, there are bound to be many cases of imperfections, and many areas of improvement should become apparent.

Also, even though everything may have seemed perfect at the planning phase, or one may have been supremely confident believing it was a perfect series of processes, the essential idea of TPS is to try to make those seemingly perfect things even better. That means *Kaizen* can be a never-ending activity.

One important thing here is to share company-wide any *Kaizen* activities developed. Any *Kaizen* must be reported to the upstream management processes in the company.

No matter how well the former 'In-advance TPS' could be carried out, it would not mean that the latter 'Follow-up TPS' is not necessary. How to include the idea of TPS as early as conveniently possible would become the key.

'In-advance TPS' can be a hard concept to follow. I suppose it came from the idea of 'Feed forward,' which is based on a system of eliminating in advance all foreseeable issues caused by any environmental changes. The thing is, how many actions can be taken in advance. If one tries to make changes afterwards, it can result in there being a lot of *Muda* due to numerous constraints that have come about in the establishment of the production process. Yet, there is also the possibility of generating 'waste' resources if issue-preventing action is taken too early. The important thing is generating useful ideas with your knowledge and wisdom and trying to reduce the amount of *Muda*.

The term '*Kaizen*' as it relates to manufacturing in Japan is known worldwide today. It's been said that Japanese people humbly admit mistakes, reflect on what they did, and try to make improvements. Under the Toyota Production System, we must pinpoint root causes of issues by asking 'why, why, why, why, why,' If this can be done within each company, regardless of the situation that emerges, that would be truly a blessing," Mr. Takeuchi closed in his remarks.

Without pausing, he announces, "From now, I am going to take any questions."

Then a designer asks,

"What **aspects of TPS** should we consider **from a designers' point of view**?"

"I will answer your question based on my general thoughts towards design," *Sensei* said, and went on as follows.

"First, be thoughtful of the *Kaizen* Activity.

That is not to say that you should try to carry out any and all restructuring proposals regarding design in attempting to adhere to the principles of *Kaizen* Activity in the production workplace. Still, even if some proposals were to be too costly to be done, try to make improvements by turning to the second best solution if necessary.

Those in charge of manufacturing at the production workplace are supposed to take the lead in ensuring that *Kaizen* principles are being followed. Certainly, they need to develop ideas based on their own department's needs, but at the same time, they should tap other departments for their knowledge and wisdom as well.

For example, the Production Engineering department also has a role in trying to ensure *Kaizen* is maintained smoothly and with the desired design, yet designers also still must take actions proactively.

Second, pay attention to particular designs in terms of the way and each step in the process of production.

Some say that design should be the primary consideration because the design factors 90% into the production processes. So it would be preferable not only to focus on the development of each product shape or performance, but also on the manufacturing processes of each product.

Though inspections of each design have become increasingly easy due to IT developments, each designer is still expected to consider each action and process at the production workplace. It is better not to leave it all up to the Production Engineering and the Production Division, but rather, TPS implementation should be approached from the stand-point of design.

Some *Sensei* insist that having less *Mura* (Unevenness) means *Kaizen*. This type of thinking comes from *Genba Kaizen*, a viewpoint regarding improvement at the production workplace. As designers who take TPS into consideration initially, trying to have less or no *Mura* (Unevenness), less or no *Muri* (Being Overburdened), and less or no *Muda* (Non-Value Additions) is supposed to be expected.

As for the production quality, the Production Engineering and Production Division are responsible for it. To follow *Genba Kaizen* at the production level, the activities by each production plays a big role. On the other hand, design departments should be in charge of predicting the increasing or decreasing qualities of a design.

Also, having some criteria in the design of particular sides of a product and insertion points for each part so that they become easier to assemble can be done with the help of Production Engineering.

It is getting more common to reduce *Muda* effectively both in each part and each step in the assembling process. For example, assembling using one screw with a snapfit fastening design is a vast improvement over the previous design that required four screws. This is an example of eliminating "*Muda* in Processing," one of the seven *Muda*. Over the long term, the *Kaizen* Activity process undergoes changes and adaptations are made.

These 'Pre-stage phases' activities are one example of 'The TPS activities coming from the Development Stage.'"

Another question from a production engineer:

"What should we consider when building up the production line?"

"A little while ago, I mentioned that some people said 90% of a whole production system would be determined by the design processes. Even though that was right, the remaining 10% would be determined by the production line. Besides, due to various conditions, such as the limitations of time, resources, etc., expecting a perfect design would be unrealistic.

Therefore, at which level is incorporating the idea of TPS on the production line considered primary, before the running or after the running of the line?

If it is after the running has commenced, it is the Production Division that should play the main role of checking the processes and make improvements to the machinery. However, if it is before the commencement of running, the Production Engineering Division should take on that role in Process and Machinery Development.

Applying TPS principles to the production line in advance will lead to the development of a much more efficient system. Besides, the production line system becomes even easier to improve after its startup.

If the system is not adequately developed due to insufficient *Kaizen* considerations and activities before the startup of running — perhaps due to expectations that *Kaizen* can simply be added afterwards on the production line — it may wind up becoming a situation where it becomes harder to make improvements later, and where there are lots of *Muda*.

The important thing is for the Production Engineering and Production Division to execute mutually by showing and sharing each other's ideas completely. Also important is developing the facility and the processes with a well-built system of Q (Quality), C (Cost), and D (Delivery)."

One further question from a production engineer:

"Can you clearly explain 'Developing new Machinery in line with TPS concepts?'"

"When a Production Engineer builds up a production line, he or she may have to consider various patterns depending on each condition with which one encounters. Yet, it is necessary to have a vision of the features of the ideal production line and to proceed with making firm decisions on the PDCA cycles.

In detail, there are three sections that need to be considered:

1. The work formation of the basic system shapes, number of workers, and size
2. The whole process of product flow and build-up
3. The whole system of logistics

For Machinery Development, the idea of *Jidoka* seems indispensable in meeting the standards of quality in each process. The goal is to have a production line with smooth mobility by making products reasonably quickly, and devising a simplified disassembling and reassembling system without unwanted massive investment towards the Machinery. Still, it goes without saying that safety comes before anything else.

Regarding some detailed conditions for achieving the ideal Machinery Development based on TPS principles, there have been features in some magazines and other sources. For example, for designing machinery, one consideration is 'Width ratio,' calculated by dividing the whole width of the machinery by the product size. That means setting each machinery width to a size which is no wider than twice the width of the smallest product is preferable. One might think that it actually seems difficult to achieve this considering the size of the smallest product. However, if there is any wasted space within the machinery, it will become too wide, leading to not only unwanted machinery space, but also waste of the number of footsteps workers must take to navigate the machinery.

Anyhow, it is essential that the basic ideology of the Toyota Production System is followed.

Mr. Taiichi Ohno did mention that TPS was not only an American style of IE (Industrial Engineering) but also one of the profit-increasing factors of IE leading directly to Cost Reduction (Profit-Making Industrial Engineering). Besides, this TPS-inspired type of IE itself is considered the 'company-wide Operations-Management-Engineering which is connected to the management.' His idea was that the Toyota Production System becomes meaningful only when it is a company-wide Operations-Management-Engineering-System achieving Cost Reduction as well.

'Company-wide' total activity is crucial in TPS. It can be said with certainty that the Designer and Production Engineer play far more important roles in the actual production."

Next comes a question from a leader who plans and manages the promotion of new overseas factories in the Production Management Division:

"I am going to be in charge of **opening new overseas factories** in Southeast Asia. What things should I keep in mind under the idea of the Toyota Production System?"

"Throughout several of my experiences as a *Kaizen* coach for overseas enterprises whose businesses were already established, I could not help but feel the necessity of having one universal concept of the Manufacturing process. Besides, it was a time when more than one factory had the chance to-start up or expand. It was then that I had decided to coach according to the 'Activity manual for the logistics of the new factory startup' I had developed based on the idea of TPS. I wanted to make each factory I produced keep to a uniform factory formation.

In particular, I tried to make it easy for improvements to be made after startup since it is difficult to develop a flawless system of machinery and processes on each production line from the beginning, despite the application of repeated time-tested techniques from Japan.

First of all, there is the attempt to set logistics within each factory based on TPS. The following is a simple summary of this idea:

Activity manual for the logistics of the new factory startup

1. Be in charge of managing the TPS activities in the factory, factory logistics, and productions as a supervisor of TPS.
2. Coach the Production Management department which is in charge of logistics, and the Production/Production Engineering department which is in charge of production.
3. Make decisions regarding the layout of each building, each factory, and each production line jointly.
4. Make adoptions of TPS that add value from the viewpoint of three types of Logistics (Procurement, In-plant, and Delivery), Components Manufacturing, and Assembly Manufacturing.
5. Drawing a 'Goods & Information Flow Chart.'
6. Drawing a 'layout chart and goods flow.' In the layout chart, showing the flow of conveyance after deciding each storage area and production processes in accordance with the 'Goods & Information Flow Chart.'
7. Putting each document into the right place.

8. Building up a detailed schedule for the acceleration of the sections above.
9. Selecting the appropriate members who can ensure the progression of the sections above.
10. According to the needs of the situation, driving the process forward in unison as a whole project team.

The points above are also a part of the 'Pre-stage phases' activities of TPS, an activity to incorporate the ideas of the Toyota Production System from the beginning."

"As a final remark," Mr. Takeuchi says as he readies to deliver his final piece of advice after answering all of the questions,

"I have been faced with many kinds of workplace situations I was really reluctant to help. They seemed to be bad businesses in terms of profit. Today, I can say with confidence that those experiences have become an essential part of my being as a TPS coach. At least, these experiences enabled me to gain a certain perspective: that one should not wilt when tackling the type of work that initially seems insurmountable or undesirable.

What I can say about Production Engineers these days, specifically those who should play an important role towards TPS implementation, is that they seem not to be strong enough to perform necessary actions when observing from the upper levels of the production system. The upper levels mean Development and Design, while the lower levels are Manufacturing and Production. It is crucial to think about how to take action in the middle of the company-wide framework.

Also, to achieve success in whatever situation, it is also necessary to have 'Innovation of production engineering.'

For any Production Engineer, it seems like it is a never-ending task to keep thinking about what the 'Key elements' and 'Key technology' in their companies are. Many people think it should be a task for the Development Division only. However, I myself think it should be both Development and Production Engineering's task.

If the Manufacturing ability within each company is poor and weak, that may attract some grave results. Though, now, it has become necessary for increasing profits and simply for the sake of surviving to adopt a way of doing productions overseas, without which it would be very hard to thrive. Moving forward, few companies can expect to survive by doing only assembling and arranging products without any core ideas underpinning operations.

In the Manufacturing field, to avoid being overtaken by competitors, and though they may come close, understanding the idea of TPS and the endless pursuit of its ideal features in the production process is essential.

Whether you are in Product R&D, Design, Production Engineering Development, or Machine Development, all of you who are in charge of any R&D for Manufacturing have to try hard to thoroughly understand the actual production line.

Refer to the principles of the Toyota Production System in addition to VA/VE or Cost Reduction activities. Take thorough looks at the next steps in the process and the production workplace.

Then, come up with effective actions. Then, the activities you are actually involved in will be more effective and meaningful. Through company-wide activities that improve performance at every level to where the entire operation can function smoothly will lead to what can be considered true, ideal Manufacturing."

19

Learning the Role of the Toyota Production System

When driving the Manufacturing forward in the midst of the global environments' increasing competitiveness, there's a certain significance in understanding the way of the Toyota Production System, and also the role of TPS. Obviously, going through a seemingly routine process with sincere effort is fundamental. Once done, the chances of achieving the desired outcome are increased. However, it often happens that great effort is expended performing these routines.

Mr. Takeuchi gives a speech with the theme of "The Manufacturing of Japan" to staff people, like Product Planners, Designers, and Sales Planners. He is giving some general ideas about attitudes and concepts toward the Manufacturing under the Toyota Production System.

-ENCOUNTERING THE TOYOTA PRODUCTION SYSTEM

It still seems surprising to me that I have been involved with the Toyota Production System for such a long time. When I was first hired by a company, I expected to be involved in the Manufacturing as a technical expert, and to have deeper knowledge of what exactly being designated "Manufacturer" entails.

Not to mention I came to realize the weight of the significance of Manufacturing as a manufacturer in terms of our role in contributing as a member of society, and understanding this more deeply has been on-going as we carry out the Manufacturing.

DOI: 10.4324/9781003323310-27

When I was learning as a TPS apprentice, I was shocked upon taking a look at the preface of an old IE textbook written long before I had started working at the East Automotive Co. It's because I found the book had already answered my question "What exactly is a manufacturer?" right at the time when I joined the company. And I am still on this journey to fully understand the Toyota Production System, which seems to come before anything else. I still feel rather powerless, as I feel I am unable to take all the refined lessons Mr. Ohno left and apply them practically.

Some people say following the Toyota Production System is like practicing a religion. It seems ironic that staff are being asked to trust TPS as blindly as they might a religion, doesn't it?

It's been said that Buddha never forced people to believe his words. Instead, he was perceived more as kind of a scientist who was guided by the principle that one should do one's own research. His teaching philosophy was said to follow the process of lecture, implementation, and discussion, despite or in response to the absence of the proper attitude of undergoing pursuits with maximum effort and sincerity.

With this consideration, I would not feel compelled to disagree if people said TPS was like practicing a religion.

Among the people who have had some unpleasant experiences while being coached on the Toyota Production System, who perhaps felt the pressure of the expectation that they be able to reduce the total number of inventory, some say TPS seems illogical.

On the other hand, when I spoke to a person overseas about the Toyota Production System being called "Illogical," the person responded by saying, "Actually, it is logical."

I imagine that an English translated version of a TPS manual may have been done well enough where it seems more logical than the original Japanese version, perhaps because of a difference in how explanations in the languages are normally structured. Moreover, in overseas coaching, no one can really appreciate the true benefit of a novel system and implement it without first receiving logical explanations.

Some people say that practicing the Toyota Production System seems easy because it should simply be a matter of following a type of flow production method based on the *Kanban* System. To me, unfortunately, it seemed difficult.

From the day I started working at the company, I have been continuously experiencing and studying the production line under this *Kanban* System.

However, I actually realized how little to nothing I knew when I tried to establish a production line by myself from scratch. I also started encountering people who pretended to know.

What's more, I had no idea how to improve an existing production line by myself based on the idea of TPS. I was clueless when I tried to practice it at higher levels.

I experienced many cases which changed according to situational changes, though I tried to pursue the ideal features at first. I've even experienced several times situations where by adjusting the line's direction by 90 degrees, we were able to produce the model shape of the product, but which allowed us to produce the products more efficiently yet still achieve the ideal features (the features in the future). The reason was I just followed each step after receiving thorough explanations in pursuit of the features to be attained. You might say that was *Muda*, but what I got in the end were pretty effective results at minimum cost, and we were still able to reach the ideal features.

Thus, the most important thing was to get each part of the process moving forward step by step, all the while thoroughly checking that goals were being met, and how to best reach the ideal features, which came from understanding the different necessary actions to take depending on the situation. Not only is it doing repeated processes as part of the means, but also understanding the means and the importance of taking actions based on the principle.

The production line we developed enabled our invention to be mass produced; we customized the machinery, and the result, after a lot of struggle, was a product ready to be sold on the market. And this came without having received TPS coaching.

No one around me knew about TPS, and the TPS instructors at that time were mainly assigned to the *Genba Kaizen* position on existing production lines, so they were far from being able to be consulted.

I remember one time when a TPS expert outside the company visited my company to give some lectures, not having then the knowledge that I have now, all of which I perceived to be a type of logic which seemed unrealistic. Therefore, I realized that I needed to either myself become an ideal coach as a technical expert by studying really hard, or I needed to, with some luck, find a really good instructor. Unfortunately, accomplishing either of these proved extremely challenging, as all of my energy at that time was spent on making the production of the invention take shape.

Whenever I look back at all of the experiences I have had, I always recall one particular production line I developed which became the trigger that encouraged me to learn the Toyota Production System earnestly. Thus, I still simulate through my head all that occurred, which enables me to see how it was the right choice to try really hard to make one flow out of the machinery prepared at that time, and if placing a "Store" in the middle of the flow, it would become identical to the ideal state Team Leader Yoshitake taught me.

Every time I refer to the books of Mr. Ohno, I always discover something new. Those ideas of our predecessors seem to be philosophy obtained in solitary on their own: at least we can never expect to be able to reach it. Indeed, surpassing this level is out of the question.

To now, I have been developing this speech with the intention of it becoming useful for beginners, especially when they are faced with tall obstacles.

I would be most delighted and relieved if you can sense and understand even at the slightest level the struggles of trying to reduce the difficulties and complexities as much as I have been able to.

Out of all the books related to the Toyota Production System published so far, though there are many good ones, there were a certain few which reminded me of a fable: "The Blind Men and the Elephant." With that, I mean the peril of staying in one place without looking at the whole picture. These books to which I refer tended to leave some matters unanswered till the end, even though they had focused on detailed explanations of the technique and examples. When trying to interpret the examples in these books, it would just result in some acquisition of the type of knowledge that would be no different from old tales or tea-chats but lacking any real-world situations related to the problems and themes within.

When we are told how it was like in the past, how are we to truly understand what we are reading without also sufficiently understanding the conditions and the situations at that time? Even though we are adopting the same concepts as were followed in the olden times, we cannot necessarily apply the exact same method now that was used then. In the cases of these books, they can be regarded as mere references. Unfortunately, they are far from able to enhance our TPS understanding.

My sincerest apologies if you felt my speech has not been any better than the books I was referring to, perhaps full of faults and generally unsatisfying due to multiple occasions where the contents were such that only the most experienced can understand, but where there were often insufficient explanations of details.

-THE MANUFACTURING WORKPLACE FOR THE JUST-FOR-YOU-PRODUCT

Next, I am going to talk about what I would like you to practice, as I am one of what can be considered a technical expert.

When I say emphatically that the Toyota Production System is all about the pursuit of the ideal features, what that means in terms of the Manufacturing is that ideally, one is able "To be able to present each item at the very moment 'Our Customers' ask for it."

And only the enterprises that can make this happen can survive. Also, the Toyota Production System has taught us there should be various routes to reach the desired features, with not only one method or one tool but a certain way of thinking permeating the job site. The source of competitiveness is the endeavor to make products with the ideal features as best as one can. Of course, the power of R&D to keep creating newer, more attractive products will be of continuous necessity. Japanese ingenuity can maintain its superiority to others on that point. I don't have any particular worries about the potential and ability to produce new things. Yet, there is a worry that we may fall behind the global competition.

On the other hand, as we continue to discuss the difficulties facing domestic production in the face of cheap labor in new developing countries, it is clear that new solutions are needed. Also to be considered are the effects of dramatic currency exchange rate changes and other economic forces, which will require Japan to continuously make adjustments as the situation calls for. With regards to commodity products (daily goods and necessities), competitive pricing is the key issue.

Out of all of that, as we have talked about it, one more key consideration regarding how one can meet "Our Customers" demands without delay is how one's superiority over other competitors will be decided.

In the world today, when people can choose products with one click, customers can easily and immediately choose another product if delivery is not soon enough. It is like there has to be a balance among all of the aspects of each product, including price and time to produce and deliver. As well, "Our Customers" must also consider the wide variety of products, all of which they may consider necessary according to their needs. We are already starting to see the kind of products that can be customized for "Our Customers" and provided to them in short order, which enables us to maintain our competitive advantage.

Both domestically and globally, in manufacturing, there is the very real possibility that delivery (D) is becoming paramount in deciding who could be considered the most superior amongst the competition.

In fact, we are at the dawn of an era whereby it is not only necessary to guarantee **immediate delivery** of purchased products, but to produce such products in – **for the customer** – desired quantities.

Therefore, what it will take is "The Manufacturing of the Only-for-You-Product," or alternatively, "**The Manufacturing workplace for the Just-for-You-Product.**"

One idea in the Toyota Production System is that "the following production process withdraws the goods it needs, when it needs them, in the exact needed amount, from the former process. The former process produces only the amount withdrawn."

Ultimately, features of that system would ideally be what I had mentioned in the beginning: "Being capable of presenting each necessary item at the moment 'Our Customers' visit to receive it," right?

The technical term is **"Lead Time Shortening" at the production workplace**, or the matter of "inventory-in-process" from the perspective of *Genba Kaizen*. That is one of the primary pursuits underlying the Toyota Production System, in addition to simply Cost Reduction.

Thus, the ideas of the Toyota Production System should be respected and regarded as crucial in discussions over how Manufacturing in Japan can remain competitive and superior to overseas counterparts.

In producing the Just-for-You-Product, each technical expert is supposed to create products that are easy to be customized later on. As a precondition, there should be the possibility of adding value as much as possible to each product, even in the final stages of the production process. From the customers' point of view, it is desirable that they be able to compare and choose among a wide variety of products.

Therefore, all company workers who work on the production line, as well as the admin staff that support them, together as one team, should always be striving to achieve the goal of being to present desired products at the moment "Our Customers" appear and make their request.

-STRIVING FOR THE IDEAL FEATURES

Japan has been facing a decline in the population and so, in the labor force. And the global environment has been changing drastically due to a stronger yen, the acceleration of overseas production, and competitive neighboring countries catching up, among other factors.

There has been much discussion recently over the challenges of staying cost competitive in the production workplace because of global competition. Despite the situation, each person involved in the production directly thinks that "we are and will continue to try to work really hard in the practice of TPS, and therefore ensure profitability. However, we do expect R&D to continue to design better products. For that to happen, we need to lend our support to the department by being profitable."

The kind of company in which "Trying-to-improve" activities can be done in the whole company would be considered a "good company," wouldn't it? Nowadays, I sense that this type of effort has been disappearing. I have personally witnessed workers at a particular company who often gave excuses and displayed a general attitude of not wanting to put forth even the slightest effort to try to make the factory operations more profitable. That should not exist in an environment whereby discussions regarding trying to stay competitive with neighboring countries on top of currency fluctuation issues also exists, among other matters.

The Japanese traditional work systems have still continued to operate well so far, even in the absence of prominent leaders. However, by visiting various companies' factories, I have also seen the work systems have been becoming rusty. Still, when looking at each production workplace, I notice many cases where there are a certain number of things that should be done and improved yet remain neglected, and thus, the "driving force for *Kaizen*" at each factory has been weakening.

Even when visiting a factory of one famous Manufacturer, sometimes points to be improved became obvious at first look. Was it perhaps they were simply not noticing the problems, or that they were so uninformed that it was to be expected that they would simply just leave things as they were, and that it spoke to the poor quality of the instructors. One can come up with a variety of reasons. The important thing is to keep searching for improvements. There are many cases of workplaces that purport to espouse being innovative, but they, in fact, are the opposite out of fear of risks.

This undertaking should be done on both the software side – like in planning and systems – and also on the hardware side at the production workplace. The optimal situation at all levels is needed to develop one ideal stream. I cannot help but hope that it will not come to be too late – as it was in the famous tale of the boiled frog, who entered what was thought to be warm water only for it to be so hot that the frog was cooked before it could know what happened – and so this level of unawareness should be avoided at work, such as when pressing a Hanko (name stamp) on each document as part of the continuous right to left processing of documents.

Also, regarding Productivity, in a book titled "*Nihon No Monodzukuri Tetsugaku* (The Philosophy of Manufacturing in Japan)" (written by Mr. Takahiro Fujimoto, published by Nikkei Publishing Inc. 2004, Page 74), the author said, "I doubt that a number of Japanese enterprises are achieving even one-third of the productivity they originally should have had, due to management that has largely neglected the production workplace."

Even though there have been more recent matters regarding the currency exchange rate and Small and Medium Enterprises (SME) when compared to the time the book was written, I still sense some similar headache-inducing problems at *Genba Kaizen*.

Also, in Big Enterprises these days, I feel that the ability or desire to look at the whole picture of the Manufacturing has been weakened due to the overwhelming number of tasks technical experts have to deal with. As a result, they have been becoming less user-oriented. Despite the high-performance potential in each technical expert, it's not been sufficiently utilized.

Thus, it would be futile to even hope for something that does not exist.

No matter what the management environment or what difficulties there are in products production, the ideas of the Toyota Production System that strengthen the production workplace and eliminate *Muda* should continue to be fundamental going forward. It is important to have sufficient ability to implement tasks by applying TPS tips and knowledge to one's own situations.

I myself feel that the Manufacturing in Japan cannot be surpassed under such environments, as long as each of us involved with the Manufacturing keep "an attitude aiming for the ideal features of the Toyota Production System."

At each department, from the planning and development of new products in the "upper flow," to production engineering in the "medium flow," to the production workplace in the "lower flow," there should be a sincere effort to maintain the aspects and corporate culture of Japanese Enterprises, and to always be in pursuit of the ideal form. It is crucial for us to keep doing those things that are thought to be as matters of course with sincerity.

The power of unity while strictly keeping to rules, yet approaching one's duties with earnestness, and strengthened by technical capabilities...these elements can be hard to encounter overseas. Therefore, we can consider it acceptable as long as we are not being surpassed by overseas companies consistently, even though they may catch up with us occasionally.

Though there was once a time when it was thought that Japan was in a league of its own when it came to production, I have been noticing lately when having conversations with European or American participants that more and more companies in their homeland have made a shift toward a management style emphasizing the Lean Manufacturing technique which they had studied in Japan.

If there comes a time when they succeed in changing management to where they figure out how to incorporate a stable corporate culture into their means of operation, it may enable them to catch up to Japan. I myself work as a coach who firmly believes we should keep competing vigorously on the global stage, so we as members of Japan, Inc. can never slow down. Once we take our foot off the pedal, we can only expect to be caught by the competition. So we need to keep up the intensity. Thus, even if we are eventually caught, we can maintain our momentum driven by a desire to not be surpassed by the competition.

The reason I have been steadfastly sticking to the principles of the Toyota Production System from the beginning is I was moved by their ideas toward the Manufacturing, as taught by mentors from Toyota itself.

If I had the ability to go back to the past, when I was in the developed production line, but with my current and more accurate understanding of the Toyota Production System, I would be able to produce the kinds of products that might be a little more beneficial to the world.

A major role of the Toyota Production System should be that each Enterprise can eventually come to contribute to society throughout the Manufacturing by using its innovations as "the interpreter of the Manufacturing."

Under the Toyota Production System, practitioners should take actions guided by an attitude prioritizing the need to keep striving to make improvements. However, to ensure output is always of the same quality, the "appeared features" of the TPS also have to keep changing.

For instance, as time goes by, things like the managing environment are vulnerable to change. Although it may seem like a simple aspect of TPS, such environmental change may result in a drastically unexpected outcome. Making an effort to change without changing the desired out-come...here lies one difficulty in adhering to the principles of the Toyota Production System.

Since the current global environment has changed a lot from what it was before, it seems that there may be no right answers in trying to follow a path that successful model cases in the past had followed. It may be risky nowadays to think the ideal features can be reached by simply trying to extend a path already followed.

Yet, I still think it to be important for us to keep doing the things thought to be matters of course with sincerity and conviction. Those "as matters of courses" seem difficult to be known and executed. Therefore, first of all, trying to execute Cost Reduction earnestly by repeating "Why?" five times at the Manufacturing workplace, then detailing the ideal features, and then aiming for the ideal way of the Manufacturing are considered to be crucial. Whether it is regarding the tangible hardware or regard-ing the intangible software, what it takes is for us to not only ensure the Manufacturing in Japan continues but to keep evolving it.

Individual manufacturing companies should specify the ideal features by not only thinking about the future of its products, but also to do so while considering all of its products, technologies, and services together.

These days, there have been many cases of so called "good" enterprises collapsing after undergoing sudden significant changes. The attitude of aiming for the ideal features relentlessly at each given position is essential for our companies to keep surviving.

⟨⟩ -CONTINUING TO LEARN

Before ending this lecture, I am going to talk about what the Toyota Production System has meant to me.

From when I first threw myself into a Manufacturing company in order to try to get some ideas on how a Manufacturer should be, it has been a long, long journey to get to where I have been finally able to realize how much TPS has guided me throughout.

How could the Toyota Production System be described academically? Some say it is a system that has already been complete, but others say it is almost complete in its maturation. On the other hand, there are also some presentations which state "this is how the system is," or "it can be analyzed as this Production Management-wise." These explanations sometimes seems to be useful.

Eventually, I came to realize that the idea of Mr. Ohno which showed how the Manufacturing should be was fundamental, and also extremely logical, though at first it seemed to be a complete contradiction. And because the Toyota Production System is principles of thinking, though those principles and how to apply them can be formed into learning material, now I am of the thinking that anything derived from them can be nothing but one case.

Henceforth, it is my wish to continue the pursuit of the ideal features under the principles of Mr. Ohno's "Profit-making IE."

With respect to human nature, it would also certainly lead to the fostering of an attitude in the workplace in which each worker can be motivated and feel joy.

20

The Never-Ending Pursuit

Both the learning activities of the Manufacturing and the pursuit of the ideal features should see no end. Keep your foot eternally on the pedal, and always keep striving to achieve better features. That should certainly be the mission among those who are involved in the Manufacturing.

 -DREAMING

Phew....

    I see Takeuchi has come up to me with some questions.

    Go ahead and ask me.

    I will answer what I can, in my own way.

    Of the things we both don't know, let's consider them together, because I myself am still on this journey of discovery.

    OK, why don't we go to an actual job site to make observations (*Genchi-Gembutsu*) first hand, and let's try to gain understanding together?

Journey Three

Implementation Journey

LEARNING HOW TO PROGRESS WITH *KAIZEN*

– Participating in *Kaizen* activity –

In this journey, the main character struggles with practicing improvement in the new environment of another company which differs in terms of products and field of expertise, so he grows into a *Kaizen* practitioner.

In order to grasp an image of TPS *Jishuken*, this story depicts a relatively big organization where the Toyota Production System has been built to a certain extent. This is the story's intention in order to avoid becoming conceptual and help you relate to the case studies used in this book. Depending on your situation, you should skip difficult words and read the story.

The story shows how support of top leadership and *Kaizen* organizations is necessary for the *Kaizen* practitioner to achieve effective results, and the *Kaizen* practitioner should practice and learn by himself.

The outline of introducing the Toyota Production System is the following procedure: top decision-making, employee's understanding, project or task force team organization, setting target item (production workplace), *Kaizen* activity, system making, object scope expansion, and continuous activity.

DOI: 10.4324/9781003323310-29

Part VII

Entering the *Kaizen* Promotion Organization

21

New Departure

Four years have passed since Takeuchi returned from production to his former position, Assistant Manager in the Production Engineering Development Division. He is going to finish the first stage of developing new foamed plastics.

A particular *Jishuken* starts at the main factory. The top management of the company has unexpectedly instructed all administrators of indirect section staff to participate in a special *Jishuken*. All members are divided into several groups and carry on *Kaizen* activities.

This special *Jishuken* which occurs for a limited period aims to deepen the understanding of the Toyota Production System. There are some people who just join the group out of a sense of obligation. Thus this doesn't look like a proper activity, even though our company professes the Toyota Production System.

Incidentally, an explanation on the details of the word of *Jishuken* hasn't been provided up to this point. We simply call the meeting *Jishuken*, but this is an abbreviated word from "The Toyota Production System *Jishukenkyu-kai*." The *Jishukenkyu-kai* in Japanese means a meeting of an independent study group or a meeting of an autonomous study group. And the *Jishukenkyu-kai* also means a *Kaizen* team activity rather than a research workshop or a meeting of study. New methods and tools are produced from the activity.

One day a main TPS leader strictly instructed us, "Never say the 'Toyota *Jishuken*' as a shortened word, because we don't research and develop Toyota but research and develop the Toyota Production System." So, when TPS peers say *Jishuken*, they think this means the Toyota Production System *Jishukenkyu-kai*.

DOI: 10.4324/9781003323310-31

The *Jishuken* recently held at the East Automotive Co. Ltd is commonly categorized into the "internal" *Jishuken* meeting or the "Manager" *Jishuken* meeting, which is formally recognized as "the Toyota Production System *Jishukenkyu-kai*." The team activity is implemented under leaders of the general manager tier and starts after they have decided themes. Members basically gather after daily tasks, so it's a burden in this respect.

"Mr. Takeuchi," Manager Yamanaka suddenly speaks to Takeuchi as soon as Manager Yamanaka takes his seat after he participated in *Jishuken*.

"TPS suffocates people. I dislike TPS."

Takeuchi replies, "Uh, what happened? I believe TPS respects others." At that time he realized it's almost time to go home, but he continued talking.

The *Jishuken* group, which Manager Yamanaka joins, handles the theme of productivity improvement in a production line. The practical implementation is to improve operators' movement. This is the first experience of Manager Yamanaka, who has grown as a staff member of the indirect section, to attend *Jishuken* and feel the activity was not good.

Takeuchi explains to Yamanaka, "I'm not sure what happened in your group, so I can't speak about your activity. But I think the Toyota Production System has a philosophy which is considerate to workers."

Takeuchi proceeds to look at the world of *Kanban* in the production workplaces. But his ability in the Toyota Production System still has to be more developed, even though he has experience in working at the production workplaces. He acquires a little knowledge of the overall Toyota Production System and a beginner's level of improving worker's motion.

Manager Takeuchi reflects back to several situations during his younger years which gave him knowledge about the improvement of worker's motion.

He joined the East Automotive Co. Ltd from university and shortly afterwards was trained at factories. The factory was in a local town. Many housewives of farmers were working a side job at his factory.

During every practice teaching, young Takeuchi worked in the Cell Production line with many housewives.

At the end of one day, he heard housewife workers cheerfully say, "We produced this amount of products today." They had to record the total number of products on the Production Control Board when the sound of closing rang. A women in charge of inspection wrote down the actual number of products on the board. The women talked with each other using a Mikawa accent saying that the day's work was better than the previous day's and they had achieved the daily target number that day. When young Takeuchi heard their happy conversation with a Mikawa accent, which was unfamiliar to him, this made a big impression on him. He realized their vitality was caused by their professional pride in the production workplace. It was the first time that he found people behave like this at the end of work.

And when Takeuchi was Assistant Manager of the production assembly line, he was looking at the motion of operators every day through Standing Observation. He observed thoughtfully while the operators were doing difficult tasks because the machinery and the equipment were not good.

The equipment was an old mechanical jig which the Production Engineering department had installed a long time ago. As he was an Assistant Manager in the Production department, he requested the Production Engineering department to repair it, but they said it is impossible.

He said that it was a design mistake of the Production Engineering department, but they said they couldn't repair it due to an issue with their repair budget. He wanted to correct such a bad system in the future.

This assembly line was designated as a specially controlled line because important automotive parts were produced on it. Partly for that reason, all female workers in the line were excellent at operation. Takeuchi thought that the women had easily operated the difficult work, nevertheless he thought that they didn't have to get tired if the jig could be corrected.

In the factory, the Production Engineering department set a standard of production man-power, so the product target number had been decided. It's natural to think a worker would like to make as many products as possible. He remembered the conversation with the Mikawa accent when being trained. Although the workers did the difficult work, when they were told that the target number had not been achieved, they would not be able to accept it. In this case, the productivity would rise with the same labor if the jig was repaired. Moreover they might work with better posture and natural motion. He thought that method of work was bad and felt that he didn't have the power to change the situation. While doing the Standing Observation, Takeuchi was thinking such things.

I'll emphasize the following perspectives of *Kaizen* regarding the motion of operators without going into detail.

First, it is out of respect for people. In other words, we make work better so as to be considerate of workers.

We should improve workplaces so workers can be "comfortable" or for them to be able to work "easily." When we make work easy, the improved standardized work sometimes looks monotonous. Easy work and monotonous work seem like two sides of the same coin.

We should refrain from equating a way which puts a burden on workers with *Kaizen*. We shouldn't follow a way which forces a working speed on workers. We should eliminate *Muda*, or waste. Then we should listen to the workers' opinion. We have to think whether we would make our own family do the work.

But in the case of an undeveloped machine or process, or for the sake of the cost performance, human flexibility of movement is sometimes needed. Then if the human flexibility of movement makes up for the task's difficulty, it also demonstrates respect for human ability.

Manager Takeuchi explains the thinking to Manager Yamanaka, "The Toyota Production System originally had the concept 'Respect for People' based on respect for humans," as shown in the previous paragraph.

He meant it is wrong that workers are forced to work only to improve the productivity in their workplaces. He wouldn't have been able to say such a thing with confidence if he hadn't practically learnt it through his own hard experiences.

-RESPECT FOR PEOPLE; THE TERM "WORKER"

Sensei appears and begins to speak.

"Takeuchi, there is a brief column which is written in my book about the term 'worker.' Let me show you it from the Japanese book, '*Seru Seisan* (Cell Production),' Noboru Takeuchi, JMA Management Center, 2006, P.124.

Management tends to consider a human as man-power. Meanwhile, members who work in a production line tend to feel like one of the gears.

When I stayed at a European factory and talked about standardized work, a local manager described this as 'working like a robot.' I immediately denied it saying, 'If a machine could do such work, it should be mechanized. But the mechanization is not easy, so we compensate for the difficulty of work with human flexibility of movement. A human is not a robot.'

The human body has a lot of capabilities. Even if human work can be mechanized, it costs a lot to make the mechanization. A time when machinery does all the human work may come in the future. But all the work which can't be done by machinery is now compensated with human flexibility of movement. In the labor-intensive industry, we will continue to depend on overseas sweat labor from now on.

We can often think there is no technology available now so we need to request people to do these simple tasks with their skillfulness. That's especially why we should respect people and we should pay the right wages for the right people. I feel this thinking is important.

Meanwhile, managers want to simplify the work in order for workers not to make mistakes, because it would become a problem if workers produce defects. So, we waver between simplified work and a work which requires skillfulness.

We sometimes call a person 'a Worker' or 'an Operator,' depending on the details of the work in a production workplace.

The word 'work' shows the concept of 'showing inherent function' and the word 'operate' the concepts of 'working effectively' and 'making things work effectively.' It seems that there are various names for workers overseas, but I call a worker 'a Team Member.' I mean I hope a member attempts to get promoted to a team leader or group leader and so forth.

In this column, I said that human beings work in place of machinery because there is a reason why the machinery can't do the work humans do.

The cost competition recently has become increasingly intense in a global society. Meanwhile a trend of thinking, in which people regard a worker as man-power, has been spreading. During this time, it is necessary for us to have a mutual respect for all people who are concerned with Manufacturing. Humans aren't a replacement for machines. I believe that the thinking of 'Respect for People' can make excellent manufacturing workplaces."

22

Transferring to the Managing Division of TPS Activities

The executive boss suddenly tells Manager Takeuchi, "Developing new foamed plastics has come to an end. You have worked hard enough. Transfer to OMCD, the managing division of TPS activities, for two years."

This personnel change is said to be a bit strange in his office. People say he knows the Toyota Production System better than anyone else in the Production Engineering department division. But this is a new journey for the Toyota Production System which Manager Takeuchi doesn't expect. He thinks many different future experiences are needed in order to further deepen the understanding of the Toyota Production System.

This year OMCD, as the managing division of TPS activities, first proposed an education system to raise up TPS leaders. The purpose of this system is "to develop TPS leaders who are the key people in the TPS activities."

Manager Takeuchi is chosen as one of TPS apprentices. He is the first TPS apprentice at a manager tier. Three managers are selected: Manager Takeuchi from the Production Engineering Center and two managers from the Production Center.

The executive boss tells Manager Takeuchi, "3 years are needed to get TPS skills, but you must return in 2 years. I have some tasks for you to do at the Production Engineering Center after you acquire knowledge in the Toyota Production System."

Manager Takeuchi has tried to deeply study and absorb the Toyota Production System within two years at OMCD which is the professional division of TPS, but as a result it was difficult for him to understand the Toyota Production System. Not only was the education system not good

DOI: 10.4324/9781003323310-32

but also the ability of the trainers was not good, which is why he has not really come to understand TPS.

It is not so difficult for us to acquire the various tools and methods, such as *Kanban*, which handle the Toyota Production System. The superficial tools can be acquired by simply studying them to some extent.

There are many workplaces where we can learn TPS, so we can have a lot experiences there. At the same time we can study TPS in many books. But it is not easy for us to fully appreciate TPS for what TPS really is. In these books, many conceptual words and phrases appear, such as "the backbone of the Toyota Production System," which don't immediately help us to grasp a deep understanding. In addition, there are trends in the manufacturing world to elevate TPS to a God-like status. Of course, we might be able to understand something about TPS after we have practiced TPS for some years.

Manager Takeuchi has read many books about TPS and practiced TPS for many years. He begins to realize that the authors of the books may possibly have only narrowly grasped the meaning of what Mr. Ohno said. He suspects that the authors had only written from experiences based on their past workplaces.

This transfer to OMCD was a start toward a time which Takeuchi thinks back to some years later,

"There are some books which just look at one aspect of TPS and remind us of the parable of the blind men and the elephant, which originated in the ancient Indian continent. It's important for us to understand the fundamental basis of TPS, and not to stick only to methods or tools (which are trivial details), because TPS doesn't work if we only imitate the external aspects of TPS. It's necessary to keep developing the right TPS ideology ..."

23

The Way to Progress the Activity: Organization for Promoting TPS

Many years have passed for the East Automotive Co. since they introduced *Kanban*. The Toyota Production System was active when they introduced *Kanban*, but it is on a plateau now. Most senior TPS practitioners who promoted introducing *Kanban* have already left our company. So our company needs to throw off the superficial Toyota Production System. And developing TPS practitioners is also an urgent business.

Manager Takeuchi has transferred to the OMCD, which is the managing division of TPS activity and has expanded from department to division.

OMCD is one division in the headquarters' functional organization, in which OMCD has a secretariat-like function to control the TPS promotion department in each factory. OMCD originated from a former *Kaizen* organization. There were IE (Industrial Engineering) specialists who managed *Kaizen* by then. Mr. Masanori Taga, who was an expert in IE, became a leader when they introduced *Kanban* with TPS. He has managed almost all TPS affairs up to now. Mr. Taga is also in charge of the TPS secretariat duty, and he serves as a lecturer of education and training in the Toyota Production System. He has sustained the OMCD up to now while our company has been in an inactive doldrum period.

On the other hand, the TPS promotion department in each factory can easily come into action, because they focus on their own factory.

OMCD is trying to develop many *Kaizen* practitioners and at the same time is growing in size from a department to a division.

Manager Takeuchi transfers to OMCD from another division as the first TPS apprentice at the manager-tier in order for OMCD to be able to develop the middle management TPS Instructors.

DOI: 10.4324/9781003323310-33

Some group leaders who were from the Production department and the Production Engineering department as the first TPS apprentices at the GL-tier had already transferred to OMCD half a year ago. Three managers and some GLs start education and training in the Toyota Production System so that they can improve the skills in practicing TPS.

Though some managers stay in OMCD, there are not enough TPS leaders in our company to maintain this training system. This TPS apprentice training system has a rule that trainees basically should be returned to their original workplaces at the end of the training. But sometimes some trainees continue to stay in OMCD.

In the Toyota Production System, it is important for *Kaizen* practitioners to practice TPS continually while growing up personally. And in order for *Kaizen* practitioners to achieve a good result, support by top management and active support organizations will be needed.

There are various analyses and evaluations about the advantage of the Japanese manufacturing industry. The organization, management, and human resources may be considered as three such advantages. As for us, we have to continue to strengthen *Genba*, the production workplace as both workplaces and products are directly connected to each other. Two important themes we then have to consider become how to establish "*Kaizen* organizations" and how to develop "*Kaizen* human resources." For example, there are many examples of companies introduced in magazines as references, such as 5S's cases. In these cases, there are good examples of teamwork which are worth imitating. And it goes without saying that soul and vision are necessary for making a *Kaizen* organization.

There are various types of *Kaizen* organization.

Now, let's briefly review *Kaizen* organization in the Toyota Production System. I don't intend to discuss about the organizational theory. This is an image of a typical organizational example, which is used in TPS activity. The *Kaizen* organization changes according to company type and company scale, and according to the situation of the company. So, readers should read through the following explanation as an organizational example.

The "Toyota Production System *Jishukenkyu-kai* (autonomous study meeting)" can be recognized as a special organization in the Toyota Production System. This is also a "*Kaizen* organization" for "personnel development," which is a system of actively developing "*Kaizen* practitioners" in corporate organizations. We can also see other types such as *Kaizen Dojo* (school), but they are a little different.

We abbreviate the "Toyota Production System *Jishukenkyu-kai*" to *Jishuken* in Japanese. I experienced someone telling me that we should correctly say the "Toyota Production System *Jishukenkyu-kai*." If we say "Toyota System" as an abbreviation which omits "Production," we might be admonished. In *Jishuken*, we persist in pursuing the better way (system) of production. And we mutually develop each other through the *Kaizen* activities of making a better production workplace. And we develop into *Kaizen* practitioners so that we can grow in our ability.

We will go into the *Jishuken* story in Part VIII.

A managing division of the Toyota Production System is generally known as OMCD.

Actually, the Japanese name can be directly translated into "Production Research Division (or Department)" in English. This translation has caused some confusion among outsiders, such as "Does the Production Research Division only do research?" So, the English name is "Operations Management Consulting Division (OMCD)" so as not to cause misunderstanding. Its tasks are consultation, guidance, and practice.

Support by the top leadership is important for a support organization such as OMCD, and support is also essential when aiming at establishing *Kaizen* organizations which have soul and vision.

Mr. Taga, who has pulled OMCD members together up to now, has been an IE specialist from a young age. He has checked many workplaces from the perspective of the production management division and the production engineering division. When conducting time study, he is really good with a stopwatch. He also has a keen eye for evaluating workers' ability.

Mr. Taga teaches Takeuchi the history of the Toyota Production System from the beginning to the present time.

He thinks we should advance the Toyota Production System based on IE. Of course, the Toyota Production System had already built in IE techniques while TPS had grown up. But Mr. Taga thinks that TPS is a little weak in terms of analytics because the Toyota Production System primarily focuses on being easy for workers to use in production workplaces.

Mr. Taga says to Takeuchi, "Some important factors in IE methods are essentially different to TPS." And he continues, "Still, the above-mentioned Japanese book, 'Shinban IE No Kiso' is so good that you should study it."

"Mr. Takeuchi, let me give you an explanation about the TPS promotion organization." Mr. Taga starts to review the TPS organization.

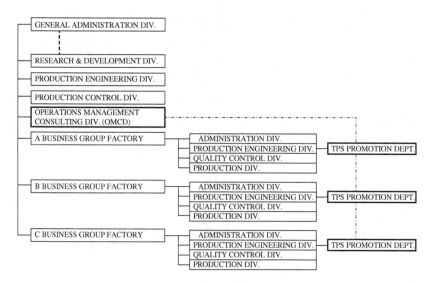

FIGURE 23.1

An illustration of organization which promotes the activity of the Toyota Production System in a company.

He explains a premise at first,

"The explanation of the organization and a function of OMCD is very complicated. This content is so technical that only a person with experience can understand it, so please get bogged down as you read it."

"First, I'll explain the promotion organization of TPS in the East Automotive Co. In this example, it is a condition that a company advances in *Kaizen* based on the Toyota Production System." Mr. Taga explains using an organizational chart. Readers take a look at Figure 23.1.

"The organization which promotes the Toyota Production System has two types: OMCD as the managing division in the headquarters' functional organization, and a factory TPS promotion department as the managing division in each factory. There are the company-wide TPS promotional secretariat and each factory TPS promotional secretariat respectively. A TPS promotional secretariat exists in both OMCD and each factory" Mr. Taga continues explaining.

"This diagram shows one type of company in which each TPS promotion department implements the TPS activity by themselves and OMCD supports their activity. The factory TPS promotion department actually advances *Genba Kaizen* in factories. Group leaders basically implement the *Genba Kaizen* at the production workplaces by themselves. But when the situation is too difficult for them to handle, they ask the factory TPS promotion department to analyze and solve the problem.

Thus the factory TPS promotion department has a section in which there are processing machines such as sheet metal processing machines and welding machines, and they make the *Kaizen* tools or simple boxes by themselves. The factory TPS promotion department promotes the management of the TPS activity in each factory. And sometimes there are people who transfer from production to the factory TPS department and definitely understand TPS."

24

What Is the Company-Wide Function of OMCD?

"Mr. Taga, I have almost understood how OMCD works in our company, but I have no idea what the important function or role of OMCD is."

Manager Takeuchi asks him about OMCD. It was Takeuchi who had thought this until then. When Takeuchi looked at OMCD from the outside, he couldn't understand the role of their organization. He got the impression that OMCD varies from the function of usual manufacturer organizations. The Japanese name for "OMCD" is directly translated as "Production research" in English. Therefore as a result, regular employees have questions about the role and function of OMCD. In addition from past, employees view OMCD in a negative light due to previous experience of a forceful management style when they first started their activity.

Mr. Taga says, "This is the role and business of OMCD." He reviews the following simple summary of OMCD:

1. **The purpose of OMCD**

   OMCD is a division which investigates various problems which occur in production jobs and takes measures against the big problems in a company. OMCD, which a company executive can directly control, implements the activity based on the top executive's judgment.

   OMCD takes part in indicating the features which our company should attain in the global production. OMCD raises issues to the production division which has the necessary implementation practitioners for *Kaizen*, and then supports their implementation activity.

DOI: 10.4324/9781003323310-34

2. The target of OMCD

Even when the company executive is absent and problems happen, it is necessary for the company administrators to be able to raise the problems to the executive at that moment somehow.

In order to make this system, it is necessary that management problems to be solved are indicated to the administrators, and that indexes which can measure problems are shared with the administrators.

All production activities in our company are implemented based on the Toyota Production System.

Management metrics in the production section are as follows;

1. Quality – quality metrics
2. Production (amount) – demand
3. Production cost (productivity) – efficiency metrics
4. Stock – stock metrics
5. Safety – safety metrics.

OMCD is in charge of (2) Production, (3) Productivity, and (4) Stock.

3. The duties of OMCD

1. Solving issues related to management
   To establish a problem-solving system that can automatically reveal problems connected to production, the productivity, and the production amount.
2. Promotion of the Toyota Production System
   a. Education and Training
      To prepare the education system and the arrangement of the human resources who have to be educated.
         To produce a corporate culture of training the human resources through the on-the-job Training.
   b. Activities for increasing the basic TPS level
      To set the necessary condition and role of the TPS General Managers who promote TPS activity in each factory.
         Education and training of the TPS General Manager
   c. *Jishukenkyu-kai*
      To attend the internal *Jishuken*, the supplier *Jishuken* and the Toyota Production System *Jishukenkyu-kai*.
         To develop the method of the Toyota Production System.

4. The human resources who carry out the OMCD duties
   1. The role of TPS General Manager
      Leader who instructs and practices TPS.
   2. Development of the TPS General Manager

-THE ROLE OF OMCD FROM THE VIEWPOINT OF COMPANY FUNCTION

"*Sensei*, I still don't understand OMCD. I guess that people outside the company understand even less." Takeuchi says.

Sensei explains the company function of OMCD using a picture depicted in Figure 24.1.

"Here is a picture which compares a general manufacturing firm to a rocket.

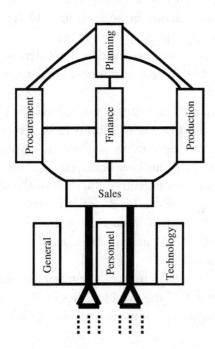

FIGURE 24.1
Five core functions and three auxiliary functions of the company organization.

(© **Noboru Takeuchi, 2013.**)

Company functions are depicted in a rocket in which five core organizational functions are driven by three auxiliary functions. I drew it just for fun, when I was young. But this is something useful now.

Now, let's give it a try to find where OMCD is in this picture.

Those days OMCD mainly focused on activities which make TPS take root in our company. After a period of time people came to not understand the activity so much, so OMCD nowadays has become unfamiliar to common people in the organization. When looking at the mission of OMCD, we feel that OMCD deviates a little from other organizational functions. But OMCD has a planning function and also greatly connects to the production function and the technology function. Thus we shouldn't regard OMCD as a simple managing division which only promotes TPS. If you say that OMCD becomes unnecessary once OMCD has completely made TPS take root in a company, you're right. However, in order to continue to investigate and pursue the higher production level, I think it is important to keep maintaining OMCD as a managing division of TPS."

Sensei is still thinking about the positioning of OMCD in the company. Takeuchi expresses his opinion about that.

"*Sensei*, I guess OMCD may seem to be a booster-rocket. A rocket can easily reach the target orbit, because there are auxiliary engines to augment the rocket capacity."

"I dare to say from a different angle, and I don't want to use a military-like word, but it is said that OMCD seems to be a corps who scouts the battlefront. OMCD members go out to the actual *Genba*, such as a supplier, first when some incidents have occurred. They investigate the *Genba* and report to the company executive. This role of the organization is the reason why the company executive directly controls. OMCD is the organization which has to act first when a company is on the verge of crisis. However, the role of OMCD becomes weakened at once TPS has taken root in the whole company.

The word logistics is a term used in war to management for movement of resources. We often find the word logistics in the side body of a truck. Fittingly, we manufacturers now use this word in the Manufacturing 'war'."

25

TPS Activity Is Mainly Implemented by the Production Division Under the Support of the TPS Promotion Department

Actual *Kaizen* or innovational activity is naturally implemented in each production line in the factory. The way of implementing *Kaizen* or the innovational activity in the production workplaces depends on the scale and situation of the company. For example, in the case of a big company which has a technicians' room in the production division, technicians support activities in the production line.

When we review organizations which promote TPS *Kaizen* or innovational activity, there are three types; OMCD type in headquarters' function, TPS promotion department/division type in a factory, and technician room (engineering section) type in a production department/division. The type of organization depends on both the company situation and where TPS practitioners are to be assigned.

People in the TPS promotion organization and people in the production workplaces work together implementing the Kaizen activity in the production lines as needed.

In the East Automotive Co., the TPS promotion department is in charge of promoting the TPS activity of the whole factory.

The *Kaizen* activities are mainly implemented in the Production Division and the Production Control Division. In other words, the *Kaizen* activities are production and logistics. It is not that the other sections, such as quality and production engineering, aren't unrelated to TPS activity.

DOI: 10.4324/9781003323310-35

It is also natural that these organizations implement their own *Kaizen* themes by themselves while they support the production workplaces.

The TPS promotion department has to have a function of the TPS secretariat because it manages all TPS activities in the factory. It creates the TPS promotion master plan which presents how to implement all the TPS activities in the factory. And then it evaluates the actual results of the activities in the factory.

Let me give you an explanation about the relationship between production and the TPS promotion department. Here, we'll assume that daily *Kaizen* activity and small group activity are implemented in the factory. For example, the "Creative Idea Suggestion System," which is a *Kaizen* proposal system, has an impressive record of achievement over a long period of history.

In the factory, targets of various metrics, or indicators, are set based on company policy for the current year. The strategic targets of a company are developed through the correct procedure of the *Hoshin-Kanri*, company policy deployment system in Japan.

The production division draws up the implementation plan for the current year with the target of metrics as follows:

1. Quality
2. Production amount
3. Production cost (productivity)
4. Stock
5. Safety

And then, this plan breaks down to the production departments and production sections in turn. The actual result is compared daily and monthly to the plan and evaluated.

In order to achieve the target, the activity is made by the whole production division. However, in reality, individual activity in the production lines or teams is a fundamental activity. The results are gathered by bottom-up in turn; the production group, section, department, and division.

The Toyota Production System is said to be a company-wide activity. The TPS promotion department is in charge of production; (2) Production amount, (3) Production cost (productivity), and (4) Stock. (1) and (5) are supported by the safety and quality division.

The production groups or the production lines draw up the implementation plans based on the factory plan for the current year. The productivity targets move from the factory tier down. Improvement of the production lines, such as reducing man-hours, are implemented based on these plans. It is desirable for people in the lines to achieve the target of productivity by themselves. But it is sometimes difficult according to their situation. Even in these difficult cases, if there is an engineering organization, we can expect a good result with their support. In the East Automotive Co., the factory TPS promotion department supports the production department effectively.

The factory TPS promotion department organizes the TPS activity report meeting which the factory manager and all parties in the factory attend. In the meeting, some production divisions and departments report their status every month in order to manage promoting the TPS activity. The factory TPS promotion department holds the monthly meeting according to the annual master schedule, so each production line has to report the TPS implementation activity in turn. These reports help to manage promoting the TPS activity and become a driving force for the activity.

The factory TPS promotion department reports the summary of the monthly TPS implementation activity of the whole factory with A3 form style documents. Evaluation of every production group and line is done through the implementation report at the meeting.

The main theme of each production line is focused on various areas, such as the improvement of productivity, quality, and so forth. There are actual themes, such as the working man-power reduction, improvement of the Operational Availability of machine, space reduction, defective rate reduction, cost reduction, and so forth. All themes will eventually connect to the cost reduction.

Therefore there is various support from the factory TPS promotion department. Sometimes it sets and leads a big theme of the whole factory, and sometimes it decides a theme from the proposed themes of the production lines, and decides the direction of activity. Practitioners in the factory TPS promotion department often support the production lines to grasp the current status of production workplaces in order to plan a *Kaizen* activity. Then the production line with the factory TPS promotion department makes a *Kaizen* activity plan which decides the direction of activity and implements three month's activity.

The production line implements the TPS activity together with the factory TPS promotion department, and the results obtained by the activity are used to improve the other lines. The development of *Kaizen* activity in the other lines is basically independently implemented by the factory production division. It's easy to implement to the other production lines because the *Kaizen* procedure is particularly effective.

This activity development is called *Yokoten*, which means "Horizontal expansion of applying similar things," so the previous sentence can be rephrased as "*Yokoten* is independently implemented by the factory production division."

The factory TPS promotion department wouldn't be able to implement such activities as these if they didn't have enough TPS human resources. Support by the indirect section like the Production Engineering department and other sections is also needed.

In the East Automotive Co., the headquarters' functional organization which promotes the TPS is OMCD. OMCD is in charge of looking at TPS activities across suppliers and global factories and promoting the company-wide TPS activities.

In the factory, the TPS activity report meeting is held every month. Meanwhile, OMCD holds the company-wide TPS meeting, which is similar to the factory meeting. The TPS meeting and workshop is held at each factory in turn every month. It aims at unifying the TPS activity in companies and being a mutual study place. Moreover OMCD organizes several global TPS workshops where members come from sister companies scattered over each global area. So it's a good place to study the TPS activities in the other factories.

OMCD is the headquarters' functional organization. The factory TPS promotion department in each factory instructs each production department in actual TPS activities. And then OMCD adopts a group system in which dedicated practitioners work for each factory. OMCD practitioners implement the TPS activity in the factory together with each of the factory TPS promotion departments. The TPS Support activity for an overseas factory is the same.

Developing the internal TPS human resources is important to sustain the *Kaizen* activity.

In the factory, training the TPS human resources is made by the on-the-job Training of the factory TPS promotion department. The production department and the Production Control department exchange the selected personnel of assistant managers or team leaders with the factory TPS promotion department members for the TPS training.

OMCD has a trainee system to train TPS systematically. It is called in-house training. Trainees should acquire the TPS understanding and practice ability through both education of TPS instructors and practice at internal and external companies, and then return to their previous workplaces. The personnel basically return to their previous workplaces, but sometimes change to a related workplace after having an interview.

OMCD had tried to establish a similar trainee system at the manager tier, but had failed with the first apprentices of Manager Takeuchi and others. That's why leadership of the company had changed. Generally, changing the company's culture is difficult.

The TPS human resources trained in these ways are being exchanged among the production department, the Production Control department, the TPS promotion department, and OMCD. They have become prospective good TPS practitioners. The TPS practice ability is being raised up in this way.

Part VIII

Implementation in *Jishuken*

26

The Institute for the Study of the Toyota Production System: Jishuken

The internal *Jishuken* meeting, which Takeuchi and Yamanaka joined as managers of the Production Engineering Development Division, was organized at the main factory.

In order to study and understand TPS, managers in the headquarters' functional sections specially joined in the "factory manager *Jishuken*," in which factory managers improve the factory workplaces together as a team. This *Jishuken* was managed by the factory TPS promotion department.

This factory manager *Jishuken* is simply called "Internal *Jishuken*" in the East Automotive Co., Ltd.

The outside company *Jishuken* organized by the Toyota-Group's companies is formally called **Toyota Production System *Jishukenkyu-kai*,** which is also simply called *Jishuken*.

The East Automotive Co. is a subsidiary company of a major automotive manufacturer. This leading automotive company organizes the "Toyota Production System *Jishukenkyu-kai*," which has the important role of promoting the TPS activity in the whole group companies.

Under the leadership of the Project General Managers (TPS *Shusa* in Japanese) at OMCD of the leading company, all TPS practitioners in the group companies mutually enhance their abilities with mutual study activities.

The previous Part VII described the internal TPS organization and activity. Now, let me give you an explanation about the outside company activity in the Toyota Production System *Jishukenkyu-kai*. The organization of both internal and external *Jishuken* activity is a good reference for forming an organization of suppliers' *Kaizen* activity.

DOI: 10.4324/9781003323310-37

Jishuken is incomprehensible to people who haven't participated, and there is also almost no explanation about *Jishuken*. We should probably regard *Jishuken* as a part of the organization or a method which promotes the Toyota Production System. The *Jishuken* activity changes according to time and situation. Thus I can only simply show the following typical explanation of *Jishuken*.

Koichi Iwaki described the dawn of the Toyota Production System *Jishukenkyu-kai* in his book: "Jissen Toyota Seisan Hoshiki," Nikkei Publishing Inc., 2005, p. 197. He noted a record of the first *Jishuken*, which started with around 15 members in 1976. In this article, we can feel a breath of pioneer eagerness at the dawn of *Jishuken* which improved know-how and developed personnel.

Keeping to the original TPS traditions from its dawn, Jishuken has nowadays become a big institute in which dozens of enterprises participate. The outline of *Jishuken* is simply summarized as follows:

1. Purpose of *Jishuken*
   1.1. Personnel development
      1.1.1. Development of administrators who can implement *Kaizen*
         - The ability to finish *Kaizen* in a short period
         - The ability to break the precondition and the constraint condition
         - The ability to practice by ourselves
      1.1.2. Development of *Kaizen* key person (Enhancing *Kaizen* ability)
         - Utilization of "Skills assessment of a *Kaizen* practitioner"
   1.2. Big outcome of *Kaizen*
      - The overall optimization of Kaizen
      - Not a tentative measure but a permanent measure
   1.3. Deepening TPS
      - Development of new TPS concepts
      - Development of method in detail
2. Features of *Jishuken*
   2.1. Implementation by members outside the target workplace
      - Various members are selected from the related workplaces
      - Developing member's ability to find problems

- Sometimes people in the target workplace cannot find problems. But members outside the workplace can easily find problems from a different perspective.

2.2. Members don't only make proposals but practice

2.3. Outcome comes from the target workplace's results

3. Attention to *Jishuken* implementation

    3.1. *Jishuken* budget should be set and estimated independently from the budget of the target workplace

    3.2. A *Kaizen* key person should be assigned as leader

    3.3. Leaders should organize the workplace in order to enable members to dedicate themselves to *Jishuken*

    3.4. Practice over theory until results come

    3.5. The target workplace needs a good attitude so that they implement *Kaizen* by themselves

4. Differences between usual *Kaizen* and *Jishuken*

People usually implement common *Kaizen* based on their needs. On the other hand, we implement *Jishuken* according to 1.. the purpose and 2.. the features mentioned above. The scale and difficulty of *Kaizen* have nothing to do with doing *Jishuken*.

Therefore we sometimes implement Jishuken with a single small theme and work to achieve it together with other workplaces.

27

Organization, Themes, and Attendees in Jishuken

The East Automotive Co. participates in the Toyota Production System *Jishukenkyu-kai* which is organized by Toyota OMCD. This workshop is an "outside company *Jishuken*" to the East Automotive Co. This is also "outside" to both Toyota and Toyota-Group's companies. Each manufacturer mutually offers each target workplace for *Kaizen*, so Jishuken helps human resources to develop themselves as a place of mutual training. *Jishuken* is also a TPS workshop in which we study the continuously evolving and deepening TPS. *Jishuken* has played an important role in improving the TPS level of all the group companies in this way.

It is necessary for us to think that the TPS *Kaizen* organization in the group companies is made of each company's organization and the Toyota Production System *Jishukenkyu-kai* outside the company. Actually, TPS activities "in and outside company" combine mutually and organically. It is effective to raise the level of the inside company *Jishuken* with the cooperation of the Toyota Production System *Jishukenkyu-kai*.

Several tens of companies participate in the Toyota Production System *Jishukenkyu-kai*. The participants are organized into several groups. For example, about 40 component manufacturers are divided into six groups and about ten body assembly manufacturers are divided into two groups. Each group decides the leader company and the sub-leader company and goes into action.

Every participating company registers a TPS promotion executive, a *Jishuken* leader and a deputy *Jishuken* leader in the Toyota Production System *Jishukenkyu-kai*. Each company forms the *Jishuken* organization with many TPS practitioners in the whole company. The *Jishuken*

DOI: 10.4324/9781003323310-38

leaders at the center of activity mutually investigate the *Kaizen* target workplace in each company and implement the *Kaizen*. As for the *Jishuken* TPS practitioners in each group company, we call them *Jishuken* members or members.

Basically, the Toyota Production System *Jishukenkyu-kai* is a yearly activity.

At the beginning of the fiscal year, each *Jishuken* group with several companies develops the group policy based on the master *Jishuken* policy. They plan an annual *Jishuken* schedule, in which each company holds *Jishuken* within about three months. The *Jishuken* members in each company mutually join in with the other company *Jishuken* and implement the TPS activities.

At the end of the fiscal year, each *Jishuken* group in the Toyota Production System *Jishukenkyu-kai* holds a closing meeting and afterwards a joint conference of all the groups is held. All *Jishuken* members assemble at the joint conference of all the groups and they report and review the summary of their activities there.

In order to start *Jishuken* activity, the workplace should attain "a sufficiently good level to enter into the Toyota Production System *Jishukenkyu-kai*." *Jishuken* is not only a *Kaizen* activity, but also requires an adequate situation for training of *Jishuken* members. Thus sometimes *Jishuken* cannot start as scheduled and its plan is shelved.

But I have experienced people being surprised at hearing they would start *Jishuken*, because people thought they had already worked hard through the internal factory *Jishuken* and finished with excellent results. People were surprised to know that there was still something to be implemented from then on in the Toyota Production System *Jishukenkyu-kai*.

TPS experts, such as the TPS practitioners who are familiar with TPS activity, *Jishuken* leaders, and deputy *Jishuken* leaders, participate and improve workplaces in *Jishuken*. So a difficult *Jishuken* theme is set so that members have to start with defining a target workplace. The theme is worth "a sufficiently good level to enter into the Toyota Production System *Jishukenkyu-kai*," and becomes a tough theme for members. This is important. A theme at a workplace which hasn't been improved yet can't reach the *Jishuken* level. The *Jishuken* theme requires difficult problems and a high level of *Kaizen* activity.

In this way, *Jishuken* has created and developed new TPS concepts and methods in detail. This part is the good point of how to evolve in *Jishuken*. When we look at a common *Kaizen* activity, we find it does not go to this level. Most *Kaizen* leaders can't attain the high-level status because of various duties.

As for *Jishuken* leaders and deputy *Jishuken* leaders, actually they are not mere *Jishuken* members. They primarily have a role of promoting the Toyota Production System in their own company. But they actually are busy in *Jishuken* activities outside the company, and don't have enough time to look at inside the company, though there are sometimes wonderful people who have the ability.

Now let's simply explain **the role of the TPS promoters who develop the Toyota Production System**.

1. Position of the TPS promoters
   1.1. The TPS promotion executive, the *Jishuken* leader and the deputy *Jishuken* leader in the Toyota Production System *Jishukenkyukai* are TPS promoters, who play the key role of promoting the Toyota Production System in the company.
   1.2. The TPS promoters should plan and promote the necessary items for the "organizational development of the Toyota Production System."
   1.3. In order to make an active organization, the *Jishuken* leader and the deputy *Jishuken* leader should be selected from the human resources who will shoulder the production division in the future.

2. Role of the TPS promotion executive
   2.1. The TPS promotion executive should take part in *Jishuken* activity inside and outside the company as the company top.
   2.2. The TPS promotion executive should personally educate administrators in the production division.
   2.3. The TPS promotion executive should intentionally select a *Jishuken* leader and a deputy *Jishuken* leader, train them, and make them recognize the role. Then he should create a good company situation and an organization which makes them implement the TPS activity with ease.

3. Role of the *Jishuken* leader

   3.1. The *Jishuken* leader should draft out a *Jishuken* plan and manage it. Then he estimates the activity outcome, and offers the TPS promotion executive a proposal for the way to advance the activity in the future.

   3.2. The *Jishuken* leader should take part in *Jishuken* outside the company, report and develop the useful contents which can be deployed to the workplaces inside the company.

   3.3. The Jishuken leader should manage the education system in the company as well as make the teaching materials.

-WHAT IS THE LEVEL OF TPS IN THE COMPANY? THE LEVEL OF THE CHANGING FEATURES OF TPS, WHICH IS EVALUATED ON A GRADE OF ONE TO FIVE

"*Sensei*, I've heard the term 'TPS level.' What do you think about it?"

Takeuchi asks a vague and simple question.

Sensei begins to explain the concept of TPS level.

"We sometimes hear an expression that the TPS level is high or low. In reality, we use these expressions only for a place where TPS is established to some extent. Now I'd like to explain the TPS level according to the thinking of Table 27.1: The level of the changing features of TPS, which is evaluated on a grade of one to five (Table 27.1).

I made several diagnoses of the factory with Mr. Taga who was an IE expert. This table was made after we had a free discussion with Mr. Taga. We collected our thoughts about TPS, so readers could see this as one example of TPS evaluation. In the factory diagnoses, we check and evaluate the factory according to the check items. Thus, we can clarify the strength and weakness of the factory, and create the items of improvement. But practical experts immediately can evaluate a factory to some extent by just looking at the workplace situation. This table is a way we can take a broad view of the factory situation. Of course, there are many evaluation indexes involved in the table, and so we need a steady activity to improve *Kaizen* items."

Takeuchi asks,

TABLE 27.1

The Level of Changing Features of TPS which is Evaluated on a Grade of One to Five

	TPS Level	Status of the Workplaces	Example of Features of the Practical Production
A	Zero TPS Company of traditional mass production	*Management isn't good. *We can't distinguish between normality and abnormality. *We have to start from 2S. *Work depends on the operator's way, and is not standardized.	Things are scattered everywhere so operators cannot find these things easily, or operators loiter on the job or leave their fixed workplaces. Sometimes things and equipment are left depending on the operators' way or their memory.
B	Cosmetic TPS Low-level Toyota Tier 2 supplier	*Kanban is not in management level. *Kanban is used as a "tag or label."	They produce in their own way for convenience, regardless of customer demand, such as the large lot sized production. Kanban is a "tag or label."
C	Full-scale TPS * High-level Toyota Tier 2 supplier * Low-level Toyota Tier 1 supplier	*Production control with Kanban *Production by each truck, synchronizing the customer demand.	They produce with the customer information on Kanban. The feature of the Toyota Production System is established as the Pull-type.
D	Sophisticated TPS * High-level Toyota Tier 1 supplier *Present Toyota	*Production control with Kanban. *Utilizing Kanban as a sophisticated tool. *Frequent production instruction and conveyance by each truck, synchronizing the customer demand.	The Heijunka Production with Frequent Production Instruction by each truck. The mixed small lot size production with Frequent Conveyance synchronized by the Production Control Section. Kanban is commonly existent in the company.
∞	Ideal TPS Ideal company	*Establishing the ideal state	The company depends on the overall optimization of operations from R&D to production

© Noboru Takeuchi, 2013

"In this case, *Sensei*, we think of *Kanban* as a standard in TPS. If groups don't use *Kanban*, how will they evaluate their performance using this concept?"

"We made Table 27.1 based on the TPS concept. This table describes the TPS level from the perspective of *Kanban* in order to make it easy to understand.

We vaguely say 'the TPS level' in the table, but instead of 'the TPS level' we can say production system level, improving level or practical productivity indicator. I think the judgment of the level has no great difference between them, because evaluation is a result of the various production activities.

We're going to evaluate the level with 5 stages as follows:

A. Lack of Management (Zero TPS Company),
B. The desired management level is not achieved (Cosmetic TPS Company),
C. Management established to some extent (Full-scale TPS Company)
D. High level management (Sophisticated TPS Company), and
∞. Ideal state (Ideal TPS company)

We set A as the lowest level for the following reason described on Figure 43.1, which depicts improving steps in the changing features level of TPS from the present level A to the ideal state. Infinity ∞ means the thinking that *Kaizen* is continuous improvement and growth never ends. The infinity sign shows the fundamental concept of the Toyota Production System.

Incidentally, artistic gymnastics defined difficulty ratings from A to C in those days. But those gymnastics were sometimes composed of skills with higher difficulty ratings than C, so the TV commentator called it 'Ultra C' at the 1964 Tokyo Olympics. Currently, difficulty ratings range from A to J."

Takeuchi askes, "Then, are you considering the TPS level E?"

Sensei explains,

"I'm sure there are many opinions against this way of TPS level evaluation. But I guess we are easily able to discuss improving our workplaces, if we can improve the thinking and evaluation standard.

For instance, when considering the global competitive situation, I think we can include another level of TPS called level E. However, we have to raise the level of TPS activity and discuss it. We are developing it now.

When we look at our factory with this diagram, we feel we can find the level of our factory. It's useful for making a benchmark for factories or competitors. If we can evaluate other competitive companies outside of us, we can establish our bench mark. Thus we have to try to do many factory visits.

I have visited many factories, so I unconsciously evaluate the factory level to some extent. I give some suggestions to them as we are shown around their factories. Of course, we can't make countermeasures for their problems unless we examine the details of their situation carefully."

28

The Activity Teams of Jishuken Are Divided into Production and Logistics

In this chapter, I want to clarify the activity teams of *Jishuken*. Think of a *Jishuken* in which a manufacturer holds a big scale conference at a whole company or factory (Figure 28.1).

In the case of component manufacturers, there are customers in the following processes of a company and suppliers in the former processes of a company. In the case of body manufacturers, selling agents can be customers.

The activity teams of *Jishuken*, or the *Jishuken* teams, can be roughly categorized into two types; "Manufacturing team" and "Logistics team."

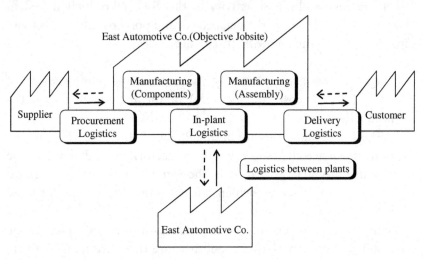

FIGURE 28.1
Classification of *Jishuken* teams.

DOI: 10.4324/9781003323310-39

They are sometimes further subdivided into some teams according to necessity and situations.

As for "Manufacturing," it is sometimes divided into "Components team" and "Assembly team."

As for "Logistics," it is sometimes divided into four types: "In-plant Logistics team," "Procurement Logistics team," "Delivery Logistics team," and "Logistics between plants team."

Actually, all the above-mentioned teams are not always created, and it depends on the scale and difficulty of them, but all themes should be improved.

I have heard of a lecture of a CEO who said, "We have been doing the Toyota Production System the whole time, but there haven't been any TPS instructors who could instruct both Just-In-Time (JIT) and *Jidoka*." He used two words in his phrases: *Jidoka* just for the manufacturing, and JIT just for the logistics.

Jidoka and JIT are interdependent in production lines, so it is wrong to say simply that manufacturing is *Jidoka* and logistics is JIT. But in reality there are many people who generally discuss it in this way. I dare to say that there is some truth in saying that manufacturing is *Jidoka* and logistics is JIT, but the important thing is to try to view our *Kaizen* situation practically.

When we review the past activity of the Toyota Production System *Jishukenkyu-kai* (*Jishuken*), the perspective and point of *Jishuken* activity seems to change in the following three stages:

- **Stage I.** The activity mainly focuses on the improvement of QCD (quality, cost, and delivery) of the manufacturing in the production lines.

  The subject factories are both TPS levels B and C. The purpose of *Jishuken* activity is to raise all the factories to TPS level C. We produce products according to the *Kanban* information of a Pull System in the factory, which has a production of one lot-sized production according to each truck's information. The priority activity is improvement of the production lines and quality. The result of *Kaizen* activity is good because there are many workers and we can easily eliminate the wasted labor. Thus *Jishuken* is mainly focused on *Kaizen* of the production lines where things are flowing. Depending on the concept of Just-In-Time and *Jidoka* with the various know-how of members, they try to increase the production line's capability. This stage is mainly for manufacturing, in which *Jidoka* aspects are large.

There are many old-fashioned leaders who are good in this area.

- **Stage II.** The activity mainly focuses on the whole factory logistics, in which we improve the logistics system.

  When establishing *Kaizen* in Stage I, the production lines are able to produce products by dispatching using the frequent production instruction, in which a truck interval time is divided into several instruction interval times. Some production lines acquire TPS level D. But conveyance is once per truck so it is a bigger lot size than production. The conveyance is incompatible with the production. People in the production lines observe that conveyance remains a big lot size and are reluctant to continue the frequent production, so they return the production line to the previous worse features of the big lot size, which was improved in Stage I.

  Sometimes there is also partial production improvement in Stage I. For example, the production lines become better, but the former and following processes become worse. In this way, we know the limitations of activity in Stage I.

  So, in order to support the production lines as well as inventory management, improvement of logistics becomes urgent business. Thus the activity is mainly focused on the whole factory logistics, in which we improve the logistics and the system. Eliminating *Muda* of logistics, we develop the *Heijyunka* system and tools so that we make both the production and the logistics develop to the higher TPS level.

  There aren't so many leaders who are good in both production and logistics.

- **Stage III.** The activity mainly focuses on deepening the Toyota Production System for the overall optimization of operations in manufacturing and logistics.

  Though some production lines return to the previous worse features, most factories acquire TPS level D in Stage II. We can see the features of factories which can be sustainable even though they need the effort of members. We establish the features of frequent production and frequent conveyance, which keeps good balance between production and logistics. In these situations, further higher quality products are needed for the market. So the company leadership instructs the company to go back to the basics of activity, saying, "We carry on activity that focuses on *Jidoka* again." This means that they target making a new and higher level of production line.

The *Jidoka* concept is important especially in the production lines. In the actual production workplaces, a keyword should be the term "*Ji-Kotei-Kanketsu* (JKK, Self-Process Completing)" which is activity developed from the thinking of "Defect Zero." This activity is a company-wide activity in which the individual workplace doesn't have quality defects in the following process. The whole company, not only production but also the indirect staff division, should execute activity based on the Toyota Production System. Individual departments target making a new and higher level of production line respectively. At the same time, they aim for the ideal state for the overall optimization of operations through the factory or the company. Then things which they think are necessary sometimes happen to become unnecessary from the perspective of overall optimization. However no one thinks that what they are doing is unnecessary and wasteful. So the important thing is to eliminate the waste to pursue the ideal state.

We are still at Stage III at present.

In this way, the Toyota Production System *Jishukenkyu-kai* (*Jishuken*) has gone step by step.

This *Kaizen* way, in which both manufacturing and logistics keep good balance and improve in level, may be one way. But I feel there are a lack of logistics perspectives in common improvement activities.

-JUST-IN-TIME AND *JIDOKA*

"*Sensei*, I'd like to know about the two pillars of Just-In-Time and *Jidoka* in detail."

Sensei says, "There are many books so far. So, I'll explain about them simply," and he gives the following explanation.

"First the thinking of Just-In-Time is to say, 'The following production process withdraws the goods it needs, when it needs them, in the exact needed amount, from the former process. The former process produces only the amount withdrawn.'

In order to achieve Just-In-Time, there are the following prerequisite condition and three basic conditions.

1. **Prerequisite condition for Just-In-Time production is *Heijyunka*** (Figure 28.2)

    Heijyunka is the overall levelling in the production schedule of the variety and volume of items produced in given time periods. The word *Heijyunka* is sometimes translated to 'Leveled Production.' I guess 'Leveled Production' can be understood as average and doesn't always carry exactly the same meaning as *Heijyunka*, so I'm recommending using the word *Heijyunka* in English.

    In lot production, the fixed quantity of the same product is produced. So, the demand information to the former processes becomes big for the individual product.

    In *Heijyunka* production, many kinds of products are produced in a queue at random according to the product item's ratio. The *Heijyunka* information of the variety and volume of items is provided to the former process so that waste is eliminated in the processes and it contributes to cost reduction.

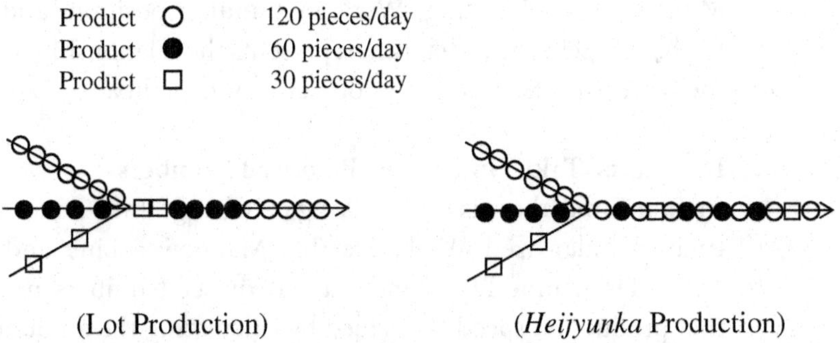

Product	O	120 pieces/day
Product	●	60 pieces/day
Product	□	30 pieces/day

(Lot Production) (*Heijyunka* Production)

FIGURE 28.2
Thinking way of *Heijyunka* Production. (Translated from Takeuchi, Noboru, *Seru Seisan*, JMA Management Center, 2006, P.133.)

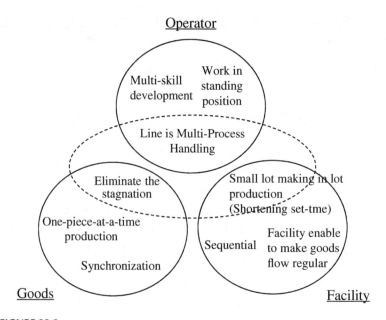

FIGURE 28.3
Thinking way of Continuous Flow Processing. (Translated from Takeuchi, Noboru, *Seru Seisan*, JMA Management Center, 2006, P.135.)

2. Principles of Just-In-Time

2.1. Continuous Flow Processing (Figure 28.3)

Goods flowing smoothly in the process without stagnation should be established based on TPS thinking, such as Sequential Layout, One-piece-at-a-time production, Synchronization, Multi-Process Handling, Work in standing position, and so forth. This schematic diagram represents the relationship using the three aspects, goods flow, operator, and facility.

2.2. Determine Takt-Time by the Required Numbers

In Takt-Time, there is the thinking of 'Change Takt-Time each time, Standardized Work, Flexible Manpower Line and so forth.' 'Determine Takt-Time by the Required Numbers' means that production speed is decided by calculating the amount of the customer (the following process) demand. Ideally the production workplace should produce at a speed which is determined by buying frequency of the end consumers, so 'purchase speed' = 'production speed.' This speed or the time which should be taken to produce a component or product is called Takt-Time. The Takt-Time is calculated as:

$$\text{Takt-Time (sec)} = \text{Total daily operating tme (sec)} / \text{Total daily Production Requirement (pieces)}$$

When producing according to Takt-Time, we can cope with the fluctuation of the demand. In order to reduce overproduction, the thinking of 'Required Numbers is equal to production quantity' is useful.

2.3. Pull System (of Production)

The Pull System was explained a lot in the previous Journey.

The '*Kanban* system' using *Kanban* is the means to promote the Pull System effectively."

Sensei simply gave the basic items of Just-in-Time.

Takeuchi askes, "*Sensei*, I'm about to be dazzled by the various TPS terminology. These should be studied as the need arises, right?"

Sensei suggests, "Absolutely, there is so much deep thinking, and you should study and practice without being impatient."

Sensei continues to explain next about *Jidoka*, or automation with a human touch, as follows.

"The **Jidoka** concept is 'Machines are made to detect the abnormal conditions and stop automatically, when abnormal conditions occur.' The most important thing is to obtain a clear understanding of the thinking of *Jidoka* to secure the product quality.

There are two **Principles of Jidoka**.

1. Quality must be built-into Process

When abnormal conditions occur, machines stop automatically with *Jidoka* to prevent producing defects. The system which detects abnormality is installed in the production line to achieve high built-in quality. Machinery should stop automatically with the installed mechanism which detects abnormalities.

On the other hand, even in manual assembly lines, there is the thinking of 'another *Jidoka*' which evolved from the original *Jidoka* concept. We established a rule that the workers themselves should push the stop button to halt production if any abnormality appears. This is the thinking of *Jidoka* in the manual assembly line.

2. Manpower Saving

In the case of automatic machines, if there is an operator who stops machines when defects occur, he may just seem like a guard for the machines. However, the operator can be utilized for another job which has added value, if the machine has a mechanism of detecting defects."

29

Learning the Ideology and the Techniques, Implementing Kaizen in Jishuken Inside the Company

Manager Takeuchi is now a member of OMCD practitioners who are dedicated to the main factory. He has been participating in the factory Jishuken which is managed by the factory TPS promotion department in the main factory.

The theme of the factory Jishuken is "*Kaizen* of Window-Switch Line."

Our company is going to offer the Window-Switch Line as a workshop of the Toyota Production System *Jishukenkyu-kai*. Both OMCD and the factory discussed and decided the line for the *Jishuken* theme. In any case, we have to improve the Window-Switch Line so as to make it "a sufficiently good level to enter into the Toyota Production System *Jishukenkyu-kai*."

OMCD and the factory TPS promotion department work at implementing the *Kaizen* of the line in addition to a regular daily improving activity. Though this is a factory *Jishuken*, the scale of it is small. The members of the Window-Switch Line feel confused about this activity. They know the workplace will become a better place, but they feel it will be hard work from now on.

Manager Takeuchi, who has become an instructor for the first time, learns and practices the TPS *Kaizen* in person as a leader from now on. This factory *Jishuken* differs from the common *Kaizen* activity which he experienced in his production workplace, because it was the beginner's *Kaizen* learned by trial and error. There are many TPS experts at the meeting, so he can be taught the way of improvement. The important thing is that we should implement *Kaizen* by ourselves. Then the practice develops personnel in TPS.

DOI: 10.4324/9781003323310-40

It is often said that TPS is all about practicing with one's own hand. It is also said that it's not good unless you are able to do it by yourself. Education of TPS is the accumulation of "training" and "practice." So you should study TPS according to your level. But, it is a pitfall to believe you understand TPS after just studying a little from a book.

Manager Takeuchi sometimes meets such people who think they understand TPS. One time, a manager in the sister company interrupted Takeuchi's explanation during the plant tour, and started to take over the presentation arrogantly and at length. The explanation by the arrogant man was mistakenly based on book learning. Another time, another manager attended a lecture on Standardized Work for a few hours, and afterwards he left the room, saying, "I fully understand TPS." Then there was also an administrator who only ever repeated one key phrase, "TPS is topdown." However, I think TPS is not so easy.

Meanwhile, there are many books which many authors wrote from different angles in order to clarify TPS. We should truly understand these books while we accumulate experience from practice. Therefore, it takes a long time to understand the Toyota Production System, and sometimes we have a lot of trouble practicing it. Many people ask us why practicing at an actual *Kaizen* workplace is necessary to understand TPS. I'm sure that a lot of effort is essential in order to acquire the true ability of TPS.

There is an inevitable reason for implementing the TPS activity of the Window-Switch Line.

This workplace has obtained the target productivity and increased profit, but there are still problems. The Window-Switch is a key product in the company and the volume of products is gradually increasing now. That's why there is a movement of customers from the old Window-Switch to the new Window-Switch. The forecast from a leading car manufacturer is that the volume of products will increase to twice the volume of products three months later. We have to cope quickly and prepare. So, we organized the *Kaizen* team for implementation.

The Window-Switch line is composed of two processes: the components and the manual assembly line. However, we are unable to increase the machines and workers immediately for the sudden volume change. And we are taught in TPS that we should cope with these cases as a result of the *Kaizen* activity without increasing workers. When the volume of products is increased, simply increasing personnel is ineffective, and endless. We should improve the workplace with wisdom and manage it with minimum investment. I experienced many activities in which workplaces were improved with such thinking for the volume increase. Those workplaces became "Strong production lines" as a result.

The *Kaizen* activity variously results in Work Time Reduction, Machine Capacity improvement, Energy Reduction, and Space Reduction. These items will also become target themes.

So, the theme of "*Kaizen* of Window-Switch Line" paraphrases to "coping with twice the volume of products three months later by improving the productivity without increasing workers and machines."

Part IX

Becoming a *Kaizen* Practitioner

30

Productivity: Apparent Efficiency and True Efficiency, Rate of Operation and Operational Availability

Purpose of *Kaizen* is mainly the cost reduction in the production workplace. People improve the workplace by eliminating *Muda* (Waste) based on the ideology of Just-In-Time and *Jidoka*. It is the activity in which they improve productivity indexes in the production workplace.

The meaning of **productivity** based on TPS is generally described as follows:

$$Productivity = Output / Input$$

For example, the productivity is the product volume per person per day when product volume per day is used for Output and personnel for Input.

TPS has the ideology of "Apparent Efficiency" and "True Efficiency."

Let's think about a case where we can produce 120 pieces per ten persons per day after a production line is improved and the former performance was 100 pieces. It must be a good efficient enhancement when the market requirement increases. However if the market requirement keeps 100 pieces as "Required Numbers," the extra 20 pieces make forward payment of materials and work expense and produce the *Muda* of inventory. So, the enhancement of efficiency can't be connected with the cost reduction.

Thus **Apparent Efficiency** occurs in the case of an increased efficiency figure where there is unnecessary production, that is to say the enhancement of efficiency is only numerical.

On the other hand, **True Efficiency**, which TPS teaches us, is the figure when producing only the necessary 100 pieces by eight persons. There isn't

DOI: 10.4324/9781003323310-42

the *Muda* of Over-production because of producing only the necessary "Required Numbers."

Takt-Time is an important factor in order to "produce only what is needed, when it is needed, in the amount needed," which is based on the ideology of Just-In-Time in TPS. Depending on the Required Numbers, it shows the speed of producing products one by one. Takt-Time is calculated by an equation;

$$\text{Takt-Time (T.T)} = \text{Working hours per day (seconds)} / \text{Daily required production quantity (units)}$$

When focusing on the productivity, we often set our index to Apparent Efficiency; how much we produce a day. But we should try to focus on True Efficiency and Just-In-Time which doesn't make *Muda* of Inventory by Over-production.

Even when we are requested to produce more or less than usual, in the future we should aim for the ideal state of "Sales = Production" where we produce only the necessary products.

However the improvement of machinery is mentioned later in this part. But firstly we have to understand the way of thinking about productivity in machinery.

It's the ideology of "Rate of Operation" and "Operational Availability" in the machine-based workplace, where the concept of "Required Numbers" is fundamental.

The "Rate of Operation" is a ratio of the actual result divided by the ability when machines or equipment are operated at full capacity. For example, it's 90% when 900 pieces is produced by a facility where the capacity is 1000 pieces a day. On the other hand, the "Operational Availability," which TPS teaches us, shows a ratio (expressed in a percentage) at which machines or equipment can effectively run under normal conditions when they are requested to be run.

This ideology of "Operational Availability" can't be understood easily. Remember, it's 100% when machines or equipment are running at their standard specification without malfunctions of operation.

Firstly what is running at standard specification? Basically it is the Required Numbers which doesn't lead to *Muda* of Inventory by Over-production.

For example, imagine the required output is 500 pieces and the ability of the facility is 1000 pieces a day. Then the facility should run for just a half day. The Operational Availability would be 100% if the Required Numbers are produced in a half day without malfunctions.

However, what happens if the facility doesn't run effectively?

For example, think about a situation where there are a lot of Frequent-Stops, Down-time, or the lack of specified ability where the running speed is decreased in order to avoid the Frequent-Stop. If the facility produces 500 pieces a day to reach the Required Numbers, the Operational Availability would be 50%, because the normal ability is 1000 pieces a day.

In this case, the report is sometimes incorrectly like "There is no problem because the Rate of Operation was 100%, even though the facility ran for a whole day." We should realize we waste a lot of resources by low Operational Availability.

Therefore, in order to achieve 100% in the Rate of Operation, the preventive maintenance of facility has to be accomplished sufficiently and the setup time of equipment has to be reduced to or become zero.

The ideology of Operational Availability is important to obtain the true performance when improving machinery or processes. And it's a way of thinking of Just-In-Time to produce only the Required Numbers using the ideal machinery for 100% Operational Availability.

It's common for us to misunderstand the Rate of Operation as true productivity. I have experienced this several times at European and American companies, where they didn't understand the problem after they mainly aimed at the Rate of Operation as a management index and produced products beyond the requested numbers.

They managed by only checking OEE (Overall Equipment Efficiency). In these cases, the Rate of Operation should be low when there is no demand. However they acknowledged incorrectly a high OEE number which has actually a low Rate of Operation in TPS. They naturally passed "The *Muda* of Inventory by Over-production."

I used to experience this many times as well that companies tried to introduce another new machine for more products without improving the low capacity of the existent machine.

31

Improvement of Work in the Production Line 1: The Muda of Work, the Ideology of Flexible Manpower Line

When trying to improve a production line, we should pay attention to three fundamental elements; People/Man, Facility/Machine and Process/Method. According to this thinking, we have to implement improvement of work, improvement of facility and improvement of process (Figure 31.1).

The Manager, Mr. Takeuchi watches the worker's movement in FEN line patiently by "Standing Observation."

Firstly he tries to take away the worker's wasteful movement or non-efficient processes in the assembly or mechanical process.

We should be careful to follow the general instruction explained in the next paragraph when observing production lines. This caution is also the same Manager Takeuchi observes when taking care of plant tours.

Firstly, we have to pay attention to safety and keep safety rules at the workplace such as wearing a protection cap, a safety glasses, and steel-capped shoes.

Secondly, we must make sure we don't disturb operators. We don't speak to operators directly and have to talk with them through a manager or a supervisor. Let's refrain from unnecessary talking.

The machine operator's activity seems to be simple repetitive work, but the difference in the output depends on the degree of skill of the worker. There is a difference in quality and also a difference in the amount of output.

Skillful operators are necessary for non-repetitive manufacturing products that are called *Ippinmono*, single items. It is also the same as operating a long process line by oneself. We sometimes say a process is deep instead of saying a process is long.

DOI: 10.4324/9781003323310-43

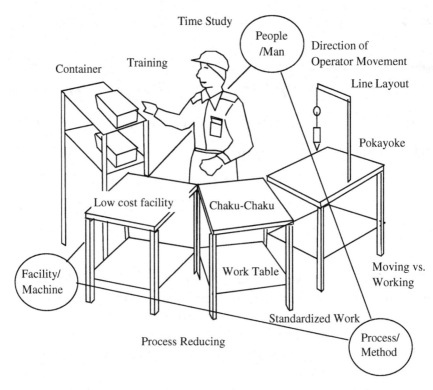

FIGURE 31.1

The image of production line. (Translated from Takeuchi, Noboru, *Seru Seisan*, JMA Management Center, 2006, P.81.)

On the other hand, we have to produce repetitive manufacturing mass products by Takt-Time which correspond to demand. It is ok if we are able to produce the daily amount with only one person, but if it is not so we should find another way to produce. One method is to add other assembly lines or another method is to apply multi-operator by dividing the production line.

So, we should divide a long process line into several segments, which are equivalent to one person's work amount calculated with the Takt-Time.

In the case of using "One-operator Manufacturing System," necessary production lines are usually added which correspond to the big daily demand. This is one type of "Cellular Production System or Method," where one operator completes a finished product in the whole process. In these cases, additional equipment will cost more money, and another skillful operator will be needed for the long process line. These should be Multi-Skilled Operators who are pretty good at all processes. Meanwhile, the Process Division Method has the purpose of simplifying the work so as not to require a skillful operator.

In TPS, there is the ideology of *Shoujin-ka*, Flexible Manpower Line. We can't understand it easily at first. On the other hand, there is a confused ideology of *Soujin*, Manpower Saving, which Japanese people pronounce similarly. Both *Shoujin* are written with different Japanese characters, and the *Shoujin-ka*, Flexible Manpower Line, is sometimes described with unique terms such as "*Menashi no Shoujin.*"

Even if the wasteful labor sums up to the value of one worker, it does not result in cost reduction when we can't actually eliminate one person.

For example, assume that a product line has the ability to complete the work with six workers. This operation must be organized with six people. If wasteful labor corresponding to one person is improved here, we can reduce the organization to five people. One person can be reduced and eliminated. It's the "*Shoujin*, Manpower Saving.*" Actually the *Shoujin* of one operator is difficult, if the work amount corresponding to one operator is not achieved after accumulating the eliminated work. In the case of 5.5 manpower on a production line, we should reduce the work load by 0.5 and eliminate one worker.

Even when demand fluctuates, the number of workers should be changed according to the Takt-Time, where the methodology is also dependent on the ideology of the Flexible Manpower Line.

When we think in terms of the quantity in proportions of manpower rather than whole number, the Flexible Manpower Line can be easily understood. This is called technically *Hasu-ninku*, **fractional manpower**. According to the ideology of the Flexible Manpower Line, we can achieve the Manpower Saving after accumulating the fractional manpower labor to one. Meanwhile, when a worker is doing only 0.8 fractional manpower labor, we can give another 0.2 work. This is called "*ichininku no tsuikyu*, **stacking fractional manpower up to 1 manpower labor**," which is one keyphrase of *Kaizen* in TPS.

When we produce goods by the Process Division Method with multiple operators, there are several cases we should pay attention to.

Even though a process is divided into several sections, multi-skilled operators are needed.

The numbers of operator are changed based on the Takt-Time, which is calculated according to daily demand. In this case, it is desirable that the operators be able to **handle the multi-processes** or the whole process. We have to train multi-skilled operators who can operate not just a single process but multi-processes. When **single-skilled operators** are trained and **multi-skilled operators** are acquired, it becomes easy to produce goods flexibly even if the customer demand fluctuates. This is the basis of establishing the Flexible Manpower Line.

We are taught to follow the slogan, **Make Baton Passing Zone**, when we use the Process Division Method. There are various operators who work quickly and slowly in a production line because they have different skill levels. In a track relay, a faster runner can make up for a slower runner in a baton passing zone. The passing zones between operators should also be established in a production line so that the quick person in operation covers the slow person, and the efficiency in the line can be improved. Then the baton passing zone should be properly understood as a cooperation zone. For example, when the quick person has an excess of additional work in the zone, the overall speed in the line becomes slow consequently. It's a case of bad cooperation which yields lesser products when the quick person operates in a baton passing zone more than necessary. There is a lot of such mistaken understanding about the method.

There's also another basic ideology: **Do Not Make Isolated Islands**. If workers are isolated here and there, they cannot help each other. If their work positioning can be arranged to combine with other work, the numbers of workers can be reduced. It's related to the ideology of *Shoujin-ka*, Flexible Manpower Line.

Manager Takeuchi is observing a FEN line from a distance where he won't become a disturbance to workers.

This line is divided into six sections of six people, corresponding to the operational speed calculated by the Takt-Time. It's a line of six-people organization, where their work has been decided to be shared in their sections.

In this way, six workers are working together to make a product one after another by the right movement.

The efficient work without waste, which is combined together with product, machine, and human movement, is called "Standardized work."

Regardless of how much workers move, it does not mean work has been done. That's because movement has to become "Working" to produce added value.

The supervisor must make an effort to **turn workers' movements into working**, where the work = working + *Muda* (waste). We eliminate the wasteful movements which produce non-added value, and improve the work to turn worker's movement into working. Mr. Ohno said, "The Japanese originated character of 'Working' explains this concept because it is composed of two elements, one element which means 'Moving' and another element which means 'person'."

In the whole work process, we should understand waste from not only the movement of worker but all of the seven wastes: (1) *Muda* of overproduction, (2) *Muda* of waiting, (3) *Muda* in conveyance, (4) *Muda* in processing, (5) *Muda* of inventories, (6) *Muda* of motion, and (7) *Muda* of making defects.

Incidentally, there is no point in trying to remember the classification of seven wastes. First, it is most important for the reader to cultivate a fine eye for *Muda* (waste). In addition, each *Muda* is mutually related and different in significance depending on the situation of the site, target, and product, so the classification of the seven wastes is not important.

Mr. Ohno said in a conference, "You can read 'there are 7 wastes' in my book, so I can't say that it is a mistake. But I was going to explain that even if we think we've gotten rid of all waste, we can still find more than 7 or 8 wastes." (*Taiichi Ohno's improvement soul*, P. 128.)

But it's better to remember it as a way of thinking when we categorize or check the wastes. In western manufacturing, the easiest way to remember the seven wastes is to ask yourself "Who is TIMWOOD?" (TIMWOOD; Transporting, Inventories, Moving, Waiting, Over-processing, Overproduction, Defects.)

Manager Takeuchi is observing each worker's respective moving in a line of six people. They must work based on the standardized works. He does a **time study**, observing their operational movement.

These works in this stage are based on the standardized work, but these are "actual or practical" works including waste. It is written **Practical standard**, which is called *omote-hyoujyun* in Japanese and expresses practical or actual standardized situations. For example, a Practical standardized work combination table and a Practical standardized work chart are written.

A standard has a property which means it changes to a Practical standard at the time it is established. It is because *Kaizen* is continual. Practical

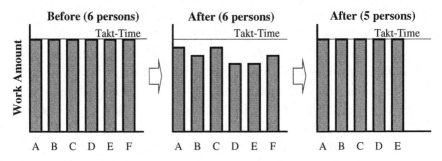

FIGURE 31.2
Yamazumi (Stack Chart) for improvement of the work.

standard – Standard after improvement – Practical standard – Standard after improvement, and endless improvements will continue.

Manager Takeuchi continues to improve the operational waste reduction in the production line. Gradually the number of improvements start to increase as a result of using many *Kaizen* case books and the past cases of companies. Sometimes he also asks for advice from experts in the factory TPS promotion division. Technical effort is necessary as well. As need arises, he gets support from designers and production engineers (Figure 31.2).

A key phrase for the improvement of work is "to consider the worker and work without difficulty."

We have to train to enhance our *Kaizen* skills which focus on workers' movement. It is important for us to cultivate a fine eye for wasteful workers' movement. Good experience makes good ability, so we have to improve our ability by "Standing Observation."

Manager Takeuchi improves the *Muda* (waste) of six workers' work.

There is a *Kaizen* group in a factory TPS promotion division. A *Kaizen* group has a *Kaizen* room where they can treat sheet metal and parts with processing equipment. *Kaizen* staff produce whatever is easy to make by themselves. Difficult goods are made by professional mechanic experts using drawings made by *Kaizen* staff.

Manpower for the improvement of work before and after six workers is shown using bar graphs of **Yamazumi (Stack chart)**, which literally means "piling up elemental works." After *Kaizen* activity, the total work fortunately results in a total of 5.0 manpower calculated by Takt-Time to achieve the Required Numbers. Then, the total work is divided into the work of five workers. As the result, a diagram of "*Yamazumi* after of 5 workers" is achieved after combining elemental works and dividing them among the individual workers. This procedure is composed of two elements: reducing the waste and piling up elemental works to each person.

Manager Takeuchi had improved each worker's respective movement in a line of six people. The work amount corresponding to one operator was eliminated based on the ideology of *Shoujin-ka*, Flexible Manpower Line, and the production line could be able to produce the needed products through the organization of five persons. It is the *Shoujin*, Manpower Saving of one operator.

A most skillful worker should be transferred like in the case of a new business when we can gain a free worker.

A Supervisor in the production workplace would be happy to make use of this operator in the production of a new product.

32

Improvement of Work in the Production Line 2: Standardized Work

Collaborating with the people in the production line, Manager Takeuchi could reconstruct the Standardized work of five workers after combining and dividing elemental works into the work of five workers.

When we try to establish a Standardized work, we have to make documents called a set of three sheets:

Standardized Production Capacity Sheet
Standardized Work Combination Table
Standardized Work Chart

And then, we prepare the training manuals for workers based on the three sheets. For example, a **work instruction sheet** and a **work manual**.

The **preconditions of standardized work** are as follows:

1. Standardized work is mainly focused on human work. It isn't focused on machines and the machine condition.
2. Standardized work is based on repetitive work. Work which constantly changes can't produce good results.
3. Supervisors have to incorporate their intentions into the standardized work by doing and showing it themselves, and then make the workers keep it.

The Standardized work cannot be established unless all of the following **three elements of Standardized work** are fixed:

1. Takt-Time
Takt-Time is the time allotted to make one component or finished product.

DOI: 10.4324/9781003323310-44

The two elements discussed below are applicable in general manufacturing, but Takt-Time is defined by the Toyota Production System. In contract to Takt-Time, a cycle time, which it is generally called in general manufacturing, is a required time in a process. It is easy to use Takt-Time when it is applied to the Process Division Method in multi-workers operation. In one-man operations, an ideal cycle time should be fixed at first.

2. **Working sequence**

The term "working sequence" means just what it says, an order of worker's operation; transporting, mounting, and removing items.

3. **Standard in-process stock**

Standard in-process stock refers to the minimum number of workpieces in a process needed for repetitive operations according to routine.

When Manager Takeuchi tries to make a Standardized work after doing a time study, he often experiences the feeling that making a Standardized work is difficult because the workers can change at any time. In these cases, the work itself could have problems because he thinks the way of making workers operate is not effective. First of all, we have to make sure that the Standardized work will be established after making repetitive work. So, training of workers is needed and *Kaizen* is also necessary for it. Then, we improve more based on the Standardized work.

-LET'S ESTABLISH STANDARDIZED WORK IN THE CASE OF THE BARBERSHOP!

"*Sensei*, I'd like to present a Standardized work that floated through my mind during dozing at a barbershop the other day. I guess it is useful to us in getting an image of the Standardized work."

Takeuchi established the Standardized work at a barbershop with the following procedure, and simplified it to make it easier to understand.

First, the work is divided into elemental works (work items) in order to do a time study.

We'll assume getting a haircut at a barbershop is performed with the following elemental works 1–9:

1. Having a customer sit down on a barber chair, and putting a cloth on him.
2. Damping his hair with a wet towel, and parting his hair with a comb.
3. Cutting his hair with scissors.
4. Shaving off his beard with a razor.
5. Washing his face.
6. Shampooing his hair.
7. Drying his hair with a dryer.
8. Putting hair conditioner on, and setting his hair.
9. Finishing his hair, and taking a cloth.

In the case of this barbershop, only a chief who is a barber Meister is having a haircut. About ten apprentices share work other than haircutting, but they cannot do all the work. They can perform only the work they are qualified for. They are not multi-skilled operators but kind of single-skilled operators. Everyone is training themselves until late evening now to pass the qualification test.

In manufacturing, a customer is equivalent to a good and a barber chair corresponds to equipment like a workbench.

The **Standardized Production Capacity Sheet** expresses the processing capacity. We can find a bottleneck process and the capacity of manual operations in this sheet. In this case, the bottleneck process is "3. Cutting his hair with scissors," because the other apprentices share the non-haircutting processes.

The bottleneck process "3. Cutting his hair with scissors" takes 20 minutes, as is indicated by the next Standardized Work Combination Table. So, 24 visitors is the capacity a day that the chief can cut hair within eight working hours. The chief dedicates himself to only the bottleneck process "3," and spends 20 minutes per one customer. The reservations for a haircut per day is also limited to 24 customers.

When the number of customers per day is 24, the Takt-Time is 20 minutes which is calculated by an equation: 8×60 minutes$/24 = 20$ minutes. In this case the barber installed six barber chairs in order to accommodate 24 customers. Considering six barber chairs, the apparent Takt-Time is 120 minutes, calculated by 20×6. On the other hand, the cycle time C.T., the haircut service time per person, is 104 minutes. This barber shop can manage 24 persons a day because they have idle time, 120 − 104 minutes = 16 minutes.

A **Standardized Work Combination Table** is drawn up by calculating the Takt-Time after observing the time used for the 1 − 9 process of the elemental work (Table 32.1).

A **Standardized Work Chart** is drawn up by writing the number of elemental work processes on the layout of equipment (Table 32.2).

Thus, this is the way to make a set of three sheets: Standardized Production Capacity Sheet, Standardized Work Combination Table, and Standardized Work Chart. Then, we prepare a work instruction sheet and a barber work manual based on the three sheets.

-IMPORTANCE OF STANDARDIZED WORK

Takeuchi asked *Sensei* a question as always.

"*Sensei*, why do you think the standardized work is important?"

Sensei answered simply, it is the basis of work.

"Everyone often talks about how it's important to establish a Standardized work.

In the book, *Toyota production system*, Mr. Taiichi Ohno positioned the 'Standardized work' as the important tool for 'Visual Control' based on the *Genba*-oriented policy.

Liker and Meier also stated in *the Toyota way fieldbook* (McGraw-Hill, 2006, P.112), 'The process Toyota refers to as 'standardized work" is so important to the overall production system that one third of Toyota's internal TPS Handbook is devoted to it.'

I educate the Standardized work first in clients, when I try to introduce the way of thinking of the Toyota Production System and the *Kaizen* activity. Even if we perform the *Kaizen* activity, we cannot produce good fruit while having no skills of establishing a standardized work. That is because there is not a defined standard.

The standardized work is one of the prerequisite conditions for having secure work and making quality as well.

By the way, I had become a chief at headquarters for production activities in the whole company, where quality, safety and OMCD divisions

TABLE 32.1
Standardized Work Combination Table in the Case of Barbershop

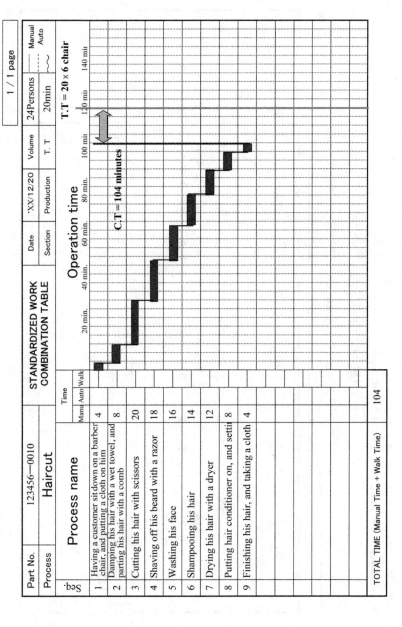

Part No.	123456—0010		STANDARDIZED WORK COMBINATION TABLE		Date	'XX/12/20	Volume	24Persons	Manual
Process	Haircut				Section	Production	T. T	20min	Auto

T.T = 20 × 6 chair

CT = 104 minutes

Operation time

Seq.	Process name	Time			
		Manu	Auto	Walk	
1	Having a customer sit down on a barber chair, and putting a cloth on him	4			
2	Damping his hair with a wet towel, and parting his hair with a comb	8			
3	Cutting his hair with scissors	20			
4	Shaving off his beard with a razor	18			
5	Washing his face	16			
6	Shampooing his hair	14			
7	Drying his hair with a dryer	12			
8	Putting hair conditioner on, and settin	8			
9	Finishing his hair, and taking a cloth	4			
	TOTAL TIME (Manual Time + Walk Time)	104			

1 / 1 page

20 min.   40 min.   60 min.   80 min.   100 min   120 min   140 min

TABLE 32.2
Standardized Work Chart in the Case of Barbershop

STANDARDIZED WORK CHART

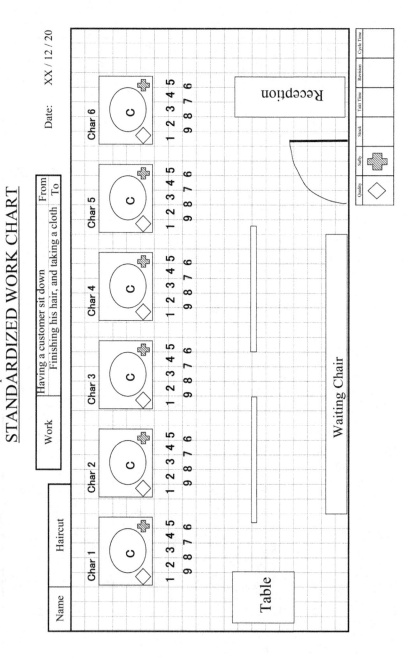

made one team. The safety, the quality and the productivity improvement are related mutually. The Standardized work has to be decided for them, and it's important to know whether abnormal work and movement are being done. That is to say, we can see abnormality at last after establishing the standardized work."

-DIFFERENCE BETWEEN TWO TERMS: STANDARDIZED WORK AND WORK STANDARDS

"*Sensei*, when someone explains, 'a work standard is – for standardized work,' it may be confusing at first."

Takeuchi asked how to remember the difference between the two phrases; "standardized work" and "work standards," which are more complicated in the Japanese language.

"The 'standard work' in Japanese means the standardized work and the 'work's standard' in Japanese means the work standards. Both words in the second half of the phrase are regarded as the subject. I guess in English, there is little confusion between the two phrases, standardized work and work standards.

The 'standardized work' is set as a standard operational method based on three elements: (1) Takt-Time (2) Working sequence (3) Standard in-process stock. Keeping the Standardized work with these procedures will safely produce efficient and high-quality products.

On the other hand, the 'work standards' is all kinds of standards defined as rules, such as work methods and management conditions, which are formalized for processing condition. Example of work standards are a work instruction sheet and a QC process chart and so on.

Bodek and Hager were talking about standardization in a book, *JIT IS FLOW* (PCS Press, 2006, P. 231), 'There are three different words: standard work; standardized work; or standardization. Which do you prefer?' The conversation about the standardized work between two authorities in this article was interesting."

33

Improvement of Machine in the Production Line

Manager Takeuchi has been seeing operators working in the production line. He observes not only *Muda* (waste) of moving but equipment as well. He solves their problems, taking out various countermeasure ideas based on his viewpoints of the system.

There are also many *Kaizen* case books and past cases of companies to improve machinery.

He takes many measures to make better works, referring to these cases, sometimes asking for advice from experts in the factory TPS promotion division, and getting support from designers and production engineers.

We have to admit that there is priority in performing *Kaizen* activity **from improvement of work to improvement of machine.**

The improvement of work is first, where we can perform the activity by using our wisdom and without money. Then we do a minimum investment to improve the machine to make work better. And finally, we perform the improvement of process or layout.

Mr. Ohno explained, "*Kaizen* (Improvement) of work is at the core of *Kaizen*. *Kaizen* is different from improvement, because *Kaizen* has another concept, that is, it can be performed by using our wisdom and without money." This is the reason why *Kaizen* is nowadays in common use in English. In this book is sometimes used the word "improvement," but most "improvement" has to be understood to have the meaning of *Kaizen*. In addition, *Kaizen* is usually translated into "continuous improvement" in English.

In many cases where improvement of machine and improvement of layout are done without performing improvement of work enough, we

DOI: 10.4324/9781003323310-45

will not be able to do it again and might spend a lot of money wastefully. Excellent fruit can be expected after we have steadily performed *Kaizen* for standardization of work.

A staff member who is or was a technical expert is prompt to remodel a machine carelessly based on his own technical ability and experience, and change the layout in order to sugarcoat his work. Such a person should perform real *Kaizen* rather than make surface level changes.

We'll advance the improvement of a machine based on the following notice 1–4, referred to many *Kaizen* case books:

1. The improvement of machines for **improving the production speed** should be advanced according to the need.
2. The *Kaizen* of **small lot sizes and quick setups** is important.
   The purpose of this item is finally for establishing the *Heijyunka* production (leveled production).

   Nowadays, it is the age of the "production of many models in small quantities," so we have to cope with many models using a single machine. In a big-sized lot production, we have to produce every product with a large stock. And in the case of needing setup change which requires time, the Rate of Operation and the Operational Availability decreases according to the increase in the frequency of setups. The smaller the lot-size becomes, the more the frequency of setups increases. Then the total time of setups increases.

   We should make production size smaller in order to establish the *Heijyunka* production. Ideally one-piece production is best, because we can produce one by one, which sequence of production comes from sales. For that reason, the *Kaizen* of the setup is so important to make the setup change prompt.

   The main *Kaizen* subject of setup is how we decrease the time of setup. It is desirable we take into account the setup process in the design stage or the process design stage as much as possible, because it becomes difficult to change the setup process in the mass production stage.

   The ***Kaizen* of setup** is explained with the following steps.

   Firstly, Non-setup, which process can be established by design change and process change, is very preferable.

   Secondly, converting In-line set-up to Off-line setup is effective. We should analyze the In-line set-up process, which has to stop the equipment or the production processes. If the Off-line setup, which can continue to run without stopping the equipment, is established, a smooth work process can occur by support of an outside line-worker.

Finally, reducing the operating time for the In-line set-up process is important. In the case of a present line, reducing the setup time should be performed with *Kaizen* steps starting from observing the current status to standardizing.

3. ***Kaizen* of reducing machine trouble** is important for improving the Operational Availability.

This is because the machine trouble retards a Just-in-time manufacturing process. Besides, we have to stock excess inventory as a provision against machine trouble. It is natural wasteful inventory.

4. There is the *Poka-yoke* system which makes machines stop when abnormalities occur. This is based on the ideology of *Jidoka*.

Mistakes that workers carelessly makes are called "human error." *Poka-yoke* is a broad concept which prevents mistakes by various devices and mechanisms. This is widely used in order to weave quality into the production process and is otherwise called Fool-proofing (FP), mistake proofing, error proofing, or fail safe.

There are so many *Poka-yoke* case books that readers can easily access and learn from as a reference. *Poka-yoke* was called *Baka-yoke* in Japanese those days, which isn't used now because it isn't preferable in Japanese. But it still comes out in documents, so I dare to mention it here. There are other words which are recommended that we shouldn't use now. But we sometimes find such words in magazines, and hear them in the *Genba*. It is difficult to lose such acceptable terms which have already spread into common language.

34

Improvement of Process in the Production Line

We should understand afresh that equipment layout *Kaizen* is after the work *Kaizen* and the machine *Kaizen*. We shouldn't change the layout which includes waste in process. There are a lot of bad examples which are implemented with the reverse sequence of procedure and have to start over again.

In TPS, the system, "Stopping the line with any abnormalities," is important. We can rephrase it with **There is no reason to fear a line stop**.

We produce with the proper power of workers which is just enough for the customer demand, and when abnormality exists, problems will surface.

Then when defects occur, we prevent generating defective products by stopping a production line with the *Jidoka* concept. In the case of machines, a mechanism which can detect abnormality is installed. Meanwhile, the manual operating line has a similar concept called "another *Jidoka*." This is where a worker can push a stop button or pull a **string switch** in abnormal situations, where an *Andon* display indicates the status of the production line.

These systems where we think "There is no reason to fear a line stop" can accumulate *Kaizen* and results in a strong line.

Let's talk closely with operators.

The quality is woven into processes together with operators.

DOI: 10.4324/9781003323310-46

35

As a Kaizen Practitioner

Manager Takeuchi grows as a *Kaizen* practitioner who practices doing *Kaizen*, and learns the basic knowledge of TPS in the beginning stages. Though he acquires actual improvement skills and tools with his gained knowledge of TPS, he doesn't feel he is able to know the Toyota Production System easily. He finds it is a profound ideology, and he feels like he is in an unfamiliar place.

"Skills assessment of a *Kaizen* practitioner," which is found on the practical TPS *Kaizen* field, has to be evaluated by the practitioners themselves.

They evaluate their own ability as a TPS *Kaizen* practitioner, and the assessment items in detail are organized in *Kaizen* tools and method. The estimated score should increase yearly by itself, because they have improved the level of their skills. But some practitioners decrease their scores yearly. Manager Takeuchi's score also has decreased. This is because he has understood the evaluation criteria more clearly.

Evaluating the TPS skill is difficult. There should be a good evaluation person who can evaluate practitioners objectively, but this is also difficult.

Thus, when we know the difficulty of the evaluation of skills of TPS *Kaizen* practitioners, we feel how endlessly profound TPS *Kaizen* is.

The *Kaizen* activity in the FEN production line has been supported by both the members in the factory TPS promotion division and the members with Manager Takeuchi in OMCD, and has achieved the current target of productivity. After achieving this we can offer our factory to the Toyota Production System *Jishuken* next year. The Toyota Production System *Jishuken* meeting will be held with *Kaizen* themes for the FEN production line, and *Jishuken* members of eight companies will come to our factory.

DOI: 10.4324/9781003323310-47

Main *Jishuken* members, a general manager of the leading automaker and the leaders and sub-leaders in the group companies' OMCD, visited our company and decided to hold a *Jishuken* meeting next year in our production workplace. It is agreed that our site has received the level required for holding a *Jishuken* meeting with group companies, where their members can learn and research a new production system.

A higher level of activity than previously is requested by the *Jishuken* meeting for the next year. It is expected that *Jishuken* activity with wisdom creates a more productive workplace.

Manager Takeuchi has grown up to be a *Kaizen* practitioner in the *Jishuken* meeting, which is held in group company's workplaces and thought somewhat special generally. But, TPS activity should be actively occurring not only in the *Jishuken* of the group company's activity but also in the individual company.

We sometimes come across executives who are all talk but no action or do things for show.

The ups and downs in TPS activity depends on the earnest mind of the company's executives. TPS is active only when the top has a strong mind of carrying on TPS activity. Manager Takeuchi found this out when he observed the company objectively outside as a *Jishuken* member. It may be the same situation not only in TPS but also in some *Kaizen* activity and innovative activity.

Manager Takeuchi was ordered by his boss to transfer to OMCD and study TPS for two years. But now he can't return to his original division, Production Engineering Center, because his company is drastically changing the organization.

He doesn't yet have the confidence to understand the Toyota Production System.

He reflects back to his past.

A big flood disaster happened this summer.

He gave everything he had to the restoration of a supplier factory.

He was very vital when he worked on inventing new products in R&D.

He was always sure of himself.

Now he has lost his confidence and feels he has no ability.

In his eyes there is no hope for tomorrow.

He also thinks he has to make great progress in his TPS ability.

It is like driving in a big downpour.

The outlook for his career is bad.

Whenever he looks around, it's always raining.

The TPS activity of OMCD in the East Automotive Co. is inactive recently. Manager Takeuchi thinks he has to continue practicing TPS and grow up to be a *Kaizen* practitioner, even if he were in bad circumstances. He also holds a firm belief that he'll return to a good situation again.

It seems as if the journey of learning about Manufacturing is never-ending.

Part X

President of Supplier Remembers the *Kaizen* Activities

36

President of Supplier Looks Back

"How can you say that? It is impossible."

I couldn't resist raising my voice.

A leader was visiting my company from the purchasing division in the East Automotive Co, Ltd. He ordered me to implement hard tasks.

"You only ever say 'Go and do it.'" I continued to complain of him giving empty orders.

Though I had remarked a little excitedly, I thought about my supplier position in the East Automotive Co.

I'm the second-generation president of a subsidiary supplier in the East Automotive Co. Three years have passed since I became the company president from my father.

I graduated from a local high school and went to a university in the capital city.

I decided to work for an electrical appliance company after graduation, as I wanted to utilize my specialty of learning.

When I had enjoyed a carefree life, I was admonished by my mother. "You should help your father."

Though I lived an enriched life in the capital city, I ended up going back to my hometown.

My father told me that I should go to work in the East Automotive Co. as an apprentice for a while. I was assigned to the design department of the technical division and did the design work of automotive components. It was the components design for the customer of leading automaker A. Sometimes I went to meetings with customer staff in charge of design in order to decide the specification.

Those works in the East Automotive Co. have since been valuable for me.

DOI: 10.4324/9781003323310-49

I had always been thinking that I needed to learn the working practices in a manufacturing company, which was my original purpose, during limited time.

Though I was assigned to the design department, I sometimes went to the production department which produced products for my tasks.

I walked between the assembly production lines together with the assistant manager, and we got to the production manager who told us to come over.

Both staff in charge of quality charge and staff in charge of shipment attended a meeting. I listened with my boss to the client complaint about the design which the production manager spoke about in detail. The cause of the issued defects was my design. Though it was my fault, it was also a valuable experience for me. I had tried to learn about the working practices through those conversations in the meeting.

I still wanted to learn a lot, but finished after several years' employment in the East Automotive Co., and returned to the company my father managed. My company has been the associate company of the East Automotive Co., so it is a tier-two supplier of the leading automaker.

We deal in assembly processing and plastic components molding.

My company which my father started holds about 250 employees now. My company has become bigger even after I started work there, but the difficulties with human resources have been endless. This was one reason why I returned from the capital city.

Most employees who joined when my father started the company have already retired. They were also senior people whose excellent talent in technology and skills we could rely on. Now I do my best to focus on managing a few staff for tasks in important departments. Japanese companies have the seniority system, even though it has been deformed. Thus, unfortunately, excellent human resources are not joining our company, though I expect mid-career people to join our company.

I became company executive when my old father retired three years ago. There was one senior executive director from during the foundation of the company. He supported me and I relied on consultations with him in many ways. It would only be another several years before he retired. My subject was how to develop the middle-tier employees.

37

President Had a Bad Time with Poor Instruction

One year has passed since I loudly said, "How can you say that? It is impossible."

There are several departments which give guidance to suppliers according to their specialized tasks at the East Automotive Co.

Sometimes we ask them "Please tell us," but this situation was not like that. Our company issued large-scale quality defects to the production lines in the East Automotive Co., and it became a production line complaint. Though we didn't have difficulty in delivery to A automaker of the final assembly lines, it might become a problem later.

The leader in charge of suppliers in the purchasing department came to my company in such a situation.

It was revealed that this quality defect was caused by mechanical processing in the assembly production line, and after this was settled there were no further problems.

An executive, who was in charge of the purchasing division in the East Automotive Co., came to our company after a while, and did an audit of quality. He judged that there was a problem as a result of management in the production line, and guided our company to be instructed continually in the future from the East Automotive Co. Thus our company signed a technical assistance contract with the East Automotive Co.

This was a *Kaizen* instruction contract.

This was the first time such a contract came into action systematically. Our company had implemented the *Kaizen* activity until then, but it had been sporadic activity which was implemented by just observing and imitating others.

DOI: 10.4324/9781003323310-50

The East Automotive Co. had been implementing TPS activity for a long time. So, I expected there were a lot of staff who understood TPS.

There is an association which organizes suppliers in the East Automotive Co. Basically, it is a supplier social club which elects a president from among the members of representatives. The club holds its meeting several times in a year.

When our company was just starting the *Kaizen* activity under the guidance of the East Automotive Co., a meeting of the association was held. I also participated in a dinner party after the meeting, though I usually refrained from joining such parties where many seniors participated. However, I thought it was a good opportunity in which I could hear about the experience of seniors having the guidance of the East Automotive Co.

Many senior presidents who were the same generation as my retired father were gathering. I told them our company was just starting TPS activity under the guidance of the East Automotive Co. This threw them into an uproar.

"Don't try to do TPS activity."

"Unreasonably, while I couldn't understand, I was reprimanded."

"A long time ago, they kicked a box with their foot, yelling 'What is this?'"

"There was a person who was intimidating."

"We did it, but it was useless."

"It is not active now."

And so on and so forth.

The presidents spoke to each other humorously about old memories of TPS leaders through whom they had a bad time or were reprimanded.

The mass media was reporting on the usefulness of the Toyota Production System, so I thought the seniors were overreacting. But I remembered what they said at the time I raised my voice at my office.

A trigger for raising questions about the guidance was the executive who was in charge of purchasing for the East Automotive Co. and had come to the audit.

He asked, "Why is there so much stock?"

I replied, "Sometimes there is a production line stoppage due to some problems. We cannot help having a big inventory, because the fluctuation of the delivery order from the East Automotive Co. is big."

The only things the executive said was, "There is too much stock, so cut it down."

Then he gave specific direction to a leader in charge of purchasing who was accompanying him.

"You guide this company and should reduce the inventory. Do it until I see the result."

The leader who was in charge of guiding suppliers in the purchasing department came to our company periodically twice a week,

He directed randomly, but didn't guide in a practical way in detail and he only asked what result had happened.

I remembered that Mr. Taiichi Ohno stated, "TPS is the system in which we realize cost reduction by thorough elimination of *Muda* (Waste), and the biggest *Muda* depends on the surplus inventory."

I have seen a picture which compares the inventory level to the water surface of a pond in order to explain the surplus inventory. In this picture, the water hides the stones during the high-water level, but the stones come out when the water level becomes low (Figure 37.1).

The surface of a pond corresponds to the inventory level, and the stones in the bottom of a pond correspond to the various problems.

When the inventory level which corresponds to the water surface is high, the stones which show problems such as defects, machine breakdown, delivery delay, work trouble, and so forth are hidden.

We reduced the inventory in order to **clarify problems** so we could find the problems easily.

TPS leaders say inventory is the worst evil in TPS. We certainly didn't have enough inventory to deal with delivery to our customers so we were afraid of not being able to deliver any more if a mechanical breakdown or

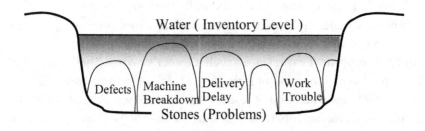

Huge water (Inventory level) hides stones (problems).

FIGURE 37.1
Relationship between inventory and problems.

quality issue occurred. And it was also a fact that mechanical breakdowns and quality troubles had frequently happened.

I understood that these situations were problems, but we couldn't solve situations of that like, so we put off dealing with them. Of course, it was desirable that we removed the mechanical breakdown and quality trouble and that we could take a countermeasure immediately even if those troubles happened.

So, I guess TPS leaders find out the hidden problems using "the way of reducing inventory first" in order to make a strong workplace. Though it might create putting a lot of pressure, I understand such thinking.

But "the way of reducing inventory" only leads to discovering problems and not solving problems because of a lack of ability in our company. However we can't improve the problem, because we don't have enough human resources who can implement *Kaizen*.

Even though I wondered if we could reduce the inventory, we reduced the stock of final products according to the leader's direction which was "Deliver without stock."

The leader directed to reduce the inventory, like his boss, but he also didn't teach how to do it. Actually, he didn't know how to do it. Unfortunately he had no ability in *Kaizen*.

In my company, we didn't have such people who could implement the *Kaizen* activity by themselves.

I've heard from the seniors of the association, "I was reprimanded by a stern TPS leader. Then I did what the leader said, even though I couldn't understand it." The seniors only followed the order, "Go and do it."

In the case that there are human resources who can implement *Kaizen*, such a strong direction might trigger good motivation to implement it, because they can achieve some success after implementing it.

When the leader says "Just do it," it sometimes implies meaning, "I don't know how to do it, even though I know what to expect in terms of results," outside the words. I experienced such a leader's saying. The leader didn't know how to do it or was not trained in a method to solve problems, even though he knew what kind of results to expect. When we are taught from such a leader, we run into difficulties. In the case of good results with this kind of leader, there are good human resources in the company.

The executive's declaration, "There is too much stock," itself sounded superficial. Such verbal or superficial knowledge was written in every book. It would be very difficult to be successful in TPS because the leader who came to our office was also inexperienced.

Meanwhile, the senior managing director whom I had great confidence in said, "I'm already at the age of retiring, so I'd like to live more freely," and then he left my company.

He shared responsibility for the *Kaizen* with me, but he was exhausted due to the leader continuously telling him, "Do it, and just do." Though I expected his assistance for another several years, his retirement became a great loss to our company.

Still I thought I would try my best. But while we reduced the inventory according to the leader's order, my company had begun to fall into a state of chaos.

My company was going to be in a terrible state.

When the variety and quantity of products in customer demand fluctuated, we were frequently unable to ship them. This created a delivery delay. We suddenly had to do overtime work and holiday work in order to cope with the trouble.

Though I had thought that eliminating the surplus assets of products was good for the company management, it resulted in increasing the labor cost as a result of overtime work. I didn't know any more why we reduced the inventory.

I guess that companies which don't have enough ability for implementing TPS are roughly separated into two cases.

In the first case, the company itself doesn't have ability. Stated quite simply, it is a case where there aren't any human resources who can cope with TPS activity. Suggestions for improvements in the small group activity are common, but TPS needs human resources who are capable.

In the second case, there isn't a good leader.

I worked for design in the East Automotive Co., so unfortunately I couldn't learn the TPS activity. I read many books, but I was not sure. Then it was necessary to ask for the help of a leader outside the company, so I expected and asked for the cooperation of the East Automotive Co.

And the leader who spoke with only superficial knowledge came to my company. In reality, he didn't have the skill to estimate the actual ability of our company.

Of course, I know that TPS is a company-wide activity so the top of management has to take part in the planning and advance the activity to the next step. But I wanted the *Kaizen* leader to ascertain the ability of our company and lead us in a suitable way.

I understood long afterwards that an excellent TPS leader considered how to advance TPS according to the objective situation. It is said that they think of the features achieved by *Kaizen* in the future and instruct us in what we should implement at the time. So they explain in detail why we should implement it.

I couldn't stand being told "What's going on with this?" and "Go and do it." Even if I was told to think something, I didn't know how to do it, because I was at a low level in TPS.

We sometimes can see queries on the overseas social media of Lean production, such as "Is there any tool or method?" Equally, our company didn't know the method.

In this way, TPS activity had gradually begun to fall into a state of chaos, because my company had a lack of power, and moreover the leader gave strict direction without any clear guidance.

We wanted the leader to tell us how to advance the TPS activity at least, and it was good if he could provide tools for the practical improvement in detail. But we didn't have an ability that could judge whether such tools and method were useful. The human resources with TPS knowledge had not developed yet in our company, but there were human resources whom I expected to have developed in the future. Therefore, I thought that a good leader who could contemplate the future was desirable.

I had guessed the leader would have an impact of creating a negative image of TPS. I knew the East Automotive had succeeded in their business, in which they advanced TPS activity. However, I had begun to think that TPS might be impossible for us.

38

Reviewing the Kaizen Activity

My company fell into a state of chaos and suddenly went into the red in a single month since we had obeyed the leader who misled us into only reducing the inventory. At that time I had a chance to attend a meeting at the East Automotive Co. I casually met a General Manager of the Corporate Planning Division in the hall. When I was working in the East Automotive Co., I had experienced his support at work.

I told the General Manager the situation of my company at that time. Then, he said,

"Leave that to me, I have everything under control. Developing the healthy suppliers is part of my work."

After a while, I received a message from a staff member in charge of the Planning department of the Corporate Planning Division saying that he would come to my company with an expert. He explained that they had come to an agreement with the executive of the purchasing division and reconsidered how to advance the activity in our company.

The staff of the Planning department, a Project General Manager of OMCD and a manager of the Main Factory TPS department visited our company.

I carefully explained our situation to them while walking in our factory.

After the plant tour, we had a meeting.

"I came to this company as a result of a request from the Corporate Planning Division. Both OMCD and the Main Factory TPS department will support your company," said the Project General Manager (TPS *Shusa* in Japanese) of OMCD. I had known that OMCD was a managing division of TPS, but I didn't expect so much at that time.

The Project General Manager, GM (*Shusa*) said "First, let's establish the promoting system."

DOI: 10.4324/9781003323310-51

Our company had already made two young employees engage in the *Kaizen* activity. And moreover, two members from the East Automotive Co. were going to be stationed at our company. They were a Sectional Manager of OMCD and a member of the Factory TPS Promotion department.

The people in charge of the activity were both me as the president and the other GM of the East Automotive Co.

We tightly made the *Kaizen* promotion organization in this way, and promoted the activity with frequent discussion. Under the lead of the General Manager, we decided the direction of all activity and then implemented it concretely.

The GM explained the aim of the *Kaizen* promotion organization as follows:

1. The structure should have staff who can implement changes by themselves.
2. The structure should be rooted in the company permanently.
3. The structure should be created to the level which won't revert back to what was done previously. The East Automotive Co. helps in order to establish such a status.
4. The East Automotive Co. will show us how to implement TPS, so the members of the organization should learn and develop it.

I thought I would be more mindful of advancing TPS.

The GM advised me, "I think that a promoting system which is suitable for that company is necessary. We will advance this way for the time being, but I hope you will make it better."

He added, "Making the organization or system for *Kaizen* is more important in overseas nations where people change their job frequently."

I guessed that our company was in a similar situation to bad companies because we were still at the first stage.

He continued to say,

"I'd like to talk about our attitude toward TPS activity.

Implementing TPS doesn't always mean that a company becomes strong. TPS doesn't work if we only imitate the external aspects of TPS. For example, superficially adopting the *Kanban* system results in failure. Firstly, truly understanding TPS is important.

We should establish a company culture in which all members from the top management to the employees understand the thinking of TPS. But it is overwhelming work to create this culture.

The company executive should take the initiative in person with the *Genchi-Gembutsu* concept.

The company establishes the *Kaizen* activity in which all the employees continuously find out problems and improve them. Therefore, it is important to develop the *Kaizen* Suggestion system and the small group activity.

Why don't you create a good corporate culture steadily?"

I was sure that the GM had shown the essentials of activity which we could see frequently in books.

"Our company as an affiliate of the tier-one supplier of the leading car manufacturer doesn't have enough human resources." I brought up an issue which I had been thinking about a long time. The GM answered strictly in saying,

"It is good if the president is able to deeply understand TPS. The employees won't follow the president if the top executive doesn't understand TPS himself.

TPS is a company-wide activity, so the employees watch the top's seriousness towards TPS, and see through people who just verbally say 'TPS is top-down.' The president surely has to become more aware and have confidence in TPS. Everyone has to practice and learn by themselves."

The GM added, "Practice is important. But, you should study the basic TPS in a classroom in order to understand it. I'll give you a class on the Toyota Production System. First, you acquire the basic knowledge through lectures."

I decided to hold the classroom where key persons and staff in the production workplaces participate in studying TPS after work hours.

The GM kept talking,

"We'd like to implement the *Kaizen* activity after we understand it with the right knowledge. Sometimes, after considering actions to some degree, people still do something that is counter to the TPS ideals. This could be from when they don't have TPS knowledge and so don't understand the explanation.

When we make the purpose clear and implement the *Kaizen* with a true understanding of TPS, we can establish a good workplace."

"Many companies failed in TPS because they considered TPS was only about introducing *Kanban*. If a wrong way of introducing TPS causes the productivity to fall, people won't be able to know why TPS was introduced to the workplace. I have many experiences of factories where people were not taught or did not understand TPS properly, though they said they were taught by TPS experts. A good TPS teacher is a leader who can instruct us about the future features according to the current situation, and has to develop members by making them think and practice. It is important to try to transform a workplace and build it into an established situation. Even if the leader thinks he has changed a workplace through forced change, if the good workplace culture and system isn't achieved, the workplace will go back to its previous condition.

This activity isn't supposed to be pressure from the East Automotive Co. We're just an aid to making a system for this company so that it can keep implementing the *Genba Kaizen*. We'd like to improve your workplace more.

We will show you how to utilize tools and methods for practicing *Kaizen*, in which you should understand the aim of them. You mustn't use tools and methods without correctly understanding them, and should understand the fundamental thinking of TPS there.

Even though the fundamental concept of TPS never changes, TPS allows for situations in which various tools and methods can be used. So, a case that practical usage and management doesn't work is highly likely, even while using similar types of tools. Sometimes, regardless of whether we use similar types of tools, cases of ineffective management and usage still occur. For example, a case might happen where methods were set correctly at the beginning but changed for the worse."

The GM had his opinion about those failures. He said there was a lot of writing about the case of failure in the Toyota Production System. When he often saw those failures, he felt they were sometimes "Just excuses" and the leaders including the president behave just like "onlookers." This behavior is not related to the result of the activity. There were some cases of failure in which factory policy or direction was reversed by a factory manager. Unfortunately, these cases were sometimes caused by a person, such as an ex-engineer, who couldn't understand the production workplace. The GM stated strongly they were just providing lip service with keywords without truly understanding.

I'm so anxious about implementing TPS with right understanding from now on, but I have decided to try to develop the ability of our company under the guidance of the GM.

Our company's particular problem was a low TPS level which was evaluated as "TPS level B" by the GM. I couldn't understand why *Kanban* hadn't been managed well, until the GM pointed it out and we noticed this was an evaluation of a "Low-level Toyota Tier 2 supplier." I had never thought of this.

Kanban was issued by the East Automotive Co., and then our company shipped the products in boxes to which *Kanban* was attached. I had thought that because we delivered products with *Kanban* we were doing the Toyota Production System.

The GM pointed out that we didn't use *Kanban* correctly and we were using it instead of a "label."

He said, "This may be harsh to say, but your company is not very different from other companies which are unrelated to *Kanban*."

Though I was not completely satisfied with the GM's suggestions, I thought that we would implement TPS activity aiming at "TPS level C."

39

Restarting the TPS Activity

Today is the first day. All parties concerned in the project including the Project General Manager of the East Automotive Co. are coming to our company.

We specially have left work early today, and all employees are assembling in the canteen. We begin a kick-off meeting which is not formal but a place where future activity is explained.

All employees should share concerns about any dangers or threats to the health of the company and then proceed step by step regarding future activity.

I explain the management status in detail. Following my explanation, the Project General Manager, GM, introduces himself with a greeting and introduces a project member from the East Automotive Co.

The meeting closes, and "TPS education" starts for our key members right away. The lecture in the classroom provides us only the basic knowledge. The volume of total lectures giving a general explanation of TPS is about two days. Several classrooms will be held after working time. Of course, I'll join in the class.

The GM said "Practice makes knowledge effective," so I'd like to eagerly understand the concrete basic knowledge of TPS.

The next day, all members of the TPS promotion organization gather.

The GM explains to us about the basic procedure of TPS as follows.

"This company has fallen into a state of chaos because you reduced the inventory unreasonably without the production ability. Surplus inventory is said to be the worst waste because it produces secondary waste, so activity of reducing the inventory is natural.

But, **we have to have the proper inventory according to our ability**. We shouldn't implement a bad way lightly such as reducing inventory by half.

This company formerly had too much inventory in the warehouse.

DOI: 10.4324/9781003323310-52

At first, we had to prepare the necessary inventory for delivery when reducing inventory. So, we should decide the proper inventory amount. Such inventory might be said as a necessary evil. Then we estimate our company's ability and the fluctuation of our customer's orders.

This might be common sense; however, we can't see hidden problems when the inventory level is huge. If we can see the problems easily and solve them, we will become a good company and be happy. When I find workplaces in factories where products are smoothly flowing and inventory is properly set, I'm sure that the factory production activity is going well."

I would also like to make such "visible" workplaces in which we can see abnormal situations. I always feel tired when we get confused about issues and can't find problems.

I want to know how to advance TPS in reality. I ask the general manager about that.

The GM answers that we should advance TPS in an orthodox way as follows:

1. First, we should recognize that the current situation of our factory is TPS level B. Here, the production workplace produces in its own way for convenience, such as producing by the large lot sized production, regardless of the customer *Kanban* demand. The products are shipped by boxes attached with *Kanban*, which is handled only as a "tag or label." So, as a result, the inventory does not become something that has been managed. This means *Kanban* is not used as a tool of inventory management and production instructions.
2. Next target is the TPS level C. We create the features of the Toyota Production System with *Kanban*, and we are very thorough on *Kanban* management.
3. Specifically, the production workplace should produce based on customer information on *Kanban*. This system is established as the Pull-type production by each truck which synchronizes with the customer demand.

Even though the GM explains his thoughts like the above, I'm seized with an uneasy feeling about whether we can do it. But, I reconsider and decided to work hard, since fortunately the East Automotive Co. supports our company. Because of this fact, I realized that I just need a bit more patience until our employees in our company can implement the activity by themselves.

40

Establishing the Continuous
TPS Kaizen Activity

The _Kaizen_ promotion team decides to draw up a blueprint.

All the team members should understand the current situation, take out problems, and define what to improve.

First, we sketch the "Goods and Information Flow Chart (Current State)," which is based on the investigation of the current state of the workplaces which are from the receiving area to the shipping area. Many problems are written in the "Current State" chart. Next, we discuss these problems and sketch the "Target State." We manage the production with _Kanban_.

In order to attain the "Target State," we have to work out a plan which we can implement specifically.

We prepare an A3 activity summary form in which we can check the progress of implementing _Kaizen_ as a planned figure and actual figure. In addition, the actual implementation items are managed in checklists in which the name of the person in charge and the due date are written.

These documents, such as the summary sheets and the checklists, are posted on boards in the workplaces.

I decide to hold a meeting in which I explain how to advance the activity to employees.

I explain and share the information to all employees so that they can understand the activity. I want to ensure the employees feel positive when they can see the achievement of activity.

Every workplace group leader explains the current activity carefully at the daily morning meeting.

DOI: 10.4324/9781003323310-53

Meanwhile, a presentation of *Kaizen* activity is held every week. There, the General Manager gives instructions and explanations in detail so that employees can understand.

Activity items are quality improvement, productivity improvement, system improvement and so forth in the whole workplace.

We make standards slowly but surely while improving the workplaces.

In this way, our workplace gradually becomes "visible" with the repeated daily activities. The objective workplace floor is now transformed beyond recognition. Next, we will deploy the activity to another floor (*Yokoten*).

The GM said TPS activity is quite orthodox; however, it wasn't easy to establish this procedure.

There are several points I learned when implementing the activity:

1. I learned "2S is surely the first step."
   When we are completely thorough with 2S of *Seiri-Seiton*, we can see whether the situation is normal or abnormal. It's important to repeat 2S of *Seiri-Seiton* continuously.
2. Even if we say that we produce based on customer information on *Kanban*, the delivery amount of the customer fluctuates. So a proper system which absorbs the fluctuation is desirable, and a proper safety stock in the Store is necessary as a buffer.
3. Structure and tools such as shelves and so forth which can easily manage "First-in, First-out (FIFO)" are necessary for the whole process from receiving to shipment.
4. Small lot sized production is essential. When we don't have any practical ability, we can't produce products with the dispatching unit of instruction by trucks. Firstly, we have to improve the productivity which is made possible by the improvement of set-up and machine malfunction. We improve them through Standing Observation, and we are very thorough about making and implementing the standards
5. In order to improve our company, we must keep employees motivated and keep the activity ongoing. Even though we are taught by the East Automotive Co., the practitioners are actually our employees. This is also true even if we use an outsider consultant. We can't keep going if we only implement what someone tells us. We need an incentive to continue the activity. Employees tend to just follow instructions.

But I want employees to feel the worth of doing something and the sense of achievement. Praise is necessary for this, so I always try to praise employees. I think they are motivated by praise for their work.

Moreover, when a presentation of *Kaizen* activity is held, we should make honorable recognition of employees' work an incentive.

Reflecting back to our activities, I aim at the features achieved through elimination of "waste of inventories with overproduction" instead of the mere inventory reduction. I sense that a company with a system which only produces the needed amount of products and doesn't have the waste of overproduction is strong. We still have to find a way to respond easily to both an increase and a decrease in production.

There is *Kanban* in our company, but even the company which doesn't have *Kanban* is in a similar situation. A system should be made with the basic tools and methods based on the TPS way of thinking. But, in our company, though the *Kanban* method was tough before reaching our current level, I think *Kanban* is easy and useful when it is well-established.

Kaizen was developed at an early stage, while I received the experienced GM's guidance. However, now I'm worried about whether the *Kaizen* activity will be well established, because I have heard of a case of a company which reverted back to a non-TPS world.

This company stopped the consulting service without understanding the consultant's expression, "I lead TPS step by step." Sometimes companies stop their consultation before the system has been completed. In this case, it is ok if the company understands that the system isn't established and can continue their activities. However, it's often difficult to continue the activities by themselves, so they revert back to their former status.

In other cases, we are frustrated by consultants who forcefully bring guidance from their surface knowledge which was seen and heard from their narrow experience. Sometimes they say they are TPS consultants and tell us what the right way is. In so doing, they force us to use improper methods.

Therefore, although it's difficult to continue using TPS in our own way, our company has to continue to learn TPS by ourself from now on.

Looking back over our activity, the quality defects in the process sharply decrease, and the production line complaints from customers get fewer. The quality level has improved because of the past activity.

The inventory has also become smaller and the empty space stands out in the factory. When we checked the inventory at the beginning, some products had 2–3 months stock. Now we only have the safety stock level as a buffer. We don't need the wasted workers and space, and the administrative expense goes down. Doing TPS results in profit.

In those days we thought that inventory was an asset, but that time is over and now the time of cash being preferable has come. Only TPS activity has a positive benefit. Yet, we have not started applying TPS *Kaizen* to the components stock area which delivers for our subsidiary companies. We will implement this step by step.

The productivity was increased so overtime work has gone.

We implemented the TPS activity in this way, then, the profit increased remarkably when we closed the fiscal year. The gained profit is divided evenly with the East Automotive Co. Our company can raise wages, and lower the unit price of products for the East Automotive Co.

But, more than that, I'm very pleased because the ability of employees who have implemented *Kaizen* by themselves has increased.

I find out that the knowledge and experience in understanding TPS has various levels. I have attained the knowledge of TPS, and I feel I'm being developed little by little, even though I have no idea how to implement TPS.

The General Manager has a stance of "Let's think over something together."

The GM says, "Someone who thinks of himself as a TPS leader tends to fail, when he says 'this is the right way,' as if it is 'the golden rule' or 'absolute truth.' A method which is useful in another company is not always the best. Even if the leader forces us to follow such a method, it doesn't work. Therefore, we should implement it in the best way at that time after we deeply think about the ideal state in the future. However, we can't move towards the ideal state, when we always follow an easy path without challenging ourselves. The Important thing is that we continuously implement TPS little by little."

The General Manager says, "TPS activity can be activated with the will and seriousness of top management."

Now, it's time to test the ability of our company.

I still feel a touch of uneasiness.

I vaguely understand why this is the case.

It may be such strong anxiety exists because I may not be able to continue this way.

I think I'll believe and keep going in the TPS activity, because there are many past cases which had success in TPS.

I have to get more understanding from people inside the company, in order to make this activity well-established. This is because there are many employees who merely do work as they are ordered. The other day, I heard from an employee in the assembly line, "I don't want to implement *Kaizen*, but I just do as my leader commands." It's a sad situation but I guess employees will be in trouble if the company goes bankrupt.

I'd like to make good teams in which all members think for themselves, but key people are still being developed now.

I'm also being developed. Yet, I haven't been able to sketch out the features of our company for the future.

I'll go around and study the actual workplaces harder than ever. I think I'll try to communicate with employees so that they are motivated.

Journey Four

Deepening Journey

VISUALIZING AND MOVING TOWARD THE IDEAL FEATURES

– Deciding the direction for ideal *Monodzukuri* (Manufacturing) –

In this journey, the story depicts the main character who is struggling with the Toyota Production System.

There is not always one way to improve the workplace. He tries to grasp actual situations, and afterwards he decides the most effective direction to create the best workplace in the future. He shows the procedure of how to find problems, how to decide a target, and how to solve the problems. The process of considering a better way is sketched out to make a better workplace.

The Toyota Production System appears with different level features. On the other hand the features of the Toyota Production System sometimes seem to be different among outsiders depending on their experience, thinking way, and viewpoint. And there are some people who affirmatively say "this is TPS" in their restricted experience.

This book finally proposes a picture of "The Features of TPS" whose concept tries to settle the above-mentioned confusion.

DOI: 10.4324/9781003323310-54

Part XI

Learning the True Procedure for *Kaizen*

41

When Absentminded

A division meeting is opening, and this is the second time since New Year.

In the division meeting held on Monday morning every week, main members report the important affairs in the last week and any pending issues. Especially as the division meeting is mainly focused on their management, it is important to communicate and discuss with others how to advance the business affairs, or how to proceed the *Kaizen* activities, rather than the general affairs.

General Manager Takeuchi concentrates patiently, and listens to the exchange between an executive and members.

He suddenly senses the executive's voices drift away to a faraway place, and withdraws into his own world where he thinks about the exchange a short while ago. The discussion has already moved to a different item, but G.M. Takeuchi doesn't hear it any more.

Five years have passed since he moved to OMCD. Meanwhile, he happened to be transferred and experienced two other divisions in two years; COST MANAGEMENT DIVISION for cost and BUSINESS REFORM PROMOTION DIVISION for white-collar productivity. Now, he has returned to OMCD again. Even when he was in the other divisions, he continued to study the Toyota Production System by making contact with his friends in OMCD. But, he has studied about TPS systematically with the practical *Kaizen* activity only for three years.

The East Automotive Co. announces the annual scheduled personnel change in January. The New Year's holidays feeling is still left over a little there. And a fresh atmosphere is also filling the room, because new apprentices in TPS have come to OMCD from the whole company.

DOI: 10.4324/9781003323310-56

In such a mood, G.M. Takeuchi gets lost in his own thought and he begins to deeply think about the essence of TPS. It is only natural that other people think he has been absentminded during a meeting.

The idea suddenly flashes into his mind. G.M. Takeuchi's tension is relieved. Now, he has a clear vision. It seems like all of a sudden the mist around him has vanished.

"Aha, I got it. 2S is surely the first one." He just had an aha moment!

Whenever he practices *Kaizen*, he is taught by senior colleagues, "*Kaizen* starts from 2S first." He thinks he has heard this many times, but it hasn't been in his mind. Then, the implication of this suddenly hits him and he understands the true meaning of 2S in TPS.

The answer is simple. He thinks he has been able to find the direction in his own TPS activity, because he has spent these several years practicing *Kaizen*.

We can say, "*Kaizen* starts from 5S." He realizes this sentence is fine but the important point is 2S is firstly essential when we try to grasp the direction of TPS *Kaizen*.

G.M. Takeuchi has seen many placards of 5S (整理・整頓・清掃・清潔・躾 *Seiri-Seiton-Seiso-Seiketsu-Shitsuke*) since he got employed by the East Automotive Co. There are quite a lot of companies which come into 5S activity for innovating production processes.

For what purpose do we implement 5S activity?

We can expect some effect after just carrying on 5S activity if the level of a company were at the level A described in the previous chapter. All results of each item in 5S should become standards. Rules will also be made clear by 5S activity, and it seems possible to improve the corporate culture. So, there are many consultants who are good at instructing 5S.

Meanwhile, we sometimes come across companies whose corporate culture of improvement is poor even though their level of 5S is ranked high.

The true goal of 5S is to make the workplace better and produce the outcome. However, in these cases, they aim at just doing 5S activity without focusing on the fruit. They endeavor to throw a lot of money about doing things for better show, and it results in 5S activity which doesn't produce profit. Or, 5S activity is sometimes put in a difficult situation where people don't know how to proceed and they can't foresee the future status.

We have to understand problems in the production workplace in order to make the place efficient using the TPS activity. We need to implement the 2S (*Seiri-Seiton*) first. This relates to the TPS level A described in the previous chapter, where we can't see the normality and abnormality of the workplace since the management is not good.

Everyone can know the normality and abnormality after doing 2S because unnecessary goods are taken away by doing *Seiri* (Shifting) and the state of goods becomes standardized by doing *Seiton* (Sorting).

Then, some of the seven *Muda* (Waste) can be found and measures taken based on being made the standardized state. Thus, in the workplace where 2S of *Seiri-Seiton* is completed, the problems of *Muda* can be easily found and eliminated, and a strong workplace is realized. We have to continue to naturally implement the following 3S of *Seiso-Seiketsu-Shitsuke*.

The *Kaizen* activity will succeed if the normality and abnormality of the workplace is found. This is the same not only when we aim at the higher level of TPS but also when we evaluate the result of countermeasures implemented for *Kaizen*. Therefore 2S is the start of every *Kaizen* activity. Even in a company where TPS level is high, they implement 2S thoroughly.

Most of the good TPS experts might have experienced such sudden flashes of ideas in their mind. Five years have passed since G.M. Takeuchi started studying TPS at OMCD. Just to make things clear, I dare to say that it will take time to understand the Toyota Production System. The situation differs from one person to another. And there are some levels of understanding and acquiring TPS knowledge at the various stages, but at the same time we need to understand and acquire the tools and methods.

Mr. Taga experienced a different situation from G.M. Takeuchi. He said, "Understanding TPS was step-by-step. I gained a lot of knowledge of significant TPS items overtime and suddenly everything clicked and it all made sense."

G.M. Takeuchi, as a TPS leader, gathered some valuable experiences, where he sketched the target state and practiced *Kaizen*. After that, he suddenly felt that he had finally grasped a part of TPS.

At the same time, he became able to explain the whole system to outsiders including visitors from foreign countries who visited the factory. And he explained the actual *Kanban*'s flow with *Genchi-Gembutsu*, and could talk with confidence.

⊕ -5S (FIVE S's)

Takeuchi asks *Sensei*, "5S comes from the five initials of '*Seiri - Seiton - Seiso - Seiketsu - Shitsuke*' in Japanese, doesn't it?"

"That's right. 5S is recently in common use as a worldwide word. *Kaizen* (continuous improvement) is also a universal language. Advancing the 5S activity should result in improving the workplace which is ranked A in the level of TPS described in Chapter 27." *Sensei* explains about 5S.

Takeuchi says, "I remembered the reverse order, '*Senketsu – Seiso*,' when I first started my company. An association taught us this order those days, but the third and fourth 'S' are now switched over."

Sensei continues to show many episodes that he experienced about *Seiso* (cleaning and washing).

"The order of 5S should be '*Seiso* (Sweeping and Washing) – *Seiketsu* (Spick-and-Span)' because we have to maintain the clean state of the workplace after sweeping and washing.

A president of a global car manufacturer in a South Asian country, who was from the mother company, was always picking up litter around the plant all the time. He continued this practice even though his domestic subordinate asked him not to do such a thing. I have often heard many such episodes, and I have experienced it a lot at overseas companies, also.

One day, a big shelf was changed. There was a lot of litter under the shelf. But no one swept it, though more than ten people were standing around the shelf. Then, the leader instructed the staff to put up a new shelf, so I interrupted his action to sweep the floor. When I started to sweep litter after taking a piece of equipment, one lady came and said, 'It's my cleaning equipment.' Then all evening, the cleaning lady was walking behind me in order to support our activity. In this domestic company, sweeping is a cleaning lady's job.

And, I was surprised that, in this country, it seems impolite that subordinates touch the senior's activity. In this case in Japan, someone who proposes to take over the sweeping for me will come out.

In overseas countries where there is a lot of mess outside the company entrance, or where there are different customs, it may be difficult to ask employees to sweep their workplaces.

TABLE 41.1

5S (Five S's)

		5S	Comment
1	*Seiri*, Shifting	Deciding what is and is not needed, and disposing of the latter.	Firstly, whoever sees, it's important that we can distinguish what is unnecessary at a glance. There is "Red tag" as a typical method.
2	*Seiton*, Sorting	Orderly storing and indicating what is needed so that things can be easily found.	Putting most simply just for a show means "Display," which is not "*Seiton*," and standardizing the right place of all necessary items. There is "Nameboard display" as a typical method.
3	*Seiso*, Sweeping and Washing	Sweeping the machinery and production line areas in the workplace and keeping it clean.	Machinery should be inspected during cleaning so that this process is defined as the "cleaning inspection."
4	*Seiketsu*, Spick-and-Span	This refers to cleanliness and order that results from observance of the above S's.	*Seiso* is to clean when the workplace gets soiled with oil and dust, and Seiketsu is to keep a clean state of workplace at all times.
5	*Shitsuke*, Discipline	The habit of acquiring 4S's skill and always keeping what is fixed right.	Administrators make members keep the work rules (greeting, the attire, cleanness, and security). When they can't keep it, they have to be scolded severely.

Source: Translated from Takeuchi, Noboru, *Seru Seisan*, JMA Management Center, 2006, P.179.

By the way, there is a case of 6S for which '*Shukan* (customs)' is added. I think 5S of *Shitsuke* can be based on the perspective of administrators, and 6S of *Shukan* can be based on the perspective of workers. It'll be important to make these 'S's for the culture of the workplace" (Table 41.1).

42

Visualize the Workplace by Initially Doing 2S, Especially in the TPS Level Grade A Company

Even in a company which had already achieved the TPS level C or D, more complete 2S activity was still an important factor for TPS.

One executive, a leader in charge of TPS activity, was walking around his plant every day in order to establish the TPS activity. He had some fixed time in his daily schedule for patrolling his plant. The executive only knew a few things about the concept of Just-In-Time and *Jidoka*, so he couldn't find a clear solution, and simply just said that something was strange. He continued to point out some items every day based on the viewpoint of 2S, which was part of the duties he gave himself. His managers couldn't deal with all of the items; nevertheless, the executive kept pointing out other items.

There was no end to the items found by the expert who has a good skill of 2S. And his subordinates had to work hard to deal with the items he pointed out.

The manager followed close behind the executive every day. He whined about his position, but still implemented the countermeasures against the items. Then, at least the result of the implementation of 2S could be good, and the following 3S could be good as well.

The company which can follow such methods is a relatively powerful company with a strong workforce.

Companies which have a high TPS level grade establish the 2S in depth, and the 5S as well, because it's fundamental to TPS. Some issues that come out as a result of 2S are accepted as items to be dealt with TPS. Then it

DOI: 10.4324/9781003323310-57

becomes easy for everyone to have a common understanding on how we shall improve the workplace.

Therefore, in the case of the TPS level grade A company, we should implement at first the 2S thoroughly. Implementation of 2S will produce a certain effect of cost reduction. For example, waste of searching for things will decrease. After we carry out 2S repeatedly, we'll be able to know today's state and set our goal to achieve a better tomorrow's state. It'll become easy for us to achieve a consensus of opinion with people whose opinion is different.

If we can't see the current status, we can't have a common understanding of what we will do. In other words, we can't sketch out the current state and so we don't know what to do to achieve the higher target. Even if a leader is talented, he won't be able to find an essential problem and present countermeasures.

There are many books which explain useful methods about 5S in detail, so we should apply it in our own.

43

Proceeding Initially to Sketch Out the Ideal State

General Manager (G.M.) Takeuchi firstly proposes items of 2S *Kaizen* at the early stage of *Jishuken* both inside his company and outside his company.

These suggested items are listed as countermeasure documents in detail and posted on the board, which include the implementation contents, their responsibility, and the due date. These items should be improved by TPS practitioners.

G.M. Takeuchi always tries to suggest 2S items. He thinks that these items might not easily be found by people in charge of the workplace and the root problem in the workplace should be appear after people implement some items. He doesn't mention surface items which only make the appearance better, because he thinks the true purpose of 2S is essentially "to make sure that normality and abnormality can be seen." Sometimes 5S *Kaizen* activity in workplaces becomes ineffective, since people misunderstand the true meaning of 2S. After the TPS level of the factory is improved with 5S activities, TPS level B can be achieved, where we can easily see the current status. Of course, companies which are ranked higher than TPS level B have to continuously carry out 2S or 5S in order to get better features.

In production workplaces which are ranked higher than TPS level B, the **current state** can be sketched out. And then we can sketch out the ideal features, or the **ideal state** that is assumed to be ideal in the long-term. That is to say, a production workplace which is ranked higher than TPS level B is at a stage where we can sketch out the ideal state.

DOI: 10.4324/9781003323310-58

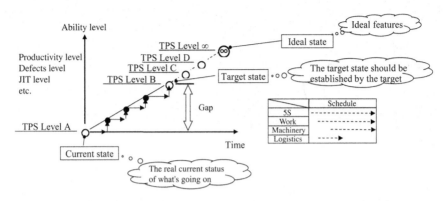

FIGURE 43.1

Improving steps in "the changing TPS features level". (Translated and adapted from Takeuchi, Noboru, *Seru Seisan*, JMA Management Center, 2006, P.175.)

© **Noboru Takeuchi, 2013**

We should also sketch out the ideal state even in a case of TPS level grade A, where we improve the current workplaces in order to find out their problems easily.

The ideology of TPS level A to TPS level ∞ is indicated in the previous chapter. In this chapter, the thinking behind **improving steps in the changing TPS features level** is simply explained (Figure 43.1).

This is **a procedure for the TPS *Kaizen* activity** which improves workplaces from TPS level A to TPS level ∞.

General TPS leaders such as G.M. Takeuchi explain the procedure below for achieving *Kaizen* under TPS:

> **Procedure 0: First, maintain 2S so that it is easy to see what's going on in the workplace.**
>
> Think of bad workplaces, where things are scattered everywhere so operators cannot find these things easily, or operators loiter on their job or go out of their fixed workplaces. Sometimes things and equipment are placed depending on the operators' way or their memory. Then work study is difficult because we can't know what operators are doing.
>
> In these cases, we can't figure out the state of the workplaces through Standing Observation. Firstly, we should implement 2S, *Seiri-Seiton*, in the workplaces so that we can see the state of them.

Procedure 1: Have a clear understanding of the current state of the workplace.

We should investigate the Goods and Information Flow of the production workplaces which is constructed from receiving to shipment, and make the current state clear.

Procedure 2: Sketch an image of the ideal state of the workplace – an image of how the workplace should ultimately be.

All practitioners who are concerned in the project should discuss and sketch out **the ideal state** of the workplaces which must be established in the future. It is the future goal of the whole plant which must be shared with all members. However, sketching the ideal state is difficult for us. And then, this ideal state tends to become the same state which is sketched with the next Procedure 3. In this case, the ideal state is perceived to be the long term target state. The situation and the purpose of workplaces always change, so it's natural that sketching the ideal state is difficult. We should sketch out the ideal state as a philosophy, then we have to drive for establishing it as our eternal goal.

Procedure 3: Sketch your image of the target state that should be established by the target date.

The target state of the workplaces are the features that should be established by a fixed day, such as the end of the next fiscal year. It is a milestone and the target of the workplaces for the time being. There are no plans which have no schedules. We fix the time, then sketch the target at that time. It is the target features of workplaces which should be shared to be implemented by all members. Here we fix the due date and the concrete numerical value. For example we chose productivity, defects, frequency of conveyance, which can be evaluated easily.

Procedure 4: Pinpoint the gaps between the current state of the workplace and the target state.

We regard the gaps as small items or a pile of problems and resolve them using individual countermeasures.

Procedure 5: Schedule in detail each step which must be taken to change a particular aspect of the workplace.

We decide each responsibility and due date for the countermeasure items. The check of the progress must always be promoted by the chief in person.

Procedure 6: Implement the targeted change to move closer toward the ideal state. Then go back to step 1 to clarify the result of changes, and then plan another change that will help you move closer to reaching the ideal state.

We manage TPS in this way, deciding a vision of the ideal state, sketching a story to achieve it, and implementing the activity. The TPS level is improved after repeating the procedure from 1 to 6. It will take a very long time, but we are able to increase the TPS level from A to D, after repeating the above cycle procedure.

Basically the important points which G.M. Takeuchi emphasizes for implementing the procedure are as follows:

1. The procedure should be run with **overall optimization** thinking, not with **sub-optimization**
2. The scope of objective workplaces should be considered according to the situation. For example, we can easily achieve a high level workplace if its scope is narrowed. Then, we expand this way as a model into new workplaces, which is called *Yokoten* in Japanese. It is important we develop the whole area in this way, because doing only the partial area is not effective in establishing a good result.
3. We should think about what is a correct goal, because we sometimes confuse the means with the end.
4. Firstly 5S, especially 2S (*Seiri-Seiton*) should be implemented in depth.
5. New improvement points will be found, when we establish the standard and observe it. We should always be flexible with change, and observe the actual situation carefully.
6. We should see the Goods and Information Flow in the workplaces. For example, if we find any stagnant stock, we know it's a problem.
7. We find a countermeasure method according to TPS thinking. There are some points which should be challenged or could be approached.
8. We should share common understanding about the direction of improvement with members. It is important to explain the target state and the due date clearly.

General procedure and important points of TPS *Kaizen* activity are shown here in this chapter. In addition, there are practical activity items shown in detail for these procedures. And it is necessary to make various documents that are recognized by members.

It is difficult to make the necessary methods and priorities for implementation, because these ways will differ according to the situation, such as scale of the workplace and the problem items. We can't put up with an improper method forced by people who insist a particular way as if their method is the only way. We are happy with excellent leaders who can foresee what will happen in the future, but sometimes we can't find such leaders. G.M. Takeuchi decides he will continue to study hard and experience a lot.

 -INDIVIDUAL TPS INSTRUCTOR EXPLAINS THE DIFFERENT SCHEDULE OR METHODS FOR IMPROVING THE LEVEL OF TPS

Takeuchi asked *Sensei*,

"The other day, I talked with a company employee whose company had been consulting with a consulting association. He asked me why TPS consultants say different ways depend on each person. However I couldn't answer his question. What do you suggest I say to him?"

Sensei gave his opinion on this question.

"This type of question is heard a lot. In the case of this association, almost all the consultants had worked in production workplaces in their ex-company, so their *Kaizen* skill was very high. I think it was a hard experience for members, and also I guess they thought their instructions were not always the same, but it depended on each consultant.

I think the ideal state and the target state must be the same among consultants. However, their immediate target, practical items and schedules are different among consultants, so members may easily misunderstand when they say various things."

"You said, 'immediate target, practical items and schedule.' What does it mean?"

"I'd like to explain with 'a procedure for the TPS *Kaizen* activity' written a short while ago. In Procedure 4, the gaps between the current state of the workplace and the target state are resolved using individual countermeasures. Then scheduling points or periods differ depending on the consultants, because it depends on whether they think in terms of the long term or the short term. In this case, we should ask the question, 'How much time will we have for what you suggested, one week, several months, or several years?'

The status of each workplace would be sketched out in various ways during the scheduled points or periods divided by consultants. There are some instructions by good instructors, which seem wasteful ways at first, because they are suggested in order to gain very good results later.

I guess the company of the questioner did not share a common target, or I guess the activity had gone on advancing without a good understanding among employees. We should strictly discuss methodology with a common target. Perhaps consultants may not have given enough explanation to members. This is one of the difficult issues which leaders have to reserve."

One day Takeuchi reported to *Sensei*.

"I talked with that person the other day. I explained, 'Trainees may easily misunderstand why consultants say various things, because the necessary action at hand varies according to each consultant, even if the ideal state and the target state are the same.' He replied, 'I got it. I'll try to think in the same way as you.'"

Sensei nodded to Takeuchi with a smile on his face.

"Even if the target state is the same among leaders, the schedule of achievement and methodology for practically improving workplaces varies. We sometimes talk about the target with our peers, and discuss our difference of opinions regarding such targets.

There are many such similar discussions in *Jishuken*.

I have one funny experience related to this, when I once went to an overseas company.

I talked with a Japanese colleague about the situation of the production workplaces there. We heard later that a local staff member who didn't understand Japanese was saying that two people were quarreling. At that time we were only quietly discussing what we should improve and what was established as the target state. I spoke quickly, so the staff member thought it was a quarrel. It's a good memory for me."

Sensei continued to talk to Takeuchi.

"Okay. The recent circumstances of our manufacturing industry is so severe that we can't respond by only the strengthening of production workplaces. Therefore I think it's important that our manufacturing industry continuously strive to only think rationally.

There are various kinds of instructors and guide books of the Toyota Production, so we should select them depending on our needs. A smart leader creates a good way depending on the situation in order to establish the ideal state."

Takeuchi listened quietly and asked,

"How do you explain a smart TPS leader?"

"I have no idea, but I have some leaders who fits my target characteristics.

I'd like to talk what I have thought about generally so far.

If we know a high TPS level workplace, we should easily expand this way as a model into new workplaces, which is called 'Yokoten' in Japanese.

A Good instructor who has a lot of experience in TPS is also desirable to teach the TPS concept and method. We can appreciate his leadership when we fix the ideal state and when we can't find a practical way of implementing TPS.

However, TPS experts in *Jishuken* are continuing to produce new methods and systems, targeting a higher TPS level, and depending on the fundamental TPS concept. Therefore, we should get instructors that can suggest not only past methods but also new creative ways.

But then there are some instructors who forcefully bring guidance from only their own experiences.

They probably only have narrow experiences in a small section of a factory, and sometimes instruct with surface knowledge which they saw and heard in the factory. Even more, there are some people who don't know how to establish the ideal state, even though they know some aspects of it. Sometimes they are not trained in a method to solve problems.

Some instructors know the TPS level D, because they had worked at a company which was ranked as this TPS level. But even if a trainee company is still ranked as a TPS level A, D level instructors can explain only the ideal state higher than the TPS level D. It takes a long time to raise the workplaces from the TPS level A to D. They don't know how to increase the TPS level and sometimes don't have experiences of training with TPS. Such instructors cannot give good guidance to level A companies and this would have a regrettable results for the trainee company.

Here I will dare to characterize various types of *Kaizen* leaders. This list doesn't communicate whether such leaders are good or bad:

1. Wild-type.... Pressure-type. A person who speaks aggressively. One of these types of leaders was fired after he kicked empty box with his foot, as he regarded it as wasteful. Another consultant spat on the floor because it was so dirty and forced the staff to clean the floor. They became legends.

2. *Genba*-oriented-type.... A person who shows his skills in a small area of workplace improvement. He sometimes tends to improve in a partial area (sub-optimization) and tends to lack a management viewpoint. And he also can't give the reason why we do something, or the way we should do something. Occasionally he changes to a wild-type instructor. We come across this type of person among old consultants.

3. Plan-oriented-type.... Planner-type, who depends on production control. He is strong in systems, but he tends to stand away from real workplaces. His methods are rooted in theory rather than real situation, because he doesn't know *Genba* well.

4. Too-high-level-type, or All-talk-type.... This type is fine for the top of a company such as an executive. This type of consultant includes a person who gets superficial knowledge from his poor experience. Such a person has previous experience in the higher level features. Even though he knows some aspects of them, he doesn't know how to get to the target state, and he has not been trained in the methods to solve problems.

These types of leaders above are mainly concerned with operational system consultancy. I think it is desirable that the Toyota Production System should be instructed by a strategic consultant, but there only are a few people who can both lead trainees and teach with the strategic ideologies.

Mr. Takeuchi, we'd like to aim to become good leaders, after we have learnt from these examples and have grown by considering both Plan and *Genba*."

⬚ -*KAIZEN* ACTIVITY PROCEDURE: SKETCHING OUT THE IDEAL STATE

Takeuchi asks,

"*Sensei*, I have heard doubts about the procedure itself of sketching the ideal state. Do you have any suggestions?"

Sensei gives him a nod.

"Think of the 'ultimate goal' deeply, when we sketch the ideal state. Confirm the gaps between the current state and the target state in the long-term vision. Think how we should improve metrics of workplaces. Confirm the past number, the current number, and the future number. What is the ideal target value in the future, compared to the current state? For example, if we assume some current variable number changes to ten times, or to half, or to zero, then the metrics number could also be changed. Think about the best way and whether their conditions are clear or not.

Thus it's important to sketch the direction clearly with the ideal state. Then we can advance the activity, as well as confirm our ability and the true status of workplaces.

For example, let's say that it's better for workplaces to introduce tools such as *Kanban* in order to aim towards the ideal state. But, even so, I don't think the activity goes well unless we confirm the current state well and share our direction with members. Even more, if we only consider *Kanban* in itself the purpose, we will move away from the ideal state. I mean we should know what the goal is."

Takeuchi asks *Sensei*,

"We have sometimes experienced that the TPS activity didn't go well even in a company which was instructed by a professional TPS expert in order to introduce the Toyota Production System."

Sensei answers,

"In short there are 2 reasons why the TPS activity doesn't go well even though the companies have a lot of ability and motivation in the implementation of TPS activity. One, members are not instructed in the right way. It is a very serious matter for members who have been working hard. Two, members don't understand correctly. In such a situation, companies consequently depend just on methodology and have a poor implementation.

There are many instances of people critical of TPS who used poor examples of TPS implementation to conclude that TPS wasn't suited to their workplaces. I think in each of these opinions there are a mix of correct and incorrect elements. However they were only focusing on one aspect of TPS. These situations were certainly difficult, but we can't say that TPS wouldn't work in these situations. It's a shame that they misunderstood TPS and then concluded not to implement it. I feel they were only criticizing TPS without looking at the positive examples of TPS implementation that had been achieved so far."

"It's also being said a lot that a surface-level imitation of '*Kanban*' doesn't work, right?" asks Takeuchi. *Sensei* said,

"Masamitsu Ishii wrote an excellent book in Japanese, 'Nyumon Toyota Seisan Hoshiki,' which explained the principle and the thinking of the Toyota Production System. In this book, he taught us that a surface-level imitation of '*Kanban*' doesn't work.

And, I won't recognize an improper way of leading, for example, the way leaders say that inventory is too much, kicking boxes, as if inventory is the golden rule. We should clearly understand that we have to have the necessary stock, depending on our ability. This is the fundamental TPS ideology.

Then, we should create the *Heijyunka* system of workplaces in the whole plant. Even in workplaces which have many times a fluctuation of daily demand or seasonal demand, there are good examples of workplaces which respond to fluctuations. We should consider the whole system which includes both *Kaizen* in *Genba* and planning, setting the man-power and the stock as the buffer. I'll explain that, when I have a chance."

"In a real situation, the reason why the Toyota production System doesn't work is because of a big demand fluctuation," said Takeuchi.

Sensei lectures,

"I think you have a good point. In particular, the home appliance industry changes the consumer products according to the season. It doesn't go well if we can't manage product changes immediately. We see the product assembly is well managed to cope with these changes. But regrettably, I guess that the system for warehouses or logistics hasn't gone well. We see even big companies haven't achieved the 5s. They struggle with getting enough parts, and with countermeasures against defects of supplier parts, before the production process ends. I also guess they repeatedly experience the same situation. Our big challenge is to establish the logistics system, which can be adapted in the short time when products change according to the season."

"Additionally, the common reasons why it is difficult for *Kaizen* activity to take root are," *Sensei* continues to lecture,

"Firstly, resources issues, such as human resources.

Secondly, motivation. For example, think of activity done with saying 'I'm on it.' These cases appear in magazines. People perform activities without any purpose and sometimes implement the activity without a due date. Then, I think, this activity won't last long. I think it is important to try to sketch the ideal state afresh in milestones, to a greater or less extent."

 -*KAIZEN* ACTIVITY PROCEDURE: *KAIZEN* OR *KAIKAKU* (INNOVATION)?

"The procedure for the TPS *Kaizen* activity explained a short while ago is akin to the problem-solving approach in QC (quality control)," remarks Takeuchi.

Sensei says,

"That's right. Total Quality Control or Total Quality Management, called TQC/TQM, is a concept based on producing quality and should be looked at based on the whole company-wide activity. The company-wide activity is basically the same as the Toyota Production System, but, I think, the commitment in TPS to sketch the ideal state is much stronger than TQC."

Takeuchi says,

"We have heard a lot about the word 'TPS *Kaizen*' until now. Here I feel like raising a query about the word '*Kaizen*.' I suppose 'innovative' action is necessary for TPS, if we are going to sketch the ideal state."

Sensei explains,

"Overseas people tend to expect that there is an epoch-making outcome in TPS. They expect some 'Production Innovation' of TPS, where the word 'innovation' is grasped as drastic change.

When we try to take measures against defects with the QC method, the biggest problem in the Pareto chart is selected to be solved first because this gives a big result.

However, in the daily *Kaizen* activity with TPS, we don't always select the biggest problem. Sometimes, the biggest one is hard to solve, and doesn't give an immediate result. Therefore, we plug away at problems every day, which are easy to solve. After some small problems are solved step by step and their results are piled up, the complex problem is gradually solved. The most difficult and biggest problem can be solved in this way.

Gradually making progress results in a great change before we notice it. Some people say, 'a small change is better than a big change.'

And someone else also recommends similar ideology: we should not think about the best way but implement the better way. This is rephrased as 'It is very effective to solve problems while running, and it gives a better result.'

So, we don't give up, and we solve easy problems first, then gradually wrestle with difficult problems. This is the royal road to establish the ideal state, which seems an innovative way.

Even if solutions are hard to find immediately, it is important for us to follow a good example like *Jishuken* where people are aiming at the highest level."

Part XII

Advancing toward the High-Level Features of TPS

44

Learning the High-Level Features of TPS, Implementing Kaizen of Production in Jishuken Inside the Company

The East Automotive Co. is a B group company in the Toyota Production System autonomous study meeting, which is so-called *Jishuken* in Japanese. B group companies are organized into eight components-manufacturers, who are in the TPS level grade C or D.

G.M. Takeuchi participated in *Jishuken* as a member at first, and he is registering as a deputy *Jishuken* leader of the company now.

The workplaces for the *Jishuken* activity in each company are all in the TPS level grade D. At this level, we can't immediately find out the bad points of workplaces. Each individual topic is established at the workplaces for the *Jishuken* activity in each company.

For example, the outline of a *Jishuken* topic, which is registered by the East Automotive Co. at the beginning of this year, is as follows:

- **Topic title: To make the JIT production system in Maia-FEN production line**
- **Purpose of topic** (middle and long-term problem):
  1. Building the model line is urgent, needed to establish the ideal state of the Manufacturing of our components.
     - The JIT level of assembly lines was raised, after the main activity focused on the assembly. But the manufacturing of components is still low.
     - Progressing to shorten the lead time by means of observing the whole process, from the manufacturing of components to customers. And promoting autonomation (*Jidoka*).

DOI: 10.4324/9781003323310-60

- Progressing to make a system where necessary components can be produced as much as necessary in a timely manner.

2. Working on making a system which is modeled on our company's core FEN product.

- **The target process outline:** Skip
- **Problem of the current status:**
  1. When die-casting components, the production lot size is big and the production lead time is long.
  2. The Operational Availability of the equipment is low.
  3. Frequent conveyance of components isn't established.

  Aim of activity and main work items:
  1. FEN components
     - Raising the production ability of components by means of information used in the next assembly process.
     - Establishing the low-cost production method
     - Improving the Rate of Operation by means of canceling the constraint of the equipment condition and doing "*yosedome* (Refer to Chapter 14)."
     - Lead time reduction by the means of "'Straightening' or 'Laminar Flow' methods using the Goods & Information concept."
  2. Die-casting components
     - Improving productivity by MT (machine time) reduction.
     - Frequent production instruction by means of shortening the set-up time.
     - Developing the small lot size of production instruction, and reducing the lead time.
     - Reviewing the system of the production instruction (establishing the lot forming, visual management).
  3. In-plant logistics
     - Lead time reduction with the frequent conveyance of components or materials from the supplier.
  4. Developing TPS instructors who can improve things in person and instruct trainees.

- **The numerical target of the activity:**
  1. Cost rate: Reducing more than 3%.
  2. Productivity: Yield (pieces/person/hour), improved by 20%

3. Inventory reduction: Within the 120% of theory stock
4. Defects reduction rate: Reduced by more than 50%.

Here the numerical target of the activity in the above outline seems to be low. But this is quite a strict target value for the *Jishuken* members, because members inside the company have already narrowed the issues before the registration.

Even if the target of the cost rate in the component plant is more than the 30%, the target of cost rate reduction which corresponds to the final product becomes 3%. So, while doing our activity, we think that our concerted effort contributes to only 3% reduction. But even 3% is a big enough number, if we think about it.

In this way, eight B group companies register their *Jishuken* topics. A Project General Manager in the leading car manufacturers, who is in charge of B group *Jishuken*, evaluates these topics together with the *Jishuken* leaders in the member company. Sometimes they don't accept the topic, and the company can't start *Jishuken* activity.

In the objective *Jishuken* workplaces, all of the *Jishuken* leaders in eight companies play a key role in studying the topic and implementing the *Kaizen*. They decide their responsibility by themselves. For example, a *Jishuken* leader in A company works for B topic of B company.

G.M. Takeuchi is registering as a deputy *Jishuken* leader of the East Automotive Co. Eight B group companies hold each *Jishuken* for three months. There are eight topics a year, and all the *Jishuken* leaders and the deputy *Jishuken* leaders of each company have their duty to participate in the main scheduled meeting of each *Jishuken*. Additionally, *Jishuken* assigns them practical *Kaizen* work in several companies. So, they have to go out of our company 2–3 days a week. Honestly speaking, he feels reluctance to stay 2–3 days in the outside company in order to practice the *Jishuken* activity.

Each *Jishuken* member in a company is organized mutually with the *Jishuken* members in all the member companies. Other company's members help the *Kaizen* in the objective of the company, and contribute to increase the level of the workplaces. This task is the duty of the member company, so someone has to fill the role of the *Jishuken* member. But, members who work outside the company are evaluated low by managers in their own company, which is inconsistent with how hard they worked.

Sometimes they are strongly asked to promote TPS activity inside the company by their executive, but they have no time to think about the inside since they are busy as the *Jishuken* leader and the deputy *Jishuken* leader. Meanwhile, they have to gain sufficient experience in order to be able to have the ability to find out the problem of workplaces. Short and insufficient experience leads to an unskilled *Kaizen* practitioner or leader.

When being in a position of leadership, he has to prioritize what produces a good result as a team, thinking with "overall optimization" thinking. Therefore, he can't focus so much on the technical areas even though he is an engineer. But he can achieve a sense of satisfaction, when they have gained a good result which can be found visibly by a big change between the before and the after. In particular, he is happy when good fruit is produced after he has tried to develop a new system which they are inexperienced in using.

G.M. Takeuchi has been visiting *Jishuken* in the West Automotive Co. one day a week from last month.

The person in charge of *Jishuken* in the West Automotive Co. was chosen at the start of the *Jishuken* meeting. The topic leader is Mr. Kosuke Kamiyama of Shizuoka-Auto. He has been a *Jishuken* peer since they were a member of *Jishuken*. He is called Kami-san among the peers.

The *Jishuken* of the West Automotive Co., whose topic leader is Kami-san, is starting three teams; assembly team, components team, and logistics team.

G.M. Takeuchi was assigned a leader of the assembly team. Meanwhile, there are matched leaders of the West Automotive Co., who cooperate with leaders from the outside to implement *Kaizen* for the topic. Both leaders sometimes assemble in scheduled meetings where they check the *Kaizen* status and confirm the direction of *Kaizen*.

The topic of the West Automotive Co. covers the whole production process, which is activity from the receiving components through to the production to the shipment. So leaders communicate with each other in the leader's meeting. G.M. Takeuchi leads the assembly team, and collaborates with both the components team and the logistics team.

The *Jishuken Kaizen* teams of the West Automotive Co. investigate the current state of the workplaces, and then sketch out the **Goods and Information Flow Chart (Current State)** in detail. This is the current state chart, in which many problems are written in the speech bubbles. For example, these are written as "Too big lot size of the production instruction," "Infrequent conveyance," and so forth.

They also proposed the **Goods and Information Flow Chart (Target State)**, together with the current state. This is a chart which sketches the target state of the workplaces that should be established by the end of this year.

The *Jishuken* members outside the company examine these charts when they start the activity of *Jishuken*. They will surely have a heated discussion on the subject covered there. Such subjects as, "Setting the target state of workplaces is too easy," "Firstly, sketch the ideal state of the Goods and Information Flow Chart," "Sketch the status of this plant that can be considered in the future," and so forth.

They mean they cannot know the target state if they cannot sketch the **Goods and Information Flow Chart (Ideal State)**. When they can sketch these, what they should implement becomes clear, and wasteful activity becomes less. The possibility of failure is eliminated.

As mentioned before, there are some member companies whose topics are not accepted and who cannot start *Jishuken*. Sometimes companies are not permitted to hold the closing meeting on the scheduled day, when the *Jishuken* activity doesn't achieve certain results. The *Jishuken* meeting is not just for show. The closing meeting is not a ceremonial occasion but a significant event of the company, where an executive in charge of the whole TPS activity attends and sometimes the CEO attends.

The numerical targets are set in the activity schedule. There are many things to do and many numerical targets to be established, but difficult problems are piled up. The *Jishuken* members need to think about and unravel these problems.

The purpose of sketching out the "Goods and Information Flow Chart" is to define the current or future workplace's state. This chart shows the goods flow such as products and components, and also shows the information flow which causes the product movement. First of all, it's important to grasp the movement of both goods and information. Therefore, in Japanese, we have to write the right word of "*Mono* (goods)" in *Kanji* for "goods," because goods are real. We should think that Information of *Kanban* is equivalent to money. Goods are also money products. Then we can reduce money by means of grasping the "Goods and Information Flow Chart."

By the way, in our group companies, there are many people who can sketch the "Goods and Information Flow Chart." In Japan, there is a book translated from an English book which I am not quite sure about. People call it "Value Stream Mapping" in English. More than ten years have already passed since publishing, and people in production want a more detailed explanation of the ideology of the "Goods and Information Flow Chart" instead of the "Value Stream Mapping." There is a lot of misunderstanding as a result of the spread of information of the so-called "Goods and Information Flow Chart" through the "Value Stream Mapping."

The name "Value Stream Mapping" in English is already spreading and an annoying matter. In Japanese translated books or other articles, they have also written the incorrect Japanese word "*Mono* (goods)" in *Katakana* for "goods." They have confused the word with the word "*Mono* (goods)" in *Kanji*, which is written for real goods. The word "*Mono* (goods)" in *Katakana* is an abstract word which indicates real goods resources in management and has a meaning of added value.

If we think that money or value exists in various places, the name "Value Mapping" is ok. But we shouldn't call it "Value Stream Mapping," because the "Value" or the "added value" never flows and just the "goods and information" flows. We should think of the concept as "goods and information flow."

We are sorry that the procedure of making the "Goods and Information Flow Chart" is not shown formally outside the group. The TPS people hate to make a universal rule for methodology and tools, because they have respect for change. So this chart has not been systematically exhibited to the outside.

G.M. Takeuchi was presented with a "Goods and Information Flow Chart" by a local person in a plant tour of a South Asian company. He regretted what they showed, because he found these documents had been made under the guidance of an uneducated trainer. He'd hoped that "Goods and Information Flow Chart" become a little more popular. He was thinking to propose the systematical chart which included the IE (Industrial Engineering) method, if he had a chance.

It isn't difficult to sketch the "Goods and Information Flow Chart" for the production workplaces, but practice in writing it is a little bit necessary. In particular, we need the ability to evaluate the production site. And it's desirable that we are trained by a good trainer.

G.M. Takeuchi joins the Assembly team as a team leader of the *Jishuken* members from the outside companies.

The "Goods and Information Flow Chart" for the production workplaces is already sketched out. And all *Jishuken* members understand the directionality of what they should establish based on the chart. They discuss a concrete way of implementation along the agreed direction.

The dual Assembly Team leaders are both G.M. Takeuchi outside the company and a manager in charge of the assembly production section inside the West Automotive Component.

The meeting is held once a week. G.M. Takeuchi comes early in the morning and goes to the assembly production line before starting the meeting. He checks with his own eyes in order to confirm their progress.

All members assemble and the meeting starts with the activity reports first. They overview the status and make decisions on what they have to do today. Then individual small task team members go to the actual workplaces after the meeting. All team leaders sometimes gather and attend a leader's meeting, where they communicate with each other and discuss the right way.

The Assembly Team investigates the production system of four lines which have been chosen as the model lines from many production lines.

The goal is basically to establish the ideal state, that is to say "After one piece has been drawn by the following process, we produce one piece." This is a right way for pursuing productivity.

They actually dispatch a production instruction every 10 minutes. They need to make the assembly lines better in order to change the instruction from every 30 minutes to every 10 minutes. Dispatching a production instruction every 10 minutes is difficult if the assembly lines don't have the capability. Therefore they solve problems which are found in the production lines one after another. This is the most important purpose of the topics.

They steadily implement the *Kaizen* activity, such as reducing the necessary man-power, reducing the set-up time, and reducing the cycle time in the bottleneck process. And they carefully check the management index such as the Operational Availability and so forth.

G.M. Takeuchi was taught "An excuse has to be replaced with a good reason," in which Japanese pronunciation of both excuse and good reason is the same in a pun.

When we try to carry out something, we often tend to think it's difficult to complete it. It surely may be difficult, but still we shouldn't excuse ourselves. If everyone sees an excuse as motivation to change the workplace and complete *Kaizen*, then we will continue to improve our workplace as our seniors experienced

This topic results in a good outcome under the appropriate guidance of the topic leader, Mr. Kamiyama.

A closing meeting is held on schedule, though the remaining items should be solved by the end of this year. For G.M. Takeuchi this was a precious experience where he pulled together the team members and led them as a team leader. Then they could advance to the goal without fail.

Here let's briefly review what G.M. Takeuchi experienced in the *Kaizen* of assembly lines, though the contents must be more carefully explained in the Toyota Production System.

Firstly, it's **after one piece has been drawn by the following process, we produce one piece.**

In this production line, the products are assembled and packed according to tote box units, so it's actually difficult to produce to the unit of piece. But then, in the case of car body assembly, the various types of cars are produced one after another in the mixed flow production.

In ordinary manufacturing companies, it is usual to produce the same models in a big-sized lot together. It's because they think that producing in a big-sized lot production is more efficient than producing with the frequent set-up change. Reducing the set-up time may be tough. But if the set-up is improved and the set-up time becomes zero, we can produce products sequentially "box by box."

This production way can easily absorb the man-power difference among products, so work moves in a steady rhythmic motion much better than big-sized lot production. A group leader in the *Genba* is amazed at achieving this improvement, and operators are pleased to experience the better operation. This is a typical *Heijyunka*, where the mixed flow production is established in the small-sized lot production and the process flow becomes good.

Secondarily, TPS teaches us, "Total set-up time should be set within 10% of the operational time" by rule of thumb.

In the Toyota Production System, we should change the product models frequently in workplaces in order to establish "the production of many models in small quantities." We can produce many models with the frequent set-up change every instruction period. Then the total set-up time may increase. So we need to decrease the individual set-up time and eliminate the frequent machine stops. After these improvements, we can easily produce products sequentially "box by box."

Thirdly, it's important to utilize human resources produced which are produced by *Kaizen* with the "Flexible Manpower Line and Man Power Saving."

We shouldn't lay off human resources produced by *Kaizen*, because employees will be reluctant to implement *Kaizen* after the layoff. And we should allocate such produced human resources to new businesses or businesses which don't have sufficient human capacity. We should avoid hiring too easily for new businesses.

We sometimes encounter workplaces where the slow work pace is permitted when demand is small. The Toyota Production System teaches us that it is important for us to implement the *Kaizen* activity especially when human resources become redundant in a recession.

 ## -THE INVENTORY IS THE OUTCOME; ONCE-IN-A-LIFETIME INVENTORY REDUCTION

"Takeuchi, you must have experienced a lot in TPS. Here I'd like to explain about ideology of inventory. Inventory or stock in TPS is a very popular topic in TPS.

First of all, Inventory is just the outcome that is produced by our activity.

Our system of workplaces results in the inventory. And it is important for us not to make the level of inventory a target, but only to seek the process of improvement to make a strong workplace.

I'd like to show a brief column in the Japanese book, 'Seru Seisan (Cell Production),' Noboru Takeuchi, JMA Management Center, 2006, P.158, as follows."

Once-In-A-Lifetime Inventory Reduction

Whenever we talk about "inventory control," we bring up the subject of "What level of maximum inventory and minimum inventory should we manage?" It is ok when the maximum and minimum inventory is properly controlled. But there are some stories with pitfalls connected to interesting management we should understand.

I have had guidance for inventory from my leader when I was an apprentice in TPS.

He said to me, "People try to reduce the inventory of workplaces before an auditor comes, and to report the wellbeing of workplaces. I think such temporary action is insignificant." Even if they can reduce the inventory, the cost reduction of the inventory happens at only one time. So my leader called the activity "Once-in-a-lifetime Inventory Reduction."

The true purpose of reducing inventory is to strengthen workplaces. People try to operate workplaces with small inventory. Then they can find and solve the problems so that they can make the workplace stronger. We also say "Inventory is the only result." We can evaluate the ability of workplaces after checking the level of inventory. So we say "big inventory" or "small inventory." The level of inventory we see is the outcome of the ability of workplaces.

Therefore when production lines don't have enough production ability and simply reduce the stock, we are going to end up with a problem. For example, in the case of a shortage of materials in the following process which didn't receive the necessary volume, there was a fake report. The report said there was no problem with the inventory management because the control was within the fixed control level.

We have to have the necessary inventory. Then we aim to establish production lines, in which we can produce with the minimum stock or with zero stock ultimately. The purpose is to reduce the lead time of production in the whole process. Workplaces should be able to cope with customer needs.

I guess that my leader wanted to say in the previous guidance, "There is no use treating only inventory. What is the true capability of your production? Does the *Kaizen* activity go well?" It's important that we not aim at the effect of "Once-in-a-lifetime Inventory Reduction," but aim for the effect of activity itself and the utilization of cash flow.

We shouldn't stick to the superficial phenomenon of "Big or small inventory." True inventory control is to aim at the ideal state so that we can produce good and cheap products as fast as possible.

-IF HAVING INVENTORY IS THE WORST TPS SITUATION, SHOULD THE TARGET BE TO BE INVENTORY-LESS?

Takeuchi asks, "*Sensei*, TPS consultants sometimes lead with saying that inventory is the worst wrong in the Toyota Production System. Here is much criticism, 'Is this guidance correct?' Do you have any thought?"

"I guess there are many misunderstandings about inventory reduction.

Difficulty will sometimes come out when leaders command members to reduce the inventory without considering the current situation. It may sometimes happen by leaders who don't have an ability to grasp the whole workplace situation.

On the other hand, when the inventory clearly results in the badness of workplaces, and if people never try to improve workplaces, it is very troublesome. In these cases, we can't blame leaders, even when leaders violently force members to implement the *Kaizen* of workplaces in order to reduce inventory. The reason for this is that apprentices will experience the goodness of workplaces afterwards. Then they appreciate the instructors' guidance. There were many such stories like this in those days."

"Then, is it possible for us to progress in *Kaizen* by means of reducing inventory?" Takeuchi asks.

"The Toyota Production System teaches us that excess inventory or overproduction, which generates secondary waste, is the greatest waste of all. Inventory causes a vicious circle of waste.

In order to explain this easily, please refer to Figure 37.1, which is a picture in which inventory corresponds to the surface of a pond.

Stones of problems are in a pond, such as Defects, Machine Breakdown, Delivery Delay, and Work Trouble. The water hides the stones during the high-water level, but the stones come out when the water level becomes low. When the inventory level which corresponds to water is low, or Inventory is small, problems occur, such as Defects, Machine Breakdown, and so forth.

We can clarify problems when the inventory is small. But we hide these problems with high levels of inventory, even though these problems could be settled normally.

The Toyota Production System also teaches us the ideology: problems come out when we reduce the inventory."

"Well, *Sensei*, you may be right; however, we can not cope with the customer demands when their orders fluctuate greatly and if we don't have enough inventory, right?"

"You are correct. In the case of a huge fluctuation or a problem which we can't solve immediately by ourselves, it becomes serious when we don't have proper inventory. We have to settle these problems with customers, but we shouldn't reduce inventory first. We have to have the proper inventory according to the situation.

The Toyota Production System doesn't introduce either its tools or the inventory reduction superficially into workplaces.

It is important for us to identify the problem of workplaces thoroughly when reducing the level of inventory. Then we aim at an ideal workplace by means of settling the problems one by one. The inventory reduction activity isn't only for the cash flow of inventory cost.

When we lower the level of inventory, our behavior, where we clarify problems and settle them, is necessary to make the production workplace strong. And," *Sensei* continues.

"Our situation in workplaces sometimes results in deciding the level of inventory.

That is to say, 'Inventory is just the outcome that is produced by our activity.'

We can't see the inventory when 2S, *Seiri-Seiton*, is not good. The bad 2S is not even worthy of consideration. However, several factors can be thought to decide the level of inventory.

For example it is the difference in timing between production and conveyance. When the interval of conveyance is too long, inventory beside the production line becomes big.

And, there is a factor of the productive maintenance PM related to the safety stock. When the productive maintenance ability is not sufficient enough to deal with machine trouble, we have to have extra inventory. In the case of two-shift production workplaces and only day-shift PM sections, extra inventory is necessary because of the machine trouble at night. This is a problem of having much inventories. We should take measures to not only deal with this issue but also other problems. Then we can establish strong production workplaces.

The structure of inventory is simplified as a relationship;

$$\text{Inventory} = (\text{management}) \times (\text{production lot}) \times (\text{conveyance lot})$$

It's necessary to investigate these three elements.
Inventory is just the outcome that is produced by our activity.
So this results in small inventory and zero inventory.
The Toyota Production System teaches us to focus on the ideology;
If it is necessary we have the 'proper' inventory, and then we strengthen the production workplaces which are the center of the Manufacturing."

Takeuchi says, "Every time a big disaster strikes, some mass media reports that the Toyota Production System is weak and not a good method because the production lines stopped."

"It is said that the production lines at Toyota immediately stopped when the Niigataken Chuetsu-oki Earthquake happened. But the competing manufacturers continued to produce for a while without stopping the lines, because they had enough materials from suppliers. We can say that they worked daily with so much waste. We understood the supply chain itself was one big problem when the great earthquake hit. I experienced restoring a plant which had stopped because of a big flood. Our group companies have experienced a lot of situations of stopping plants because of unexpected disasters. But we still have an unwavering belief in the ideology; we have the proper and the smallest inventory, and continue to strengthen the production workplaces which are the center of Manufacturing."

45

Learning the High-Level Features of TPS, Implementing Kaizen of Logistics in Jishuken Outside the Company

The *Jishuken* in the West Automotive Co. got through the process without any problems.

The next *Jishuken* is held in Shizuoka-Auto where Mr. Kamiyama, or Kami-san, works as a General Manager of OMCD. Kami-san is also a chief leader of *Jishuken* inside the company.

G.M. Takeuchi takes part as the leader of the logistics team. He investigates the topic of logistics and implements the *Kaizen* in Shizuoka-Auto while sometimes discussing with Kami-san who is very reliable. The topic of logistics is focused on the whole in-plant process from the entrance to the exit. We should improve the whole system. Then we can get good fruit and the achieved system will be set.

G.M. Takeuchi became one of the operators instead of being an absent operator, although he was a sectional manager as administrator in the former production workplace. Then he experienced managing the instruction *Kanban*. Managing the instruction *Kanban* was one part of the *Kanban* system and a function of logistics. Logistics is still difficult for G.M. Takeuchi who is an engineer though still not a fully developed one.

Here explains the thinking and the practical knowledge of logistics.

We wonder what Just-In-Time Manufacturing is like.

When G.M. Takeuchi had begun to study the Toyota Production System, he thought it was just a production workplace which produced goods by assembly, based on the *Kanban* information. This is exactly true in that TPS is based on the Pull-system, but he had begun to think that

DOI: 10.4324/9781003323310-61

Just-In-Time Manufacturing was based on logistics. Logistics is in the center of JIT Manufacturing.

As it was previously explained, logistics is generally divided into Procurement logistics, In-factory logistics and Delivery logistics. Of course, we should think that production workplaces are at the center of Manufacturing, and production is controlled with instructions of the Production Control Division that is in charge of these three logistics.

In the case of automobile manufacturing, it is said that the total length of production lines come to several kilometers if we combine the whole process from components manufactures to finished car manufacturers. Aside from whether this number is valid or not, we should be able to produce automobiles basically in a single combined line.

In the old days, an automobile body was assembled with automobile components around the body. This is like producing a ship at a boat dock. This style of production was transformed into the conveyor line by birth of the Ford system at the beginning of the twentieth century. The conveyor line achieved the mass production which assembled automobiles efficiently and inexpensively.

Even now, production at one place, which regularly and continuously flows on the conveyor line, is desirable. But, nowadays it is difficult to build all processes into one place, because there are many conditions such as the growth of the independent automobile component manufacturers, and employment. Therefore instead of a conveyor, there is conveyance, which is made by trucks and ships outside the plant, and by carts inside the plant.

In the TPS activity, we say, "Like a string stretched tight" for describing the synchronization in process. This saying imagines a situation where there isn't inventory-in-process and goods are regularly flowing one by one.

It's the features of processes without wasteful stock, worker's waste, defects, and machine stops. In the same way, the conveyance, which means the logistics here, should perform the similar important functions of a conveyor, which flows regularly. In other words, it is as if the line at the automobile component manufacturer connects to the line at the automobile manufacturer.

Most *Jishuken* member companies manage the Manufacturing, using special processes and facilities. So, those companies have a specialty and keep ahead in their industry. And, they sometimes create special logistical methods in their logistics. The basis is the same, but particular tactics are necessary. This is the role of *Jishuken* members.

Thus there are so many items which should be explained about the logistics in the Toyota Production System. Here, several topics in the factory have been simply explained.

When we do the Standing Observation in the logistics *Kaizen*, how do we see "flow of goods?"

The Japanese original word for logistics can be directly translated into "goods flow," and this could be "physical distribution" or "the supply and distribution line." But in TPS, we use "logistics" in the generic meaning.

A leader taught us, "We shouldn't focus on the flow of goods. The goods themselves can't communicate anything to us, so we need to look at human movement." It is good if we can see the flow of goods. In other words, the goods don't move by themselves. Movement of the goods are done in some way by operators unless the machinery is fully automated. So we observe the movement of operators carefully. This is the same as operators of assembly process and parts processes. Thus in the case of *Kaizen* of the parts supply work and the products withdrawal work, a practitioner follows an operator. Then he finds out both the difficulty and the waste of work, and improves it. The work improved is standardized as a standardized work.

Does logistics mean only conveyance of things so as to flow regularly?

The communication method for information like electronic *Kanban* (e-*Kanban*) has recently been changed because of the development of IT, so below is an explanation of the basis.

In the Toyota Production System, the Pull System is principle.

Kanban as the information tool is brought from the following process to the former process. And *Kanban* is attached to the corresponding goods in the former process. Then the goods are conveyed to the following process with *Kanban*.

So, the work of logistics workers is to manage a series of logistics cycles, in which they bring *Kanban* from the following process to the former process, attaching *Kanban* to goods, and conveying the goods to the following process. Thus, one of the important works of logistics workers is to instruct the production to the workplaces by means of managing the *Kanban*. This is an important work of information communication by *Kanban*.

The "Electronic *Kanban*" was not common in those days. Truck drivers brought back the paper-based "Returnable *Kanban*" from the customer, and then the production workplaces were able to know the details of *Kanban*. Though the difference among trucks is small because it was

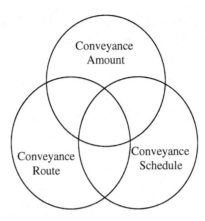

FIGURE 45.1

Three elements of conveyance. (Translated from Takeuchi, Noboru, *Seru Seisan*, JMA Management Center, 2006, P.150.)

levelized by *Heijyunka*, sometimes we were surprised at receiving the demand of very rare products.

The thinking of **Three elements of conveyance** was proposed in the Japanese book, "*Seru Seisan* (Cell Production)," Takeuchi, Noboru, JMA Management Center, 2006, P.150 (Figure 45.1).

1. Conveyance Amount: Man-power based on the amount and the numbers of things.
2. Conveyance Route: Way of conveyance, direction, and so forth.
3. Conveyance Schedule (Time): Diagram, timetable, and so forth.

The three elements are correlated with each other. For example, when "1. Amount" is decided, "3. Management time" of things is decided. When "2. Route" is decided, "3. Time" for movement is decided. When "3. Interval" of picking becomes longer, "1. Amount" of treatment becomes larger. Thus, we can standardize the conveyance work with the three elements.

Also in *Jishuken* activity, standardized work is established as a cycle of "every 10 or every 30 minutes" **frequent conveyance** work.

We also make standards with the thinking of the three elements in truck conveyance.

We shouldn't convey only the loaded boxes and only the empty boxes separately by big lot sizes.

There is a **loaded-empty container exchange system** of conveyance which is called "Mi-Kara" in Japanese; an actual cargo box is called "Mi" and an empty box is called "Kara."

One cargo box is exchanged for one empty box as a rule of conveyance. Several rules are needed for it. It is easy to establish the loaded-empty container exchange system by means of using the frequent conveyance which conveys a little bit at a time without carrying many boxes together.

The loaded-empty container exchange system is a very important topic in *Jishuken*. This is because there are many companies which can't establish it as well as the frequent conveyance.

Think of the loaded-empty container exchange system in the case of a beer box in a liquor shop. This is an example which changed in business activity from a liquor shop to a convenience Store over time. This convenience Store also does work to deliver alcoholic drinks to restaurants by pickup truck every day. Empty boxes with empty bottles is loaded onto a depot facing the Store. It is like a mountain and overflows to the road. It's a stagnant inventory of empty boxes. We can't know how many days' stocks there are. Truck drivers come and deposit the boxes here. They bring not only plastic boxes but also cardboard boxes. The cardboard boxes are folded after they become empty. So a few plastic boxes should stay if the truck drivers withdraw them.

The obstructive empty box should be put away, if the loaded-empty container exchange system is running thoroughly. But we are not sure who the owner is. Because the inventory of empty boxes doesn't create added value, it may be troublesome for the convenience Store. Or, the shop may want to have them, and so on. In this way, we think deeply about the rules of the loaded-empty container exchange system.

-WHY SHOULD WE PRACTICE THE PRODUCTION OF SMALL LOT SIZES OR THE CONVEYANCE OF SMALL LOT SIZES?

"*Sensei, Jishuken* members often use an expression, 'frequent production and frequent conveyance.'"

"That's right. It means 'frequently produce in a small lot size, and frequently convey in a small lot size'.

Finished products sell one by one at shops, and the process flow connects to our production workplaces. The components which are assembled to make finished products randomly flow in the production workplaces, depending on the variety of finished products. It's an image like a string stretched tight. Then we have an image of various components flowing randomly. This is called '**Production of many models in small quantities.**' Some people incorrectly call it Production of various models in various quantities. But we produce our products depending on the *Heijyunka* Production, so this is an image of the Production of many models in small quantities.

Carrying out one-piece-at-a-time production is necessary, when trying to establish 'frequent production.' Actually, we produce and convey products by the box."

"Is it 1 box per 1 *Kanban*?" Takeuchi asks.

Sensei continues the conversation.

"Yes. One *Kanban* per box or per package is the principle. After dispatching the *Kanban* as a tool of the production instruction, the production workplace produces products depending on the information of the *Kanban*. The number is specified on the *Kanban*. As one *Kanban* is a minimum unit, the production becomes a big lot size production when the number is big. Therefore, one of the big topics in *Jishuken* is sometimes to reduce the quantity of the *Kanban* or box. Moreover, production by gathering several sheets of *Kanban* becomes a big size lot production."

"Even if I recognize the thinking of 'produce one by one, and convey one by one,' I don't know why it is good."

"It is good if we can produce products in selling speed by frequently changing the type of products and producing in small quantities.

Conveyance of carrying many models in small quantities is easier than carrying things in a big lot based on the truck's shipment. Think of the relationship between the conveyance interval and the conveyance amount. Then conveyance in small quantities at a time becomes easy work for us.

In a company of South Asia, several people were conveying a cart very slowly with very large iron component boxes which looked like a mountain. Suddenly the boxes fell down on the aisle in front of us. We were amazed at the large crash. The conveyance method with several people was not good. In this case especially the conveyance distance was very short, but they spent a long time carrying the items. They should have conveyed a small load of boxes by individuals using a cart.

There is a hidden concept about the thinking, 'frequently produce and convey in a small lot size.' The production workplaces must have strong lines if they try to produce each product one by one with the instruction of each *Kanban*. Therefore we should make strong production lines, in which there are no defects and no machine stops after we improve them. This is the true purpose.

A logistics person takes an active role in controlling the production speed, or the Takt (Time), by means of conveying goods with *Kanban*. This thinking may be a bit difficult, but we should make the strong production lines in this way so products flow regularly. In a plant where such a situation is established, we can find they produce products with a small stock beside the lines.

Inventory is just the outcome that is produced by our activity."

-IS IT CORRECT THAT THE FILL-UP SYSTEM OF PRODUCTION IS A FUNDAMENTAL PRINCIPLE IN THE TOYOTA PRODUCTION SYSTEM?

"*Sensei*, I've heard someone said 'The Fill-Up System is a principle in the Toyota Production System'" Takeuchi asks.

"It must be a misunderstanding. The Pull System is a principle. Therefore, there is 'Store' certainly as a finished goods place beside the production lines. Logistics persons withdraw the needed goods here. Then, the production lines produce goods of the amount withdrawn and restock the Store with them. This is the 'Fill-Up System.'" *Sensei* explains and goes on to say,

"I also saw a person who incorrectly said that the Fill-Up System is a principle of the Toyota Production System. It was at a high TPS level company, where they located Stores beside lines and produced products of the amount withdrawn.

In terms of principle, we should say that the Pull System is a principle. The Toyota Production System is the way of production: 'The following production process withdraws the goods it needs, when it needs them, in the exact needed amount, from the former process. The former process produces only the amount withdrawn.' Generally, if we are asked whether it is the Push or the Pull, we say the Toyota Production System is Pull-type production. In the Pull-type production, the amount withdrawn = the amount produced. Meanwhile, there are few production lines which can produce the needed products at the moment of withdrawal efficiently. So, we locate the Store for finished products and implement the 'Fill-Up System,' in order to establish the 'Pull' production system."

"*Sensei*, how do we manage the Toyota Production System when the daily demand and shipment fluctuates sharply?" Takeuchi asks.

"This is a way to manage finished goods which are stocked at the shipping area.

Shipping information becomes the *Heijyunka* information which is instructed to the production workplaces, and then the production workplaces produce products according to the information. A procedure to execute this process is simply explained as follows:

- First, have a certain amount of finished products as the stock of the Store/Shop in a shipping warehouse.
- The Store is managed as a buffer of the finished goods which should cover the demand and shipment fluctuation.
- Assume the Store is your customer. Shipping information of the store becomes the original data to the production workplaces.
- Then, the arranged data which is calculated by the *Heijyunka* method is instructed to the production workplaces.
- This is a typical example of a Fill-Up System in the Store of a shipping area. However, the process overall is the Pull System where the production workplaces produce according to the information of shipping from the Store of finished goods."

46

Implementing the Activities in a Different Culture Where a Practitioner Develops the Ability to Find Out the Problem

General Manager (G.M.) Takeuchi has quit as a member of the external *Jishuken* meeting which is held outside the company.

He's devoting himself to the TPS activity inside the company.

In the East Automotive Co., it's urgent business to raise the TPS level of the suppliers and the global sister companies, so he travels around world as a person in charge of global TPS division.

As he can't tend to look at all business units, he only makes a business trip to a unit which requests his support. He especially deeply guides the overseas business unit which has trouble with their finances.

G.M. Takeuchi thinks he will make every overseas business unit establish the same features of Manufacturing. Even if the condition, equipment, and buildings are different, it's ideal to make the basic system the same. It is a global standard system.

Therefore, he has established a system of launching new plants with his subordinates. It interweaves the ideologies of TPS, in order that the plant members can easily implement TPS activity.

All layout drafts of new plants and buildings always pass through G.M. Takeuchi now. In the interval of overseas business trips, he is sometimes asked for a consultation about a new plant plan. Someone says, "Fortunately, you are here today. I can't present this document if you can't approve it." Unfortunately, his company hasn't made a rule yet in which such a TPS matter should be checked and permitted by OMCD. But in

DOI: 10.4324/9781003323310-62

reality, the approval by OMCD is needed, because the boss of an executive in charge of TPS promotion never permits TPS documents without first checking with OMCD.

After a while, G.M. Takeuchi mainly begins to visit two factories from the East Asian unit and the European business unit alternately for in-plant consulting.

As the mother plant of two plants is the same, the products and the buildings' status are similar. But, there was a time difference in establishing overseas the relatively old East Asian unit and relatively new European unit, and the topics and problems discussed and solved are different as well.

He greatly worries about how to advance in implementing *Kaizen* in both plants. It takes about three business trips to create a sense of direction for them.

He looks at the workplaces carefully, finds problems, and then decides which point is most effective to solve.

In particular, the improvement of the profit and loss of the company's finances is urgent business for the European business unit. It is a priority to eliminate waste which directly connects with production cost.

On the other hand, the East Asian plant is requested to be the model for the other East Asian companies.

The mother plant in Japan has supported both business units up to now, and also OMCD which is in charge of global TPS is expected to raise the level of TPS urgently.

G.M. Takeuchi has to raise the TPS skills of himself too.

There are various conditions in the global sister companies, such as procurement from Japan. Here, he intends to increase his ability to find out problems, while developing a way of looking at things. Thus, he grows his ability to lead the approach and advance the *Kaizen* method.

Mr. Chen is a person that has been in charge of TPS Activities in the East Asian business unit since the factory's establishment. He has grown with TPS while managers from the parent company have taught him. The TPS level of assembly is high, and there are a lot of example cases for the mother factory from East Asia.

It is really a secret mission to train Mr. Chen. G.M. Takeuchi is told by his boss to raise the TPS level of the East Asian business unit, because their TPS activity is stagnant and still has many problems. However, it's far away, so he can't take actual action there. So, G.M. Takeuchi takes a trip to the factory and confirms the progress once every two months or once a month if he can.

One theme that come out from the East Asian plant is logistics from a receiving place to a shipping place.

The TPS level of the assembly is good, but the goods flow is not good from the entrance to the exit. The level is not good compared to companies of the same scale in Japan, because the circumstances are different.

In particular there is often a shortage of components. When they suddenly know that there are no components, a logistics person take a trip to Japan by airplane and returns from the airport as soon as he receive goods. G.M. Takeuchi also experienced carrying components when he made a business trip. It is called hand carry.

The East Asian factory only has a few parts processing in the plant, and mainly purchases products from local manufacturers. But, a considerable number of functional parts are imported from Japan. Then, both local and imported parts are stocked in the parts warehouse. A 10-ton container comes from Japan once or twice a week. Logistics people unload and unpack the loads, and stock boxes on shelves. So, the receiving area and the receiving work are essential for logistics.

G.M. Takeuchi clarifies problems in the East Asian business unit as follows:

- Works of shipping are not standardized.
- Works of picking in the parts warehouse are not standardized, and missing parts are not easily found.
- Works of part supply to the production workplaces are not standardized.

Manuals are based on the whole logistic operation, but the actual operational methods are not good. The logistics people convey goods in a large lot, and place goods in large lot temporarily. This is why a standardized work cannot be established.

Then, the following *Kaizen* is implemented in order to establish a scheduled work of conveyance.

- Shipping time is managed by the Shipping Control Board, which visualizes the schedule for the individual shipping lane.
- Reconsideration of the work of picking in the parts warehouse.

- Reconsideration of the layout of parts shelves.
- Reconsideration of the work of parts supply to the production workplaces.
- Remodeling of the handcarts. Elimination of the relay points of conveyance.

The purpose of the above items is to establish the scheduled conveyance using frequent conveyance.

It takes three years to establish TPS level C from B in both the assembly and the logistics.

Mr. John is a person that has been in charge of TPS Activities in the European business unit.

G.M. Takeuchi is called Take-san by John.

When he took a trip to this plant for the first time, he walked on a plant tour along with his executive boss who was in charge of promoting TPS. The boss directed him to teach the local people the way of Japanese TPS. After that he decided to stay there for three weeks every three months as a business trip. He always communicated with the plant manager and two Japanese who had been sent there.

First of all, he points out problems in 2S (*Seiri-Seiton*). He advances *Kaizen* in this way, but people cannot easily understand problems in this plant. So we need special skills to find problems. Although the TPS level of this plant is evaluated as A, the 2S activity was already very good, a big English slogan of 5S with explanations is displayed on the wall of the clean room.

There is sometimes a shortage of parts, and the missing parts sometimes can be found in unpacked pallets because of bad management. A lead time by a shipping service is eight weeks, so enough parts are stocked as safety stock. Thus it is rare to use an air flight conveyance unless there is an emergency. But the logistics system in the warehouse has to be improved.

G.M. Takeuchi clarifies some problems in the European plant, which are mainly the in-plant logistics around the assembly line.

The productivity is bad. The way of picking goods by in-plant logistics people has a problem. Although the daily shipment is stable, stock of the finished goods warehouse don't become stable. Therefore a production manager calculates the amount of stock, then he instructs the production lines every day. The Production Instruction *Kanban* is not working.

In order to restructure the system of the in-plant logistics around the assembly line, the following measures are taken for the problems listed above:

- Reconsideration of the moving line of the in-plant logistics persons in the clean room.
- Reconsideration of the layout of the production lines and the Store beside the production line.
- Reconsideration of management of the production instruction *Kanban* to production lines.

The purpose of the above items is to fix the system first, so that people convey and produce frequently.

It takes two years to establish the TPS level B from A in both the assembly and the logistics.

G.M. Takeuchi feels that he can't avoid looking at the cultural differences. He also feels that we can understand each other to some extent in intercultural communication but there is an invisible barrier between us. He believes that even though we may have cultural differences, if the goal is correct, various ways to get there are all fine.

One example was with an experience connected to Feng Shui, which is a traditional method for positioning of buildings, rooms, and objects to achieve harmony with nature. When he pointed out the layout *Kaizen* of both a receiving area and a shipping area in South Asia, his opinion was rejected due to Feng Shui.

His colleague had also experienced such a similar rejection before at the same plant. Then the next best layout plan was adopted.

Sometimes in other countries even cleaning around machinery can't also be made operator's work. This routine tries to train operators, but he guesses it's difficult because the culture is different. Meanwhile, there are good cases where cleaning around machinery can be made operator's work. These cases may depend on the rule of the company in the end.

A person who was sent to sister companies several times from Japan talked to G.M. Takeuchi about the culture. He said, "I thought religion lay at the root of all thinking, when I talked with various nationalities and I felt that there was an invisible barrier." G.M. Takeuchi doesn't have enough experience by which he can judge this opinion. But he guesses it comes from the difference between thinking of "labor as a burden" and thinking "every honest occupation deserves esteem." He feels the difficulty of improving the workplaces in various environments where there is intercultural communication.

If we think the Toyota Production System is based on the human system which is described in the next part, TPS would have the features of the human system based on universal thinking. On the other hand, a system called Lean which was introduced in the West has a different approach and ideology. And Lean is particular about methods or techniques. He wonders if Lean doesn't have the features of the human system, or doesn't penetrate the Japanese thinking.

He thinks Japan is probably different from other nations. Even though recently if the Japanese Lifetime employment system has been difficult to continue due to changes of circumstances in Japan, most Japanese people want to sustain this system. But then overseas people change their jobs frequently, and it is difficult to establish their job in the same company. So it is important to make a system which can be done well even if workers frequently change. Focusing on forming or changing the corporate culture to implement *Kaizen* may be difficult. At that time he establishes a system with some procedures first in order to quickly make workplaces stable.

It is said in the TPS guidance that leaders have to know the corporate culture first.

Some leaders announce how great TPS is and then push an understanding of TPS on people. G.M. Takeuchi doesn't accept that approach. If Manufacturing takes place against a background of human behavior, the guidance also should be done based on humanity. It won't go well, if only Japanese ways and thinking is forced.

Then, when items depend on a deep thinking in TPS, only an item which can be changed to a system of methods can be fixed. Thus Visualization (Visual Control) is easily accepted in the West. Even if it is suggested to managers to go to an actual *Genba*, they don't easily leave from their floor with a nice view of skyscrapers. But they like the management system. We sometimes come across messages in social media which request some formats regarding TPS tools and documents.

But, when establishing a system in order to make workplaces stable, if we make the system only by advancing in the methods, we will fail in establishing it.

The Toyota Production System teaches us that we have to think about what the purpose is, because method changes whenever the situation changes. Even if we advance the methods, it is important to create permanent methods in the future.

If elements of the situation such as: (1) time, (2) Viewpoint, and (3) materials, change, the outcome will change. We have to deeply think of the relationship between method and purpose.

For example, "Pull System" is a principle which can be generally thought as a Method, a Tool, or Thinking.

A principal tool in Pull System is *Kanban*. When *Kanban* started, *Kanban* for supplier was basically paper-based "Returnable *Kanban*" conveyed by truck drivers. The traditional *Kanban* changed to e-*Kanban* and the lead time of published e-*Kanban* must be the number of conveying trucks between the supplier and customer. Thus, while changing from the returnable *Kanban* to the electronic *Kanban*, the essential purpose did not change, but the methods and tools changed.

-MANPOWER POWER SAVING AND HUMAN RESOURCES; MAY LAYOFFS HAPPEN AFTER IMPROVEMENT?

Sensei appears and begins to speak.

"Takeuchi, there is a brief column which is written in my book about the Manpower Power Saving and the utilization of Human Resources. Let me show you it from the Japanese book, 'Seru Seisan (Cell Production),' Noboru Takeuchi, JMA Management Center, 2006, P.202, as follows.

May Layoffs Happen after Improvement?

I have read an interesting preface in a foreign book which became popular before. The main point in the preface said; a company laid off unnecessary human resources who were produced and made redundant after implementing *Kaizen*. When employees improve their workplaces, companies fire them from their jobs. Meanwhile, layoffs never happen at companies which don't do improvement. This is a contradiction in *Kaizen*.

I thought about such unexpected occurrences that happened in a foreign country. In Japan, we are taught that we should allocate the redundant resources to new businesses after doing *Kaizen*. Those days there were not many cases in which we heard of workforce reductions. Social systems are different among countries, so we cannot say that foreign companies are the same as Japanese companies. But anyway, staff of overseas manufacturers seem to have the thinking mentioned in the previous preface.

It's because I had a surprising experience at the European plant after I read the book. When I advised a production manager on operations, he replied, 'I am reluctant to implement *Kaizen*. My company hasn't done Layoffs, since I joined this company. I didn't want to lay off people.' I was really surprised.

In this company, the business was so good that the company increased profitability and scale. Even though the company had enough room to utilize personnel which was produced from *Kaizen*, it continued to increase only the number of personnel without implementing *Kaizen* well. Then the financial situation of the company got worse.

First of all, *Kaizen* should be implemented in order to make workers be able to operate easily. Then human resources are produced as a result. If we make a mistake in the thinking of *Kaizen*, work will become excessively intensified. This situation is not considerate towards people.

Thus, you must be really shocked, when the production manager said, 'I am reluctant to implement *Kaizen*.'

Even more, there is a misunderstanding that the Toyota Production System is a method of personnel cuts. And when there are labor surpluses, we tend to think that *Kaizen* will create even more extra personnel. In these global circumstances, the driving force for doing *Kaizen* is often weaker.

The Toyota Production System teaches us that during such times we have to do *Kaizen*. We should aim at a true Toyota Production System."

47

Changing Features of the Toyota Production System

General Manager (G.M.) Takeuchi works at OMCD, and is responsible for the instruction of TPS Activities to suppliers and global sister companies.

His senior colleague supports him to instruct the domestic suppliers carefully, so he doesn't have any concerns. Meanwhile, most overseas plants should be good because they were established based on TPS, yet they still remain at the low TPS level. Then G.M. Takeuchi has to guide TPS in person.

While basically there is a general rule that all business units should be guided by the mother plant, G.M. Takeuchi has to focus mainly on a few plants which have management problems.

One day his executive boss who was in charge of promoting the company-wide TPS activity ordered him to take a trip to the European business unit.

He met another executive who was in charge of the mother plant and stayed in the European plant by chance. Then the executive outrageously told to G.M. Takeuchi, "You can't return to Japan." It was the day before his return.

Kaizen should have advanced with the responsibility of each business unit until then. G.M. Takeuchi thought, "This is his responsibility of implementing improvement." He remembered the executive who had been all talk and no action from his young age. The executive didn't work with actual action in *Genchi-Gembutsu*.

The executive said "TPS is top-down" in words only. The key phrase was correct, but he didn't know TPS. He was the all-talk-type which was listed

DOI: 10.4324/9781003323310-63

as a type of leader (see Chapter 43). He was also the pressure type. He was an executive, so he was equal to the task.

G.M. Takeuchi thought that OMCD hadn't supported unifying the global TPS activity of overseas business units. OMCD didn't have an ability to unify the overseas TPS activity then.

When the overseas plants expansion had started, our company should have unified the TPS activity with the headquarters' function. But our company had no choice other than to advance forward, because TPS management hadn't been established as a company-wide activity, while OMCD, which was not the Operations Management Consulting Division but the smaller OMC-Department, was still acting on a small scale.

Therefore, although G.M Takeuchi thought in his mind that the executive was all talk and no action, he advanced the TPS *Kaizen* which was implemented as part of his mission on the overseas business trips. OMCD wasn't involved in the overseas business units until then, and all the members of the overseas business units and mother plants didn't know how to advance. Not every TPS person can do it.

It also wasn't his duty at that time, so there was a choice for him not to be involved in the overseas business units. But he complied with a request from the Corporate Planning Division.

There are various features of TPS.

In the case of plants which have already implemented TPS to some degree, we can't know at first how to improve the plant.

After we think deeply about what we are aiming at, we come to the conclusion that we need to go back to the basics. It's to return to the basics of the Manufacturing.

Actually, we make good use of various "TPS techniques" to improve. So Lean also aims to try to use techniques. But, those techniques and tools are not always suitable for particular situations. If we don't evaluate this, the outcome will be bad. For example, when we superficially use *Kanban*, we can't understand the true purpose of it and will fail in introducing *Kanban*.

This book explains that the Toyota Production System appears with different level features. But then, the features of the Toyota Production System sometimes seem to be different among outsiders depending on their experience, thinking way, and viewpoint. There are also some books which seem correct at first sight but the logic progresses with clear mistakes. And there are some people who affirmatively say "this is TPS" in their restricted experience.

There are many books which write about the Toyota Production System. These books are respectively excellent with good content, but the explanation parts are sometimes different. The basic difference is whether the thinking or the methodology is emphasized.

For example there is an excellent book: Jeffrey K. Liker, *The Toyota way*, McGraw-Hill, 2004. This book says the Toyota Way and the Toyota Production System are the double helix of Toyota DNA; they define its management style and what is unique about the company. This book describes 14 principles of the Toyota way. However, some principles seem to belong to the methods, so it is not easy to understand them.

When we find that there are many books on the Toyota Production System, we can't understand TPS at first reading, and we are unable to understand the Toyota Production System. A main point of this book is to show the whole forms of TPS, so this book doesn't describe the techniques so much. There are a lot of TPS methods which are written in general books, and also there are high TPS techniques which aren't common knowledge. Only certain knowledge of TPS techniques is open to the public.

It's not that this book doesn't introduce the techniques. But it's necessary to explain in detail with clear premise or purposes, because methods are often contingent on the situation. So, we shouldn't just look for tools or methods, but we should think about our unique situations and create methods ourselves.

The Production System, which is made based on the concept of the Toyota Production System, changes the features depending on the status of the company and what stage we have progressed to. The features of TPS must be the same form.

But, the features of TPS appear in various ways.

Then, even if we think of a way to make our workplaces much better, we can't know how to progress well.

G.M. Takeuchi had an experience where an idea suddenly flashed into his mind, "Aha, I got it. 2S is surely the first one." He spent several years practicing *Kaizen* in order to be able to find his own way in his TPS activity.

There is not always one way to improve the workplace. He tries to grasp actual situations, and afterwards he decides the most effective direction to create the best workplace in the future. He thinks about how to find and solve problems with deciding a goal in mind.

The best solution, he thinks, is that we should respect humans and stand on this fundamental ideology. We have to start with the fundamental ideology and then think about the better way in order to produce the better workplaces.

In order to survive in increasingly competitive global marketplaces, at the core of TPS is understanding the value of employees. Often, companies emphasize cost and efficiency and lose sight of the activities of their employees. This often leads to a host of problems that perplex companies who are unaware that the root cause lies in their flawed philosophy. Companies should acknowledge the contributions and potential of their employees, as the workers themselves could be considered stakeholders wishing for the success of their workplace.

When graduating from university, G.M. Takeuchi got a job and had a purpose of looking at: "What is a manufacturer?" He entered the world of the Toyota Production System by chance. As he was promoted to be a leader after his personnel transfers in the company, he gradually began to think that he shouldn't stick to the framework of the company.

When he got a job, he thought that he wouldn't quit the company and would continue to work at the same company under the Japanese employment system. This was because he thought technology everywhere was the same.

Still G.M. Takeuchi retires from the East Automotive Co., Ltd., and chooses to follow the path of a freelance consultant. And he continues to teach and learn again the ideology: "we will keep pursuing the ideal features of true Manufacturing which is considerate of people."

Part XIII

The Features of TPS

48

The Features of TPS (Global TPS: Schematic Diagram of the Toyota Production System)

When a novice in TPS tries to study a book about it, the objectively and systematically written books become useful to understand the basics of TPS. But there are some books which seem to have been written without a good understanding of TPS, with a perspective given only from outside the production site, often from the perspective of the so-called headquarters' operations of a company. And then there are some books which just look at one aspect of TPS, and that brings to mind the parable of the blind men and the elephant, which originated in the ancient Indian continent. While attempts to teach TPS through such types of books seem noble, none offer sufficient enough insight to truly understand the breadth and depth of TPS. The reason is because the authors only explain the trivial details of tools and methods that they experienced in various situations at former worksites. TPS should exist at various levels of production and with various features. However, the features of TPS sometimes appear different among different outsiders depending on their experience, way of thinking, and viewpoints, so it is a major challenge for them to truly grasp TPS.

GM. Takeuchi summarizes and emphasizes the ideology of *Monodzukuri* (Manufacturing).

In the features of *Monodzukuri*, the philosophy is the core, which is supported by some principles. And moreover, practical human behavior and techniques, which is equated to the tools or methods, are based on these principles. The practical activities based on this ideology in the workplace result in the features of *Monodzukuri* we are able to see.

DOI: 10.4324/9781003323310-65

In order to explain schematically the above ideology of *Monodzukuri*, Takeuchi proposes a diagram called "The Features of TPS." This conceptual diagram, similar to an Earth cutaway diagram, gives an overview of the outline of "The continuously changing features of the Toyota Production System" (Figure 48.1).

As for explaining the diagram, **The Features of TPS (Global TPS: Schematic Diagram of the Toyota Production System)**, the nine articles below are summarized in detail:

1. *Monodzukuri* consists of four layers:
   - Layer 1. Philosophy (Core Concept)
   - Layer 2. Principle (Complementary Concept)
   - Layer 3. Component (Practical Behavior and Technique)
   - Layer 4. Emerging Features (Features of Manufacturing)

   In Layer 4, we can see the features of Manufacturing where the philosophy in Layer 1 comes out through Layers 2 and 3.
2. The four elements of production are generally called, "Man, Materials, Money, and Information."

   Here, to make the argument concise, the following three elements of production are macroscopically rearranged, which is taken to be each of the three axes of a rectangular coordinate system.
   - **First element of production: Human system**

     This essentially corresponds to "Man," for example, culture, corporate culture, employee, supplier, shop, manager, and stockholder which are abstract and intangible.
   - **Second element of production: Knowledge and material system**

     This essentially corresponds to "Material," for example, technique and products-which are concrete and tangible.
   - **Third element of production: Management system**

     This essentially corresponds to "Money," for example, organization, management, and information.

   In the following argument, we try to grasp the outline of *Monodzukuri* through the first and second element of production. The third element of production, the management system, has been left for later on, because it is complicated and should be divided into various elements.
3. Toyota way 2001 and the Toyota Production System emerged formally from Toyota.

Toyota way 2001 identifies and defines the values and business methods that all employees who work in Toyota should embrace. It is the basis of internal human resources development in Toyota.

The Toyota Production System was systematized by Mr. Taiichi Ohno based on the *Genba* oriented policy and philosophy of humanity, so the thinking of Taiichi Ohno is fundamentally included in the Toyota way.

4. The contents from Layer 1 to Layer 4 are organized into both "First element of production: Human system" and "Second element of production: Knowledge and Material system."

5. Layer 1. Philosophy (Core Concept)

"Layer 1. Philosophy (Core Concept)" of "First element of production: Human system" is "Sharing the Toyota Way Values: Behave oneself according to the two main pillars, 'Continuous Improvement' and 'Respect for People,' which identifies and defines the management philosophy, the values and business methods in Toyota. And this helps foster a corporate culture which enhances the creativity of individuals and strengthens teamwork."

"Layer 1. Philosophy (Core Concept)" of "Second element of production: Knowledge and Material system" is "TPS Concept: Base actions on the two main pillars: Just-In-Time and *Jidoka*, where we realize cost reduction by thorough elimination of *Muda* (Waste), and continuously secure long-term profit."

6. **Layer 2. Principle (Complementary Concept)**

"Layer 2. Principle (Complementary Concept)" of "First element of production: Human system" is "Respect for People and Continuous Improvement, which the Toyota Way 2001 identified and defined."

"Layer 2. Principle (Complementary Concept)" of "Second element of production: Knowledge and Material system" is "Principles of Just-In-Time and *Jidoka*, for example, *Heijunka* production."

7. **Layer 3. Component (Practical Behavior and Technique)**

"Layer 3. Component (Practical Behavior and Technique)" of "First element of production: Human system" is "Mindset of basic behavior."

"Layer 3. Component (Practical Behavior and Technique)" of "Second element of production: Knowledge and Material system" is "Basic technique (TPS tools)."

In addition, there is a *Kaizen* domain: "Mindset of *Kaizen*" and "Procedure of *Kaizen*," which is related to both "First element of

Human: Features of the thinking process and the emerging behavior

(Sustainment) Execute a daily routine smoothly

(Improvement) Change the manner of action when the situation changes, and standardize it

(Evolution) Decide your action based on a long-term concept, and though you may eventually stop it, you won't revert back to what was done previously.

(Business Process) Pursue the best process with the perspective of the customer in mind.

(Scope) Optimize performance in the whole process; next, self, former process

Stratified Role)

Top: Act and instruct with Genchi-Gembutsu

Administrator: Define the gap between the vision and the current status, then decide and justify a plan of action.

Front-line supervisor: Manage the workplace in a position of "CEO of genba," and carry out tasks utilizing your team and teamwork.

Workplace (Man, Machine, Material);
Features of the work processes and the organizational behavior

(Organization) Work with Design, Production Engineering, Production Engineering etc.

(Training) Learn by TPS Training in Design, Production Engineering etc.

(TPS Activity) Share the information, and make a line based on TPS concept.

* TPS concept should be woven into new product introductions
* Build new factory based on TPS Concept.
* Achieve high built-in QCD before building machine and process.
* Facilities should be flexible, low cost, and human-oriented so that Kaizen is easy to be implemented
  (Create small machine and don't introduce half-baked automation)

(Organization) Organize the task force team who can support Kaizen activities.

(Training) Develop the Kaizen practitioner by practicing in Genba.
 (TPS training, Training Center (Dojo), Jishuken)

(TPS Activity) Organize the daily Kaizen activities.

* Eliminate Muda (Waste)
* Continuous improvement
* Continuous standardization and revision
* Improve equipments everyday
* Work improvement and logistics improvement   and so on.

(Organization) Effective organization composed of small groups for Kaizen.

(Training) Long-term human resources development by OJT and OFFJT.

(TPS Activity) Produce better quality goods by Heinyunka production based on demand.

* Always grasp hidden issues.
  (Distinguish between normality and abnormality)
* Daily management based on the metrics of defect, productivity and delivery.
* Be thorough "Visual Control" with "Genchi-Gembutsu"
* Stop the equipment immediately, when a problem occurs.
* Keep thorough the Five S's.

Features of the initial workplace	Features of the improving workplace	Features of the workplace that is evolved and can be maintained

Layer 4. Emerging Features
(Features of Manufacturing)

Mindset of basic behavior

* Basic TPS activity on humans. * Respond to change without being afraid of change * Continuously pursue the ideal state over the long term * Concentrate on the Genba oriented policy with Genchi-Gembutsu * Be vigilant in finding and solving problems * Don't pass on issues to the next step in the process

Mindset of Kaizen (Put "wisdom" into Kaizen)

* Start with needs * Find the root cause, then apply a countermeasure without using temporary coping measures * Apply countermeasure with holistic systems-thinking (Make sure systems flow smoothly) * Accumulate small Kaizen (Small change is easier to gain benefits than big change) * Improve manual operations before improving issues with the facility (The proper order) *Fast action is better than being careful but late (Speed)

Kaizen domain

Procedure for Kaizen

"The changing features of the Kaizen activity cycles"

(Step1: Implementing 2S) Implement firstly the 2S necessary for TPS Kaizen. (Step2: Finding Muda (Waste)) Work process and goods flow can be seen, so any abnormality and waste can become reasons for improvement. (Step3: Implementing the countermeasure) Finding the root cause with the 5 Whys, then apply the countermeasure. (Step4: Establishing a standard) Standardize the workplace, complete the visual control, and develop in other areas.

Utilizing the Information Technology

Basic technique (TPS tools)

1	One-Piece-At-a-Time (Production)	
	Synchronization	
	Multi-Process Operation System	
	Multi-Skill Development of Operator	
	Standing Operation	
	Equipment Layout according to the Process Sequence	
	The small lot sizes	Shortening the setup time
2	Change Takt-Time each time	
	Standardized Work	
	Flexible Manpower Line	
3	Kanban System	Kanban
	Frequent Conveyance	Good & Information Flow Chart
4	Equipment or System capable of detecting abnormality	
5	Separation of human operation and machine work	

Layer 3. Component
(Practical Behavior and Technique)

Guiding Principles

Respect for People: We respect all stakeholders, and believe the success of business is created by individual effort and good teamwork	Respect
	Teamwork
Continuous Improvement : We respect all Toyota stakeholders, and believe the success of our business is created by individual effort and good teamwork	Challenge
	Kaizen
	Genchi Genbutsu

Principles of Just-In-Time and Jidoka

Prerequisite Condition:

JIT : Manufacturing and Transportation of only what is needed, when it is needed, in the amount needed	Heijunka
	Basic Principle-1: **Continuous Flow Processing**
	Basic Principle-2: Determine **Takt-Time by the Required Number**
	Basic Principle-3: **Pull System (of Production)**
Jidoka : When abnormal conditions occur, machines are made to detect these abnormal conditions and stop automatically	Basic Principle-4: Quality must be **built-into Process**
	Basic Principle-5: **Manpower Saving**

Layer 2. Principle
(Complementary Concept)

Sharing
the Toyota Way Values

Behave oneself according to the two main pillars, 'Just-for People' and 'Continuous Improvement'

This helps foster a corporate culture which enhances the creativity of individuals and strengthens teamwork

The Toyota Way 2001

TPS Concept

Base actions on the two main pillars, Just-In-Time and Jidoka, where we realize cost reduction by thorough elimination of Muda (Waste), and continuously secure long-term profit.

TPS Concept &

Layer 1. Philosophy
(Core Concept)

Abstract and Intangible | (Human system)

Concrete and Tangible | (Knowledge and Material system)

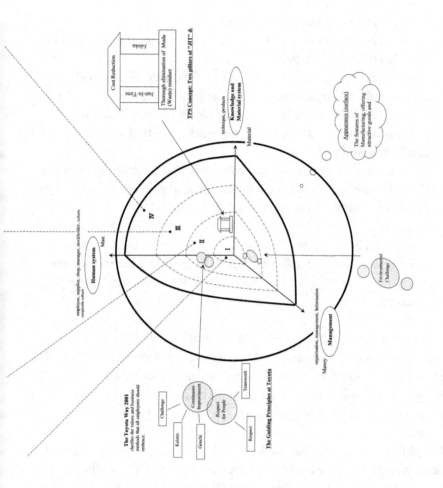

FIGURE 48.1

The features of TPS (Global TPS: schematic diagram of the Toyota Production System).

© Noboru Takeuchi, 2013

production: Human system" and "Second element of production: Knowledge and Material system."

8. **Layer 4. Emerging Features (Features of Manufacturing)**
"Layer 4. Emerging Features (Features of Manufacturing)" is the features of *Monodzukuri* (Manufacturing) as resulting from activities that are based on Layers 1, 2, and 3.

Two features of *Monodzukuri* appear:

Features as human activities, "Features of the thinking process and the emerging behavior."

Features as the workplace situation, **Features of the work processes and the organizational behavior**, which consist of three phases, **Features of the** initial **workplace, Features of the improving workplace**, and **Features of the workplace that** is evolved and **can be maintained**.

It is not easy to divide the daily workplace's activities into the above three phases, so it must be understood as the function or the dividing of duties in the organization.

9. Summarizing 1 to 8 above, *Monodzukuri* of the Toyota Production System can be stated by presenting an overview of both the two elements: "Human system" and "Knowledge and Material system," and four layers: Philosophy, Principle, Component, and Emerging Features.

"The Features of TPS" really resembles the structure of the earth.

The earth's inner core corresponds to Layer 1, the outer core to Layer 2, the lower mantle to Layer 3, and the upper mantle to Layer 4.

The globe cutaway is specified by using the X-, Y-, Z- axis of the rectangular coordinate system, in which the cross sections of Layer 1–4 are drawn.

The philosophy of the Toyota Way and TPS concept covers Layer 1, which is a solid base, like a core of a hard ball. The principles of the Toyota Way and the concept of the two main pillars in TPS cover Layer 2. The practical behavior and the technique cover Layer 3. Layer 4 is the activity based on Layers 1–3.

The contents of the Human system and the Knowledge and Material system are very complicated like the yarn which is wound around a core of a hard ball. The "*Kaizen* Domain" particularly seems to be inseparably interwoven yarn. The surface of Layer 4 ultimately corresponds to the appearance of *Monodzukuri* (Manufacturing) that outsiders can see. It is like the leather of a hard ball, or the thin surface of the earth's crust.

The features of *Monodzukuri* are the activities of Layer 4, which is grounded on the items in layers 1–3. Based on observations of the status of the workplace, that is Layer 4, the TPS level is judged to be Level A, and so forth. Our activity is to make a better Layer 4 of the workplace. The Layer 1 of Philosophy sometimes might not be strong. On the other hand, there may be a manufacturing workplace where a certain status is achieved beyond the contents organized here. Thus, if a new philosophy is added in Layer 1, it's also said to be a true deepening of *Monodzukuri*.

Here, this diagram deals with only the two systems, the Human system and the Knowledge and Material system. However, if we think about the Management system, some philosophy might be at the core of the system. For example, today's ideology of protecting the environment might be considered.

Even if there are any concerns about the descriptions in Layers 1 and 2, the contents could be correct, but a heated discussion by readers especially about the contents in Layers 3 and 4 will be appreciated.

TPS is discussed a lot in a vague way, for example, "TPS is a tool," "TPS is an ideology itself" and so forth, and TPS is sorted into the four Layers of "The Features of TPS" in this book: "Philosophy," "Principle," "Component," and "Emerging Features." Thus this book shows the ideology, which will give you an answer to solving the uncertainty of understanding TPS, so any thoughts readers could graciously share with me will be greatly appreciated.

At least, the outline of "The Features of TPS" will make it easier for readers to understand their particular area of study on TPS. It can indicate the positioning of the reference literature that explains the Toyota Production System.

For example, "Ishii, Masamitsu; *Nyumon Toyota Seisan Hoshiki* (Basic Toyota Production System)" (Chukei Publishing Company 2005) comes under "Layers 1 to 3" of "Second element of production." The category of *Kaizen* books almost completely belongs to "Layer 3." And weekly magazine articles such as: "–in Toyota" may be focused on "Layer 4."

Thus, it probably becomes easy to understand the positioning of TPS literature when readers compare them with the contents of the "The Features of TPS." And afterwards, readers can clarify the items of TPS which should be understood in more depth.

⬯ -THE MEANING OF "THE FEATURES OF TPS": THE NARROWLY INTERPRETED TPS AND THE BROADLY INTERPRETED TPS

Takeuchi asked, "*Sensei*, I think I understand the outline of TPS by using 'The Features of TPS.' The argument over whether it's right or isn't right is another matter. It's difficult, but in order to understand TPS, I acknowledge 'The Features of TPS' as one ideology, and I'm going to find a simple explanation for it."

"When I had begun to instruct TPS in foreign countries, I was informed by a TPS instructor that there is a secret ideology in TPS. It is in the 'Mindset of basic behavior' of 'Layer 3,' and is stated as 'Continuously pursue the ideal state over the long term,'" *Sensei* answers and continues.

"When I participate in discussions among Lean Manufacturing members and *Kaizen* members in foreign countries, I feel they are apt to stick to techniques in TPS. Although I agree with my senior instructors' opinion that it is inevitable they stick to techniques because of their situation, I sometimes feel they miss the quintessence of TPS. Thus, I think that various opinions, like 'TPS is the only technique or *Kaizen* method' or 'TPS is grasped as a strategic tool,' nowadays results in chaos.

I tried to organize these opinions, and this led to a diagram of 'The Features of TPS.' I utilize it when I am consulting others in order to explain the outline of TPS. The diagram is titled aptly '**Framework of the Features of TPS**'" (Figures 48.2 and 48.3).

Takeuchi tries to describe it more succinctly: "It eventually teaches us that the Toyota Production System is conducted by *Monodzukuri*, which is based on the Toyota Way as a code of conduct, and Just-In-Time and *Jidoka* as the two main pillars."

Sensei then defines the scope of the Toyota Production System.

"I am in a position to recognize the starting point where Mr. Taiichi Ohno wrote his management philosophy in his book, *TOYOTA PRODUCTION SYSTEM*. He taught us the importance of continuing to keep the *Genba* oriented policy.

Here, I dare attempt to present TPS restricted within narrow limits, '**The narrowly interpreted Toyota Production System (TPS)**.' In this case, TPS is regarded only as a means of improvement in the production workplace. Thus, TPS is generally trivialized as knowledge which has

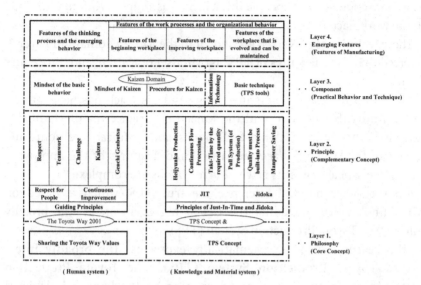

FIGURE 48.2

Framework A of "The Features of TPS".

© Noboru Takeuchi, 2013

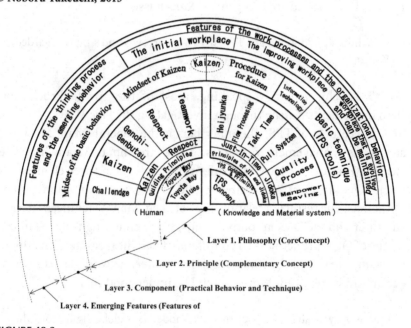

FIGURE 48.3

Framework B of "The Features of TPS".

© Noboru Takeuchi, 2013

a narrow scope, so many people think of TPS as simply a *Kaizen* technique in the workplace.

These techniques of *Kaizen* are shown in the *Kaizen* domain in Layer 3, referred to in 'The Features of TPS' as 'Mindset of *Kaizen*' and 'Procedure for *Kaizen*.'

Mr. Ohno has taught us many things and his teachings have spread. These words that he used and the *Kaizen* experience manifests in this domain as techniques. Almost all books about *Kaizen* are confusing in two of the layers: '*Kaizen*' in Layer 3 and 'Features of the improving workplace' in Layer 4. This is why *Kaizen* books are complex.

On the other hand, I reference the true TPS, which is based on Mr. Ohno's spirit, including the *Genba* management, as 'the broadly interpreted Toyota Production System (TPS).'

'The Features of TPS' schematically expresses '**The broadly interpreted Toyota Production System (TPS)**.' The Toyota Production System is constantly evolving and deepening. So, the diagram is depicted to try to easily understand TPS by explaining the outline of the Toyota Production System."

Takeuchi then asked about a general *Kaizen* issue.

"*Sensei*, how should we regard TPS, if TPS is narrowly and simply regarded as *Kaizen*?"

"Mr. Takeuchi, generally speaking, most of the Toyota Production System implements *Kaizen* through investigating the Five Whys.

In 'The Features of TPS,' the inner part is the general 'Man, Machine, Material' as management resources. These are input. Meanwhile, the 'Emerging Features' of Layer 4 result in the contents of three elements of demand: Quality, Cost, and Delivery reflects the success in production of the products. The result is a relationship between 'Man, Machine, Material' as an input and QCD as an output. Thus, if the emerging features in the outcome of QCD are actually so far different from the ideal state imagined, we have to implement the *Kaizen* activity to alter the workplace to where the ideal can be realized. *Kaizen* should be understood this way."

Sensei, were you able to depict the TPS model as a globe right from the beginning?

"Mr. Takeuchi, I called it 'The Features of TPS' here. When we say features, it's a part of the face or an appearance. But in this case, it should be called 'earth-shaped TPS' or 'globe of TPS' because Figure 48.1 shows the entire structure of TPS. Therefore, 'The Features of TPS' could be called 'Global TPS,' which has a similar meaning to global TPS' activities in a global company.

I explained this decades ago by using the same typed document as the upper table in Figure 48.1. It has four cascades of structure: Philosophy, Secret concept, Technique, and Action. And I guessed there were other emerging features on the outside of the production activity. Afterwards, during the process of organizing the document by 'Human system' and 'Knowledge and Material system,' I noticed it happened to take the same shape as the earth. It was not my intention at the beginning for it to take the shape of the earth, but it became an easily comprehensible structure to readers.

Volcanos explode on the earth's surface (crust). It is similar to various issues in *Monodzukuri*. So we can explain that *Kaizen* is to countermeasure the issues which are shot out from Layer 4, and to make a better workplace."

Takeuchi asked,

"*Sensei*, would you tell me what we should pay attention to when looking at 'The Features of TPS'?"

"Firstly, the 'Emerging Features' based on the inner 'Core Concept' comes out on the surface. So, you should think *Monodzukuri* appears as the result of the mechanisms under that surface – the inner layers. Then you can easily imagine that the emerging features transform when they evolve and deepen. When you analyze some situations in the workplace, it's very difficult to analyze only by means of observing the appearance, so you should think about Layer 3. Thinking only in terms of what is observed at Layer 4 might result in a compound phenomenon. If you can analyze only with Layer 3, TPS can be explained in terms of mindset or technique that might depend on the field of 'behavioral science.' For example, if technique, which develops human ability by 'mental practice,' could be achieved, TPS would become a means similar to the Lean manufacturing system. I'm not sure about that, but I'd like to see such a trend in the future.

Secondly, in addition to the principles, the roots of TPS are in the core of the two systems: 'Human system' and 'Knowledge and material.'

Thirdly, the Toyota Production System includes activities 'in advance' at upstream stages like R&D or production preparation, although people generally understand that TPS is useful in the 'follow-up' activity of *Kaizen* in the production workplace. It is not only essential for us to keep improving the existent product line, but also to interweave the ideologies of TPS as much as possible. Thus, the production activity consists of three stages: 'the initial workplace,' 'the improving workplace,' and 'the workplace that is evolving and can be maintained.'

Fourthly, it's desirable for us to successfully use the Information technology IT resources in order to advance work efficiently, although you shouldn't stick to only the means. In order to get a better workplace in the long term, it's necessary to organize the IT and the workplace system together."

Takeuchi asked,

"How do you explain adding human behavior principle to 'The Features of TPS'?"

"Mr. Ohno taught us that manufacturing is based on human behavior, while it is similar to the thinking of *Jidoka*, whereby human capabilities are transferred over to machines. He didn't explain TPS as just tools, but that humans are part of the basis of TPS. Therefore, 'The Features of TPS' consists of the two roots. It is not the two main pillars, but the two roots."

Takeuchi spoke about one idea from an authority in Japanese manufacturing.

"Professor, Dr. Takahiro Hujimoto published, '*Nihon no Monodzukuri Tetsugagu*, or Japanese *Monodzukuri*'s Philosophy' (Nikkei Publishing Inc., 2004), and in this book, he explained the Japanese manufacturing industry and proposed 'the integrated *Monodzukuri* system.' He stated that Toyota Motor should be emulated by other companies. He explained that other *Monodzukuri* systems after World War 2 were also 'the integrated *Monodzukuri* system.' He also explained that the Toyota Production System could be the foremost *Monodzukuri* system for us to follow, and then major companies' systems, such as the 'Cellular Production system,' could subsequently followed as well."

Sensei nodded, and shared his thoughts about *Monodzukuri* based on the human system.

"*Monodzukuri* is particularly necessary to keep the human system ideology.

When we say *Monodzukuri* or TPS is deep, we mean that it might be based on the ideology of the human system behavior. And saying Japanese culture or corporate culture also touches on this area would be proper as well. There are very Japanese features even in the current *Monodzukuri*, such as sophisticated things seen by a mechanical (*Karakuri*) doll that was produced many years ago, and characteristics such as Japanese modesty, sincerity, and seriousness. I guess that the typical Japanese *Monodzukuri* forms the basis of something like the Japanese soul that is written in the famous English book, 'Bushido: The soul of Japan,' by Inazo Nitobe. Training centers are sometimes called Dojo by manufacturers in the West. Dojo is a Japanese term which literally means 'place of the way,' and it originally referred to the training halls in martial arts.

But, if Japanese manufacturing is tied to Japanese culture or the ways of thinking based on, say, religion, I think, it might become a barrier to truly understanding *Monodzukuri*. So far, I have explained specifically about the meaning of words like *Monodzukuri*, but the reason for this is because you have to understand the true meaning of it before proceeding in trying to understand TPS.

The processes of learning and practicing the methods in TPS, which many advanced companies are trying to do, is useful for beginners. But, it may not always work if the current system is changed based on purely the desire to apply methodology. Efficiency is taken as a top priority in society now, and a short-term result is desired in particular. However, it's crucial to pursue the ideal state. You should investigate the true cause of issues by means of the Five Whys while you are continuing to eliminate *Muda* (Waste). Human resources development in *Kaizen* is achieved through experiences where the desired result is able to be obtained by such processes. Thus, the most important thing in TPS is to create a corporate culture which keeps developing human resources who continuously engage in the *Kaizen* activity."

Overview of the Toyota Production System (TPS): "Three Keys," "Four Behaviors," and "the Features of Monodzukuri (Manufacturing)"

Let's summarize the overview of "The Features of TPS (Global TPS: Schematic diagram of the Toyota Production System)," then we can more easily understand the Toyota Production System. These outlines are based on the concept "The broadly interpreted Toyota Production System."

The overview of TPS, including what senior practitioners have experienced, is summarized in three categories:

- "Three Keys" for understanding the Toyota Production System
- "Four Behaviors" for implementing the Toyota Production System
- "The Features of *Monodzukuri* (Manufacturing)," which appear in the Toyota Production System

THREE KEYS FOR UNDERSTANDING THE TOYOTA PRODUCTION SYSTEM

i. **Practical Viewpoint**
   Understand that the Toyota Production System is the ideology itself of the company-wide management.
   - The Toyota Production System is based on a philosophy which powerfully influences the features of *Monodzukuri*.

DOI: 10.4324/9781003323310-66

- The Toyota Production System is a company-wide process which starts from "Our Customers" and ends with "Our Customers."
- The Toyota Production System can be adjusted and made appropriate for any situation a company may face.
- Even if the product changes in manufacturing or in the service industry, the ways of thinking in the Toyota Production System can be applicable to it (this book's story mainly focuses on the manufacturing industry).

ii. **Total Structure**

Understand that the Toyota Production System consists of four layers:

Layer 1. Philosophy (Core Concept)
Layer 2. Principle (Complementary Concept)
Layer 3. Component (Practical Behavior and Technique)
Layer 4. Emerging Features (Features of Manufacturing).

- It is important to understand that the Toyota Production System has a structure which consists of 4 layers. Other production systems also seem to have a similar structure.
- The core concept of the Toyota Production System exists in "Layer 1. Philosophy." It is the philosophy of TPS which is "Behave oneself according to the two main pillars, 'Respect for People' and 'Continuous Improvement.' This helps foster a corporate culture which enhances the creativity of individuals and strengthens teamwork," and "Base actions on the two main pillars: Just-In-Time and *Jidoka*, where we realize cost reduction by thorough elimination of *Muda* (Waste), and continuously secure long-term profit."
- The complementary concept of "Layer 1. Philosophy" is "Layer 2. Principle." It is both the guiding principle "Respect for People and Continuous Improvement" and the principles of "Just-In-Time and *Jidoka*."

- The practical behavior and technique based on "Layer 2. Principle" is "Layer 3. Component." It is "Mindset of the basic behavior" and "Mindset of *Kaizen*" in the Human system, and the "Basic technique" and "Procedure for *Kaizen*" in the Knowledge and Material system. Both the "Mindset of *Kaizen*" and "Procedure for *Kaizen*" are inside the *Kaizen* domain.
- "Layer 4. Emerging Features" is the feature of *Monodzukuri* (Manufacturing) that result from activities that are based on Layers 1–3.

iii. **Formation of Features**
   Understand that the features of the outcome based on the Toyota Production System vary depending on the situation and the TPS level in the workplace.
   - In the Toyota Production System, the philosophy is the core, which is complemented by some principles. And then the practical activities based on these principles in the workplace result in the features of *Monodzukuri* we can see. These features of *Monodzukuri* (Manufacturing) are only the result of what we implement.
   - The activities in the Toyota Production System depend on both the mindset of behavior in the Human system and the technique in the Knowledge and Material system. Then, the various features appear-depending on the situation and the TPS level.
   - The essence of TPS can't be understood easily. The reason is because the emerging features of TPS sometimes seem to be different among outsiders depending on their experience, way of thinking, and viewpoint. The instructors often only explain the trivial details of tools and methods that they experienced in various situations somewhere.

FOUR BEHAVIORS FOR IMPLEMENTING
THE TOYOTA PRODUCTION SYSTEM

iv. **Mindset of the basic behavior**
Be always mindful of the Mindset of the basic behavior in the Human system when practicing the Toyota Production System.
- Base TPS activity on humans
- Respond to change without being afraid of change
- Continuously pursue the ideal state over the long term
- Concentrate on the *Genba*-oriented policy with *Genchi-Gembutsu*
- Be vigilant in finding and solving problems
- Don't pass on issues to the next step in the process

v. Mindset of *Kaizen* (Put wisdom into *Kaizen*)
Be always mindful of practicing the Mindset of *Kaizen* with the Mindset of the basic behavior in the *Kaizen* Activity.
- Start with needs
- Find the root cause, then apply a countermeasure without using temporary coping measures
- Apply countermeasure with the overall optimization thinking (Make sure systems flow smoothly)
- Accumulate small *Kaizen* (Small change is easier to gain benefits than big change
- Improve manual operations before improving issues with the facility (The proper order)
- Fast action is better than being careful but late (Speed)

vi. **Basic technique (TPS tools)**
Be always mindful of practicing the Basic technique (TPS tools) in the Toyota Production System, which is based on Just-In-Time and *Jidoka*.
- The Basic techniques based on Just-In-Time are as follows:
- One-Piece-At-a-Time (Production), Synchronization, Multi-Process Operation System, Multi-Skill Development of Operator, Standing Operation, Equipment Layout according to the Process Sequence, Small Lot Sizes,

Change Takt-Time each time, Standardized Work, Flexible Manpower Line, *Kanban* System, Frequent Conveyance etc.

- The Basic techniques based on *Jidoka* are Equipment or System capable of detecting abnormality, Separation of human operation and machine work, and so forth.
- Quality concept is certainly woven into the ideology of *Jidoka*. We need to pay attention to the ideology of TPS, where activity for the sake of quality in TPS is not the main objective, but it is a prerequisite and also an outcome. TPS differs from some other production systems regarding this point, although quality assurance activities are very important.

vii. Procedure **for *Kaizen***

Be always mindful of practicing the Procedure for *Kaizen* with the Basic technique (TPS tools) in the *Kaizen* activity.

- *Kaizen* activity in the Toyota Production System is organized according to the following operation cycle called **The changing features of the *Kaizen* activity cycles**, which is based on the basic technique.

The changing features of the *Kaizen* activity cycles

(**Step 1: Implementing 2S**) Implement firstly the 2S necessary for TPS *Kaizen*.

(**Step 2: Finding *Muda* (Waste)**) Work process and goods flow can be seen, so any abnormality and waste can become reasons for improvement.

(**Step 3: Implementing the countermeasure**) Finding the root cause with the 5 Whys, then apply the countermeasure.

(**Step 4: Establishing a standard**) Standardize the workplace, complete the visual control, and develop in other areas (*Yokoten*).

- Return to step 1, and repeat.
- Transform the workplace gradually into the ideal state of Manufacturing by repeating "The changing features of the *Kaizen* activity cycles."
- Practice the Toyota Production System in the actual workplaces. Understanding of the technique is deepened only

through practicing, where your knowledge of TPS has to be rooted in practice, not only theory.

- Don't stick only to methods or tools which are trivial details, because TPS doesn't work if you only imitate the external aspects of TPS. The techniques of TPS can vary depending on your situation.

THE FEATURES OF *MONODZUKURI* (MANUFACTURING), WHICH APPEAR IN THE TOYOTA PRODUCTION SYSTEM

viii. **Human and workplace; The Features of *Monodzukuri* (Manufacturing)**

"The Features of *Monodzukuri* (Manufacturing) in TPS appear in the features of humans, machines and the product, which are the outcome of activity based on actual behavior and technique. In order to pursue this ideal state, grow the personnel who are advancing the Toyota Production System. Thus, create a workplace of the Toyota Production System where the following features of three stages are woven in: 'Features of the initial workplace,' 'Features of the improving workplace,' and 'Features of the workplace that can evolve and be maintained.' It's, for example, creating a system where you can distinguish between normality and abnormality, and implement action where the manner of management changes depending on the situation."

- In the Toyota Production System, human resources development tries to make sure that all members, from the company's top down to all employees, should have a thinking process whereby the ideal state of *Monodzukuri* is pursued, and where they are capable of implementing the process themselves.

(Sustainment) Execute a daily routine smoothly.

(Improvement) Change the manner of action when the situation changes, and standardize it.

(Evolution) Decide your action based on a long-term concept, and though you may eventually stop it, you won't revert back to what was done previously.

(Business Process) Pursue the best process with the perspective of the customer in mind.

(Scope) Optimize performance in the whole process: following process, self-process, former process.

(Stratified Role)

Top: Act and instruct with *Genchi-Gembutsu*.

Administrator: Define the gap between the vision and the current status, then decide and justify a plan of action.

Front-line supervisor: Manage the workplace in a position of "CEO of *Genba*," and carry out tasks utilizing your team and teamwork.

- In the Toyota Production System, the features are depicted in three stages; "Features of the initial workplace," "Features of the improving workplace," and "Features of the workplace that can evolve and be maintained." Activities of these stages could be pursued the ideal workplace which depends on human, machine, and material.

The contents summarized here should be understood as one example of an overview which depicts the Toyota Production System, even if there may be different opinions among TPS practitioners. Readers can realize deeply the Toyota Production System after understanding the three categories listed above. By doing so, you can take more appropriate actions based on the ideology of the Toyota Production System.

ⓛ -THE NEVER-ENDING JOURNEY AS A TPS SPECIALIST

Phew….

Takeuchi is continuing to do his best.

Takeuchi was told by a TPS expert, "With TPS, eventually, you should be able to find an appropriate method somehow," and hearing this made him disappointed.

It was the impetus to begin his struggle to learn TPS.

He eventually learned the Toyota Production System through experiences in the workplace.

It is an eternal journey where we pursue the ideal features of *Monodzukuri*.

Takeuchi is still learning as a TPS specialist.

We always keep practicing the never-ending activities of TPS.

The TPS journey is a continuous endeavor.

Glossary

Japanese Originated Term	1:*hiragana* 2:*katakana* 3:*kanji*	English Description in This Book	Note or Simplified Meaning
Andon	3 行灯	*Andon*	Attention-calling lamps or display
Genba	3 現場	*Genba*, production workplace	Actual workplace, shop floor, shop workshop
Genchi-Gembutsu	3 現地現物	*Genchi-Gembutsu*	The actual thing in the actual place
Haken-Giri	3,1 派遣切り		"*Haken-Giri*" literally means slashing temporary workers
Heijyunka	3 平準化	*Heijyunka*	Leveled instruction, leveled production and so on
Hoshin-Kanri	3 方針管理	*Hoshin-Kanri*	Policy deployment
Jidoka	3 自働化	*Jidoka*, autonomation	Automation with a human touch
Ji-Kotei-Kanketsu	3 自工程完結	(Self- Process Completing)	*Ji-Kotei-Kanketsu*, JKK, literally means "Self-Process Completing"
Jishuken	3 自主研	*Jishuken*	Meeting of an independent study group, or Meeting of an autonomous study group
Just-In-time	2 ジャスト・イン・タイム	Just-In-Time	
Kaikaku	3 改革	innovation	
Kaizen	3 改善	*Kaizen*, continuous improvement	Continuous improvement or never-ending improvement
Kanban	2 かんばん		See Figure 10.1
Karakuri-Ningyou	1,3 からくり人形	mechanical doll	"*Karakuri*" means a special mechanism
Keiretsu	3 系列	series	Group, subsidiary
Monodzukuri	1,2 モノづくり	*Monodzukuri*, Manufacturing	Manufacturing with Japanese soul ("*Monodzukuri*" has a spelling "dzu" at the center)

(Continued)

Japanese Originated Term		English Description in This Book	Note or Simplified Meaning
Muda	3ムダ	*Muda,* Waste	Non-value added waste, Unnecessary activity
Mura	3ムラ	*Mura,* Unevenness	
Muri	3ムリ	*Muri,* Overburden	Being overburdened, or unreasonable
omote-hyoujyun	3表標準	Practical standard	*Omote* means practical or real
Poka-yoke	3ポカヨケ	*Poka-yoke*	Fool-proofing (FP)
Sensei	3先生	*Sensei,* coach, professor, TPS instructor	Teacher, Guru, Japanese consultant
Seiri	3整理	*Seiri*	See Table 41.1
Seiton	3整頓	*Seiton*	*Ibid.*
Seiso	3清掃	*Seiso,* Sweeping and Washing	*Ibid.*
Seiketsu	3清潔	*Seiketsu,* Spick-and-Span	*Ibid.*
Shitsuke	3躾	*Shitsuke,* Discipline	*Ibid.*
Shikumi	3. しくみ	*shikumi* (system)	Software-like, Structure, Makeup, the way it works
Shikumi	1,3仕組み	*shikumi* (system)	Hardware-like, Construction
Shoujin-ka	3 少人化	Flexible Manpower Line	*Menashi no Shoujin:* "Menashi of少" means "small (省without 目)," and "人" means person
Shoujin	3 省人	Manpower Saving	"省" means "elimination"
Yamazumi	1,3山積み	Stack Chart	
Yokoten	3 横展（開）	*Yokoten*	Horizontal expansion to apply similar things

Note: Japanese writing system primarily uses 3 kinds of character: *kanji, katakana,* and *hiragana.*

Bibliography

[JAPANESE LANGUAGE LITERATURE]

Fujimoto, Takahiro; *"Nihon No Monodzukuri Tetsugaku,"* (Nikkei Publishing Inc.), 2004
Fujita, Akihisa; *"Shinban IE No Kiso,"* (Kenpakusha), 1978
Ishii, Masamitsu; *"Nyumon Toyota Seisan Hoshiki,"* (Chukei Publishing Company), 2005
Iwaki, Koichi; *"Jissen Toyota Seisan Hoshiki,"* (Nikkei Publishing Inc.), 2005
Nakayama, Kiyotaka; *"Jikiden Toyota Hoshiki,"* (Diamond, Inc.), 2005
Nikkan Kogyo Shimbun; *"Ohno Taiichi No Kaizen Damashii,"* (The Nikkan Kogyo Shimbun), 2005
Ohno, Taiichi; *"Toyota Seisan Hoshiki,"* (Diamond, Inc.), 1978 Translated to English edition, Taiichi Ohno; Toyota Production System, Productivity Press, 1988
Takeuchi, Noboru; *"Seru Seisan (Cell Production),"* (JMA Management Center), 2006
Tanaka, Masatomo; *"Kangaeru Toyota No Genba,"* (Business-Sha, Inc.), 2005
The Japan Society for Production Management; *"Toyota Seisan Hoshiki,"* (The Nikkan Kogyo Shimbun), 1996

[ENGLISH LANGUAGE LITERATURE]

Hiroyuki Hirano; *"JIT is Flow,"* (PCS Press), 2006
Jeffrey K. Liker; *The Toyota Way,* (McGraw-Hill), 2004. Translated to Japanese edition, Jeffrey K. Liker; *"Za Toyota Wei,"* (Nikkei Business Publications, Inc.), 2004
Jeffrey K. Liker and David Meier; *The Toyota Way Fieldbook: A Practical Guide for Implementing Toyota's 4Ps,* (McGraw-Hill), 2006

Index

Note: Page references in *italics* denote figures and in **bold** tables.

Printed in the United States
by Baker & Taylor publisher Services

Printed in the United States
by Baker & Taylor Publisher Services